HARRIS COUNTY PUBLIC LIBRARY
3 4028 03906 8664

C0-DKN-366

WITHDRAWN

HISTORIC TOWNS of TEXAS

Volume II

HISTORIC TOWNS of TEXAS

Volume II

- GONZALES
- COLUMBUS
- JEFFERSON

By Joe Tom Davis

Photos by J. C. Hoke

EAKIN PRESS ★ Austin, Texas

FIRST EDITION

Published in the United States of America
By Eakin Press
A Division of Sunbelt Media, Inc.
P.O. Drawer 90159 ★ Austin, Texas 78709-0159

2 3 4 5 6 7 8 9

ISBN 1-57168-044-6

Library of Congress Cataloging-in-Publication Data

Davis, Joe Tom, 1938 —
Historic towns of Texas/by Joe Tom Davis : photos by J. C. Hoke.
p. cm.
Includes bibliographical references and index.
ISBN 1-57168-044-6: $18.95
1. Cities and towns, ruined, extinct, etc. — Texas — History. 2. Cities and towns — Texas. 3. Texas — History, Local. I. Title.
F38.D38 1996
P76.4 —dc20 91-17276
CP

This book is dedicated in memory of my father-in-law, John Hastedt, Jr., a true Southern gentleman whose family settled in the Columbus area in 1848.

Contents

Acknowledgments

I could not have written this book without the assistance of three colleagues and friends at Wharton County Junior College. I am truly indebted to Mrs. Pasty L. Norton, director of the J. M. Hodges Learning Center, and two members of her excellent staff. My reading and research always begins in the Hodges Learning Center, where an extensive collection of Texas history titles has been acquired since 1964 through the generosity of the Raymond Dickson Foundation and proceeds from the book, *The History of Wharton County*, by Annie Lee Williams. This book was written in collaboration with Assistant Director J. C. Hoke, who is also an outstanding photographer. Mr. Hoke accompanied me on three trips and provided all of the on-site photos in this book along with numerous photographic reproductions. The quality of his work has truly enhanced my writing. A special word of thanks is due Mrs. Cynthia Huddleston, circulation technician, for promptly obtaining the 1943 book, *George W. Littlefield: Texan*, through an interlibrary loan.

I want to thank Mrs. Mary Bea Arnold, curator of the Gonzales Memorial Museum, for giving Mr. Hoke and me access to photos of pioneers on display there. Hugh Shelton, owner of First Shot Photographics, Gonzales, generously donated four important photos for the Gonzales chapter. Mrs. Pat Marvin, secretary of the Gonzales Chamber of Commerce and Agriculture, provided promotional brochures and pamphlets in helping us find our way around town.

I also appreciate the assistance of Antonio Martinez, assistant director of the Victoria Public Library. Mr. Martinez kindly provided working space during the two days I took notes from *The History of Gonzales County, Texas,* an out-of-print book in the Local History and Genealogy section of the library. I am also grateful to the members of the Gonzales Art Group. Their book, *Gonzales,* is an invaluable source of information about eighteen historic structures in the city. Special thanks is also due to Mrs. Mary Blundell, a former resident of El Campo, who gave me copies of the *Gonzales Inquirer* "Come and Take It Days" Celebration supplements for 1988 and 1989. They provided very useful local biographical material.

Bill Stein, archivist of the Nesbitt Memorial Library in Columbus, was especially helpful. He provided both working space and access to the Stafford Family file, the Fannie Darden file, the Tait Family file, and the William B. Dewees file. Seven scholarly articles that Mr. Stein either wrote or co-authored in the *Nesbitt Memorial Library Journal* were a superb source of information. He also gave Mr. Hoke and me access to numerous photos from the library archives collection. I am truly grateful to Bill Stein for sharing his considerable expertise and knowledge of the history of Columbus with me.

I also wish to thank Mr. Bob Tait for allowing Mr. Hoke and me to visit and take photos of the Tait plantation house and the Tait family cemetery.

Mrs. Joyce Loessin of Columbus allowed me to borrow numerous issues of the *Nesbitt Memorial Library Journal* and a copy of the book, *Come Reminisce With Me: A History of Glidden, Texas,* by Dorothy Jean Heine. I am also indebted to Mrs. Mildred Campbell of Columbus, who gave me a copy of William H. Harrison's book, *Alleyton, Texas: Back Door to the Confederacy.* My study of Columbus was made more complete by knowing the history of these two nearby towns.

I also appreciate the assistance of Allan and Jane Miller Hill of Columbus. They graciously provided information about the recent history of the Stafford-Miller House and allowed me to photograph this historic home.

Mr. Tex Rogers, editor of *The Colorado County Citizen,* kindly donated darkroom facilities, supplies, and labor to provide numerous prints for the Columbus chapter.

My fascination with Jefferson, Texas, dates from 1983,

when Minnette Carpenter of the Excelsior House was kind enough to send me promotional material about the famed hotel and Jefferson along with a copy of the booklet, *A History of Jefferson, Marion County, Texas 1836-1936.*

I am greatly indebted to Dr. Fred Tarpley, longtime professor of English at East Texas State University. Dr. Tarpley wrote the first documented history of Jefferson in 1983. His definitive book, *Jefferson: Riverport to the Southwest,* provided a wealth of both information and book and periodical sources for my chapter on Jefferson.

When Mr. Hoke and I visited Jefferson to take photos in July 1994, we were warmly and graciously received. One unknown lady even stopped her car in the middle of a block to offer directions when she noticed our camera and tripod.

I wish to thank Martha Ford, desk clerk at the Excelsior House, for allowing us to photograph various portraits and drawings displayed in that storied hotel.

A. M. Bower of the Jefferson Historical Museum granted me advance permission to photograph certain published museum pictures. On the day of our visit to Jefferson, Mrs. Adelaide Green allowed us to make photos of additional pictures we discovered while browsing through the extensive museum collection.

I am also grateful to Mrs. Fances Ford, who gave us a personal and unscheduled tour of the Ruth Lester Memorial during our visit to Jefferson.

A special thank you is due my very talented niece-by-marriage, Mrs. Penny Grissom Bonnot, who designed the attractive book cover. Mrs. Bonnot is an art teacher at Town Center Elementary and Coppell Middle School East at Coppell, Texas.

Most of all, I want to thank my wife, Kathy, who provided an environment that enabled me to do my writing at home. Her tolerance, patience, and understanding truly made this book possible.

Introduction

This is the second volume in a series of books about historic towns of Texas. Volume II covers a town renowned for valor and sacrifice, a center of culture and civility taken hostage by two bloody family feuds, and an inland East Texas port whose prosperity sluiced away in 1873. These towns have evolved into tourist centers today because their residents would not allow a rich heritage to die.

Unlike most town histories, this book focuses on individuals rather than institutions. The life of a town is much more than a litany of general stores, hotels, banks, clubs, and churches. The flavor and spirit of a town develop from the dreams and deeds of its residents. Thus I have chosen to emphasize the achievements and exploits of the town founders, builders, and prominent later residents.

Gonzales, the capital of the DeWitt colony, was founded on the Indian frontier in 1825. The Minuteman statue on Texas Heroes Square recalls the special valor displayed by the men of Gonzales during the Texas Revolution. The first battle was fought there. The only response to Travis' plea for help at the Alamo came from the thirty-two martyrs of Gonzales. Indeed, this remote outpost was "The Cradle of Texas Independence."

In the 1840s, Matthew "Old Paint" Caldwell led a new generation of Gonzales men in repelling Indian depredations and Mexican invasions. Rebuilt from ashes, Gonzales had an impressive business district, a respected newspaper, and a highly regarded college by the 1850s. During the Civil War, the Gonzales area provided two generals and twenty-two volunteer companies for the Confederate cause. The town could also boast of the only Confederate fort commissioned to be built west of the Mississippi River.

In the postwar years, new fortunes were made as such Gonzales cattlemen as George W. Littlefield, the Dilworths, and the Houstons drove herds up the Chisholm Trail. Some of their grand homes still grace St. Louis and St. Lawrence streets. Such landmarks as the old Gonzales jail (1887) and the Gonzales courthouse (1896) are impressive reminders of a colorful — and often violent — past.

The cattle and poultry businesses dominate the local economy today, but tourism has grown steadily in Gonzales since the annual "Come and Take It Days" Celebration began in 1956.

Columbus has a population of some 3,400, yet it has fifty-seven historical markers within the city limits, including a National Historical District. The history of Columbus is tinged with irony: its founder died an indigent ward of the county; a sedate town proud of its culture and civility was the focal point of an abortive slave revolt, a lengthy reign of terror involving two family feuds, and a mob lynching of two teenagers.

Columbus can boast of the first drugstore in the Republic, the first castle built in Texas, and the first railroad hospital. For a time it was a major hub for stagecoach service and a railroad terminus. Over the years the town has been home to two cattle barons, an important planter, two early chroniclers of Texas history, a renowned poetess and writer, three prominent Confederate leaders, a lieutenant governor, and an attorney general.

A turning point in the history of a stagnating town came in 1961 with the formation of the Magnolia Homes Tour and the subsequent restoration of an ornate old opera house. Since that time tourism has become a major focus due to the efforts of a band of dedicated and energetic Columbus residents who promise visitors that "the past is our present to you."

Walking the streets of Jefferson, one feels suspended in time. Only Galveston can claim more historical markers than the sixty-five found in this tiny town of some 2,200 residents. The forty-seven-block Jefferson Historic District is a National Register District showcasing fifty-six restored buildings dating from the 1850s to the 1890s.

Surveyed in 1841, a freak of nature made Jefferson the state's largest inland port and a major steamboat terminus. During the Civil War, this "Belle of the Bayou" was a major supply depot for Confederate armies in the West. Tragedy haunts her past: a steamboat disaster, a famous murder trial, and a sinister curse are all associated with Jefferson. The town is the home of a singer dubbed the "Father of Country Music," a renowned novelist, a prominent Texas historian, the designer of the famed Kelly Blue Plow, and a governor of Texas.

Wall Street wizard Jay Gould is still the town villain, but it was a nytroglycerin charge, not his mythical curse, that sent Jefferson into a dizzying decline after 1873. The town was in a moribund condition in the 1950s when a handful of determined women began to view its many historic — and seedy — structures as an economic asset. Thus began the oldest historical pilgrimage in Texas. Since that time tourism, including the bed and breakfast industry, has brought renewed prosperity and a national reputation to Jefferson.

Delving into the history of old Texas towns has been a fascinating learning experience for me. I have discovered that these three small — and seemingly insignificant — towns offer an architectural treasure trove for the Texas history buff. Their grand past has been nobly restored and preserved, and our "now generation" is richer for it. I trust that the reader will share my newfound appreciation of these town founders, builders, and preservers. Of course, I take full responsibility for any errors made in telling of their accomplishments.

I

Gonzales: The Lexington of Texas

Gonzales, the first Anglo-American settlement west of the Colorado River, was founded in 1825. The remote outpost suffered more Indian raids than any other town. Of all early Texas towns, Gonzales made the greatest contributions — and sacrifices — to Texas independence. The first battle of the Texas Revolution was fought there; the first council of war was organized there; forty-one Gonzales men died at the Alamo; Gonzales was burned by General Houston's retreating Texas army.

A proud military tradition continued as Gonzales sent two generals and eleven companies to fight in the Confederate army. Over the years such legendary names as Almeron and Susanna Dickinson, Matthew "Old Paint" Caldwell, Ben McCulloch, Thomas Waul, Thomas J. Pilgrim, George W. Littlefield, John Wesley Hardin, and Gregorio Cortez appeared in the saga of Gonzales.

Since the mid-1950s, Gonzales has actively promoted her glorious past with the annual "Come and Take It Days" Celebration, the Pioneer Village Living History Center, two fine museums, and walking and driving tours of preserved historic homes and majestic buildings. Tourism has thus joined the cattle and poultry businesses in providing economic development.

Green DeWitt, the founder of Gonzales, was born in Lincoln County, Kentucky, on February 12, 1787. When he was an infant, his father moved the family to Spanish-held Missouri. At age eighteen Green was sent to Kentucky, where he spent two years finishing his education. Soon after returning to Missouri, DeWitt married Sarah Seely, a cultured and refined woman whose parents migrated from Brooks County, Virginia, and settled in Saint Louis County, Missouri. At the time of their marriage, Sarah owned a considerable amount of property.

During the War of 1812, DeWitt rose to the rank of lieutenant in the Missouri militia. After the war he served as sheriff of Ralls County, Missouri. Upon hearing of Moses Austin's Spanish land grant in Texas, he traveled to Mexico City in 1821, hoping to receive a similar grant. During a three-month stay there in 1822, Green never formally petitioned for a land grant. Although his trip proved fruitless, he was greatly impressed with Texas as he traveled to and from Mexico City.

After hearing news of the Mexican General Colonization Law of August 1824, DeWitt returned to Texas carrying a letter of recommendation by Judge William Trimble. From his first meeting with Stephen F. Austin, who was carrying on his dead father's Texas enterprise, Green placed great trust in Austin and continually sought his advice and assistance.

In December 1824, DeWitt was in Saltillo, the capital of Coahuila-Texas, where he presented his petition for a land grant. The next month Austin wrote the Baron de Bastrop, the Texas representative in the state legislature, asking him to aid DeWitt and to use his influence in obtaining the grant.

On April 15, 1825, *Empresario* DeWitt was authorized to settle 400 families in an uninspected area within the following land boundaries:

> Beginning on the right bank of Arroyo de la Vaca at a distance of the reserved ten leagues from the coast, adjoining the colony of Stephen Austin on the east, the line shall go up the river to the Bejar-Nacogdoches road; it shall follow this road until it reaches a point two leagues to the west of the Guadalupe River; thence it shall run parallel with the river down to the Paraje de las Mosquitos; and following the inner edge of the ten-league coast reservation, it shall close the boundaries of the grant at the point of beginning.

For each one hundred families DeWitt introduced within six years, he was to receive "premium land" consisting of five leagues

(22,140 acres) and five labors (885 acres). The entire contract would be void if the *empresario* failed to introduce the minimum of one hundred families. Above that number, his land compensations would be reduced proportionately.

When there were one hundred families in the colony, DeWitt was to inform the state government, which would appoint the needed commissioner to issue land titles and establish a town.

The law also provided that the *empresario* was to organize and command the militia with the rank of colonel.

After leaving Saltillo in late April 1825, DeWitt's colonial project was delayed when Peter Ellis Bean charged him with misappropriating public funds. The charges were heard at San Antonio by the *jefepolitico* (political chief), who appointed Austin to investigate the matter. Once Austin found him innocent, DeWitt was exonerated from the charge on October 17, 1825.

In January 1825, DeWitt appointed James Kerr as his surveyor-general. Kerr was the former sheriff of St. Charles County, Missouri, and had served in the state senate. The first Anglo-American settler west of the Colorado River, Kerr probably did more to hold the precarious DeWitt colony together in its formative years than did the *empresario.*

James, his wife Angeline, their three small children, and seven slaves left Missouri in February 1825. After traveling down the Mississippi River to New Orleans, the Kerr party reached Brazoria on a coastwise packet in May. A month later, Angeline Kerr died while encamped west of Columbia. Within weeks little Ison and John James also succumbed to the hardships of the journey. The bereaved husband then left his three-year-old daughter, Mary Margaret, in the care of Mrs. Pettus at San Felipe.

Kerr then set out to select a site for the capital of the DeWitt colony, taking with him Erastus "Deaf" Smith, Bazil Durbin, Geron Hinds, John Wightman, James Musick, and Mr. Strickland. Choosing a location two and a half miles east of the junction of the Guadalupe and San Marcos rivers, Kerr and his small party built a few crude cabins on Kerr's Creek, a mile east of the present town of Gonzales, in August 1825.

When the Kerr party surveyed the townsite and the four leagues of land assigned to each capital, James named the site Gonzales in honor of Don Rafael Gonzales, the provisional governor of Coahuila-Texas. The town plan was sent to the political chief on December 12, 1825, and approved by the state governor on March 10, 1826.

Initially, Kerr's surveying party survived on wild game, bread made from Indian corn, honey, and a soon-depleted supply of coffee.

Within a few weeks, Francis Berry and his family arrived from Missouri and settled on Kerr's Creek, bringing two grown children of Mrs. Berry by a previous marriage, John and Elizabeth Oliver. This raised the population of old Gonzales to fifteen colonists and three Kerr slaves — Jack, Shade, and Anise. Other settlers who visited that fall included Capt. Henry S. Brown, Edwin Morehouse, Elijah Stapp, and Frost Thorn.

In late October 1825, *Empresario* DeWitt arrived at Gonzales and stayed three or four weeks before returning to Missouri by way of New Orleans and the Mississippi River. En route he met Frost Thorn, who had evidently provided some financial assistance. DeWitt reimbursed Thorn with $200 in "Guadalupe land office money," land scrip which was the first form of paper money used in Texas. When he needed funds, DeWitt issued this handwritten currency in denominations of five, ten, and twenty dollars. The notes soon became transferable and were used as a medium of exchange. Among the holders was historian John Henry Brown, who accumulated eight of DeWitt's bills.

By early 1826, DeWitt was back in Missouri advertising his colony. In April he departed for Texas with wife Sarah, their two sons, Christopher Columbus and Clinton, and three of their four daughters, Naomi, Evaline, and Minerva. The youngest daughter, Eliza, was left in New London, Missouri, to finish school and joined her family two years later.

The DeWitts were accompanied to Texas by the Stephens, Lockland, and Reynolds families. The group chartered a schooner in New Orleans to carry them to the mouth of the Lavaca River on the Texas coast. By July 1826, they were anchored in Lavaca Bay. When DeWitt observed Indians in the area, he sent word seeking Kerr's assistance.

On July 2, 1826, Comanche and Wichita Indians carried out a horse-stealing raid at Gonzales. At the time, James Kerr was at Brazoria, and Smith and Hinds had gone on a buffalo hunt. Durbin, John and Betsy Oliver, and a slave named Jack left Gonzales by horseback that very day to attend a Fourth of July celebration at the Atascosito Crossing on the Colorado River. Musick, Strickland,

and slaves Shade and Anise had gone to spend the day at Francis Berry's place a few miles away. Thus only John Wightman remained at the Gonzales settlement. During the raid he was killed trying to defend his cabin. No buildings were burned, but the Indians took all the horses along with papers, books, and surveying instruments.

The small party heading for the Atascosita Crossing was encamped fourteen miles east of Gonzales when they were attacked at midnight. Durbin was badly wounded by a musket ball in the shoulder but managed to escape to a nearby thicket as did the others, who were unharmed but badly shaken. The Indians took their horses, blankets, and goods.

By noon the next day the group arrived back in Gonzales, where they found Wightman's scalped body. Upon reaching Berry's deserted cabin, they saw on the door written in charcoal: "Gone to Burnham's on the Colorado." They followed as quickly as possible, making the trip in three and a half days. En route Durbin's shoulder wound was treated with mud and an oak juice poultice to prevent gangrene. They arrived at Burnham's on July 6 and were welcomed by the others. Smith and Hinds joined them a few days later.

As a result of the Indian raid, James Kerr decided to find another site nearer the coast for the DeWitt colony. Since the new location, "Old Station," was only six miles up the Lavaca River and within the ten-league coastal reserve, Kerr had to travel to San Antonio to seek permission for the change. The *jefepolitico,* Jose Antonio Saucedo, agreed that Old Station could serve only as a temporary port of entry to receive DeWitt colonists, but not as a permanent settlement.

When DeWitt's small party arrived on the Texas coast, Old Station consisted only of a few blockhouses. By October 1826, however, the settlement was well-established with forty colonists, who built cabins and planted a corn crop. The *jefepolitico* appointed James Norton as temporary *alcalde,* but no land titles were, or could be, issued.

Upon his arrival Green DeWitt contracted the services of the fifty-ton schooner *Dispatch* for four years to bring immigrants and cargo to the colony. He also built a warehouse near the mouth of the Lavaca and constructed a thirty-by-twelve-foot flatboat to shuttle colonists and cargo from the *Dispatch* to the shore.

DeWitt soon came into conflict with Don Martin De Leon, a

neighboring *empresario* to the southeast, over the issues of land claims and contraband trade. En route to inspect his colony capital of Gonzales, Green was surprised to find the center portion of his grant occupied by twelve Mexican families of the De Leon colony, who had already cultivated crops and organized the flourishing capital of Guadalupe Victoria in October 1824. In April of that year, Don Martin had obtained an informal grant from the Provincial Deputation of San Fernando de Bexar to settle Mexican families on any unoccupied lands between the lower Lavaca and Guadalupe rivers. In October 1825, the De Leon grant and land titles were sanctioned under the Colonization Law. Don Martin's grant thus predated that of DeWitt, who was required by law to respect existing land claims.

In July 1826, while on his way to assist DeWitt, James Kerr found a destroyed boat of a DeWitt colonist on Garcitas Creek. Kerr maintained that De Leon or one of his sons was responsible and convinced DeWitt of that fact. He also informed Austin that De Leon was guilty of ill-treating and robbing a Mr. Stout.

It was the issue of contraband trade, however, that triggered an open conflict between DeWitt and De Leon. In October 1826, Thomas Powell, a DeWitt colonist from Missouri, landed at the mouth of the Lavaca and received permission to store his cargo of goods at Old Station. Powell's trade goods included a large quantity of proscribed tobacco, which was not exempt from import duties. A Dr. Oliver, a Frenchman and officer in the Mexican army, befriended Powell and offered to assist in selling the cargo. It was probably Dr. Oliver who informed the *jefepolitico* at San Antonio, who in turn authorized Don Martin to investigate the contraband matter.

De Leon, his son-in-law, Capt. Rafael Manchola, and the Mexican garrison at La Bahia then paid a visit to the Old Station amid rumors that they intended to stamp out the settlement. De Leon took his sword along and boasted that he intended to return with DeWitt's head tied to his saddle. When the Mexican party approached, the cool-headed Kerr persuaded the settlers not to fire on the garrison. Don Martin's search party then disarmed all the DeWitt colonists, confiscated *all* of Powell's cargo, arrested Green DeWitt, and took him and the goods to La Bahia.

After Kerr asked the *jefepolitico* and Austin to intervene in the matter, the entire proceeding was dropped, and DeWitt was back at the Old Station on December 13, 1826. The unnerved *empresario* blamed De Leon for the whole affair, contending that Don Martin's scheming effort was designed to ruin his colonizing efforts.

When the Fredonian Rebellion erupted at Nacogdoches in December 1826, the uprising was condemned at a meeting of the DeWitt colonists. The resolutions were signed by chairman Byrd Lockhart and secretary James Norton. This strong stand against an abortive independence movement was influenced by James Kerr, who led a three-man commission sent to negotiate with leaders Haden and Benjamin Edwards. Ultimately, direct military action was taken to crush the revolutionary uprising.

On July 14, 1827, DeWitt gave Kerr power of attorney to manage colonial affairs. During the next two months, the *empresario* attempted to recruit more colonists in the United States. It should be recalled that DeWitt needed to introduce one hundred families by 1831 or else he would lose his contract and the "premium lands."

In September 1827, DeWitt returned to his colony to find that *jefepolitico* Saucedo had just ordered him to move the colony from Old Station to Gonzales within one month. Saucedo also suggested that new immigrants should no longer arrive by way of the Lavaca River. This would result in a major setback to the DeWitt colony since this shorter route — New Orleans to Lavaca Bay by way of coastal schooner — would no longer be available. If prospective colonists were required to take the longer overland route, immigration was sure to be adversely affected.

Kerr immediately took DeWitt's appeal for an extension and a colonial petition to San Antonio. After Saucedo granted an extension of time until December 1, Governor Jose Maria Viesca extended that deadline until June 1828.

In early January 1827, DeWitt had sent Byrd Lockhart and a number of colonists to the Gonzales site to begin construction of a fort. Work stopped the next month after the men became fearful of renewed Indian attacks. They were told that a party of Comanche and Waco Indians had defeated a band of Lipans and Tonkawas only nine miles away on the San Marcos River. Once Lockhart persuaded his work party not to abandon the site, the stockade was completed in April on block 3 of the inner town, later the site of the Gonzales Cotton Oil Manufacturing Company. Lockhart then reported that all had been quiet in the area since the Indian skirmish.

By December 17, 1827, DeWitt and his forty colonists abandoned Old Station. When he returned to Gonzales, he settled on the south bank of the Guadalupe River opposite town. During the next year the colony almost doubled in population. The official census of 1828 showed thirty-four adult males and thirty-seven women and children. A good majority — forty-five out of seventy-one — came from the Upper South: Tennessee, Kentucky, Missouri, Arkansas Territory, and portions of West Virginia and North Carolina. Only seventeen came from the Lower South. Arthur and Sarah Burns were the parents of the first child, Arcus, born in Gonzales in 1828.

The new site of Gonzales was on the east bank of the Guadalupe three miles below its juncture with the San Marcos River. By early 1828, the settlers completed "log pens" for living quarters. These crude cabins were constructed of unhewn logs with the cracks and joints filled with clay or mud. Each cabin had a door and one window fitted with a wooden shutter. The log pen floor was either clay or wooden planks. Nearby was a small corn field and corral.

The settlement consisted of six or seven such log pens built near the fort. Almost all of these houses were located along two tiers of blocks near Water Street on the riverfront.

By mid-1829, the colony more than doubled in size to 158. Much of that increase came in March when Byrd Lockhart brought in fifty-five new colonists, bringing the total to thirty families and thirty-four single men. By the end of the year, the colonial population reached 186.

During 1829, two roads were built to facilitate transportation to Gonzales. Unfortunately, these new routes were also used by traders of contraband goods bound for San Antonio. DeWitt, who was fearful of being blamed for the illegal traffic, informed the *jefepolitico* that although the trade was substantial, his colonists were not taking part in the activity.

In October 1830, Almeron Dickinson and his new bride, Susanna Wilkerson, left Hardeman County, Tennessee, to join a party of forty-eight settlers bound for the DeWitt colony. Almeron was a blacksmith by trade, and Susanna was a simple, illiterate country girl who was a great cook and seamstress.

On February 20, 1831, Almeron petitioned for a Mexican headright, a league of land located on the San Marcos River above the mouth of Mill Creek in present Caldwell County. On May 4, he received title to this land near the northern limit of the DeWitt colony.

After Byrd Lockhart surveyed four square leagues of land for the new townsite of Gonzales in 1832, town lots 1 and 2 in block 16 were assigned to Dickinson. Since he was a mechanic, he received these two "in" lots free of charge and set up a gunsmith shop.

By the end of 1830, the population of the DeWitt colony reached 377. In the first three and one-half months of 1831, 154 entered the colony. The Colonization Law of April 6, 1830, prohibited further Anglo-American immigration to Texas. Although the DeWitt colony was exempted from the law, the flow of immigration was obviously affected by it: there were no new arrivals after April 1, 1831. The total population of the DeWitt colony reached 531 at that time, making it the second most successful *empresario* endeavor in Texas.

Since there were over one hundred families in the DeWitt colony — the number required before land titles could be issued — the state government appointed Jose Antonio Navarro as land commissioner in January 1831. He then began his most important task: issuing and registering land titles. In April, Navarro appointed Byrd Lockhart as surveyor-general of the colony, a position given to James Kerr by DeWitt in 1825. When the colonists returned to the Gonzales site in 1827, Kerr chose to remain on land he held title to in the Lavaca district. At that time, he appointed Lockhart, a trained surveyor, as deputy surveyor, and he performed all such work after 1826.[1]

Byrd was assisted by Charles Lockhart and received $8 for each league of land surveyed, $3 for each labor, and $1.50 for every town lot surveyed. Since money was scarce, he was paid in either goods or services. Byrd Lockhart was also granted four leagues of land for his skills in surveying and building roads into the Gonzales area.

Land Commissioner Navarro recorded the first four land titles on April 15, 1831; the last of 189 titles was issued to William B. Lockhart on September 17, 1832. *Empresario* DeWitt's contract expired on April 15, 1831, and was not renewed.

As the site of Gonzales continued to grow, the temporary log pens were replaced by one-story, one-room houses that were typically twenty-five feet long and eighteen feet wide. After the timber was cut and hauled by oxen, it was hewed with a foot adze, a hoe-like instrument used to scrape and shape the timber into four flat surfaces. The "house raising" usually took only one day. Most of these houses had one heavy cutout door and one window twelve inches square and covered by a hide curtain. A thick wooden shutter or iron bars were added for protection.

Most of the Gonzales settlers raised beef cattle which were allowed to range freely. Hogs were also allowed to roam, feeding on the mast in the timber bottoms and prairie roots. There was also a plentiful supply of deer, antelope, turkey, and bear.

Once Indian corn or the soft white Mexican variety was planted and harvested, it was most often roasted. Corn also provided meal for bread. Since wheat was not planted extensively, flour was scarce and considered a luxury item. Milk came from goats, not milch cows. The daily menu consisted of corn bread, fried pork, wild game, honey, and coffee with no milk or sugar.

David B. Edward, a Scot and former academy principal at Alexandria, Iowa, came to the DeWitt colony in 1831 and established a "seminary." When Edward wrote *The History of Texas* before the Revolution, he referred to himself as the preceptor of Gonzales Seminary. He described the settlers as being indolent, filthy, and intemperate. The first trait was blamed on the fertility of the soil and an abundance of wild game. Typical dress included a leather hunting shirt and a pair of buckskin breeches, an outfit good enough for the mud and briers. Edward blamed intemperance on the lack of literary amusement, "religious excitement," and enjoyments. He noted that the settlers often visited with their friends in grog shops. Other pastimes included dances, horse races, and rifle contests.

Protestant ministers and churches were prohibited by Mexican law. Few of the colonists were Catholics, however, and there were no Catholic priests or churches in the Gonzales area. As a result, the Sabbath was considered only as a day of visiting, not of worship.

Sumner Bacon, a Protestant missionary, was sent to Texas in 1832 by the Cumberland Presbytery of Tennessee. This circuit-riding preacher held camp meetings and prayer meetings in the Gonzales area. He also met no governmental opposition when he distributed Bibles in English and Spanish at his own expense. During the Texas Revolution, Reverend Bacon joined General Houston's army, purchasing and transporting ammunition.

Legalizing marriages in the Gonzales area was a practical problem since there was no priest or church. Traveling to San Antonio or San Felipe was simply too far for couples wishing to marry. To solve the problem, *Empresario* DeWitt was authorized to perform marriages by bond. On March 5, 1829, he performed the first such ceremony between John Oliver and Nancy Curtis. The two were held and bound to each other in the penal sum of $10,000. The said parties agreed to faithfully appear before some priest or person legally authorized to solemnize marriage as soon as circumstances would permit, then the bond was forever void. Witnesses were H. S. Brown and H. Frisby.

Gonzales never suffered a major Indian attack, but it suffered more scattered raids than any other Anglo-American settlement in Texas. To make matters worse, the DeWitt colonists had been disarmed by Mexican commandant Rafael Manchola during the contraband controversy of 1826. The few weapons that were returned in January 1827 were in poor condition and were practically useless. Early that year James Kerr asked Austin to assist in obtaining a heavy caliber weapon from the government arsenal for protection against the Indians. Although the request was denied, the Mexican government promised that a Mexican garrison would be stationed there after the colonists moved from Old Station to Gonzales. All the families were there by early 1828, but the Mexican troops did not appear.

In December 1828, some 500 horses were stolen from trader Henry Stevenson Brown on the road between San Antonio and Gonzales. Brown immediately went to Gonzales and organized a futile "expedition" to assist in recovering his horses. His force was gone for thirty-two days, traveling 200 miles northwest into Comanche territory as far as present Brown County.

In March 1829, several Tonkawa raids occurred near Gonzales, prompting DeWitt and seventeen colonists to pursue some thirty warriors toward Goliad. During the chase the Tonkawas were joined by another raiding party of forty braves with fifty stolen horses. When four colonists located the much larger force hidden in a thicket, DeWitt wisely ordered a slow retreat under cover of darkness. Luckily for him, the encounter was not with Comanche or Wichita warriors.

At this time the *empresario* suggested stationing a "company of rangers" drawn from the settlers to patrol the area between the Colorado and Guadalupe rivers. The idea was never acted upon. It should be noted that DeWitt never organized a formal militia company as he was required to do by law.

When another Tonkawa raid occurred in April 1829, DeWitt and some of his colonists again gave chase. This time he resorted to diplomacy after overtaking the Indians. When he asked why the Tonkawas had raided his settlement, they replied that pressure from the Comanches to the north had interrupted their hunting, forcing them to raid rather than face starvation. The Tonkawas reminded DeWitt that they had harmed no one, taking only corn, cattle, and hogs.

Acting on the authority of the *jefepolitico,* DeWitt suggested that the Tonkawas become farmers; they would be given horses, corn, hoes, and axes and be assigned four leagues of land for a town. Although this idealistic plan was never put into effect, the DeWitt colony encountered no more problems with the Tonkawas.

In 1830 there were more Comanche and Wichita raids than ever in the Gonzales area. Colonist George Singleton was killed in one such attack on a mill only three miles from town. When DeWitt again requested Mexican troops in January 1831, he also asked to borrow an artillery piece that would be returned whenever the authorities requested it. Two months later a six-pound, unmounted cannon was made available, and DeWitt sent a wagon to San Antonio for the weapon.

In June 1831, a Mexican detachment began to patrol the road between San Antonio and San Felipe to prevent contraband trade. On August 18, fifteen of these troops were attacked by a war party of nine Comanches, who killed two Mexicans and took thirteen of their horses. A month later the Mexican patrol was withdrawn to San Antonio.

In 1832 a French peddler camped with his wagon at a pool near the home of John Castleman fifteen miles west of Gonzales. After the trader was murdered near daybreak by Comanche and Wichita warriors, eighty of the braves paraded single-file past Castleman's window showing off their loot. A posse of twenty-seven DeWitt colonists led by Dr. James H. C. Miller then undertook an offensive campaign against the raiding party, pursuing them for three days as far as the hills of the Blanco River. During the chase Miller's men killed several of the savages and recovered some of the dead peddler's stock.

On April 4, 1831, Ramon Musquiz, the *jefepolitico* of the Department of Bexar, instructed Commissioner Navarro to resurvey the Gonzales town tract according to Kerr's plan of 1825. Assisted by surveyor-general Byrd Lockhart, Navarro laid out the townsite in a grid pattern with the same number of lines running east-to-west as north-to-south. In the center of the grid was a main square or plaza measuring 333⅓ feet on each side. Plazas to the north, south, east, and west were designated for a market (block 4), military square (block 26), church (block 32), and municipal square (block 18), respectively. There was also a jail plaza (block 24) and cemetery square (block 46) established at the extreme western and eastern edges of town, respectively. The survey was completed on May 26, 1832.

The streets, all at right angles to the plazas, were 55½ feet wide, and the distances between all streets was 333⅓ feet. The streets were named for saints of the church calendar such as St. Joseph, St. Paul, St. Matthew, St. Andrew, and St. Michael and are still so-named today.

The areas formed by the intersecting streets were town blocks. Each of the forty-two town blocks measured 333⅓ feet square. Each block contained six lots, each of which was fifty-five feet wide and 166 feet long.

All of this area was known as the "inner town," which was located in the extreme southwestern portion of the town tract. The inner town made up only a small fraction of the four square leagues in the town tract.

The "outer town" made up the remaining portion of the town tract. Water Street formed the western boundary of the inner town and was extended to provide a dividing line between the two types of lots in the outer town. Lots to the west of this line were 1,400 square feet, divided into smaller lots half that size. The entire section was divided by streets seventy feet wide running north-to-south and east-to-west. Many of these larger lots were irregularly shaped since they fronted on the banks of the winding San Marcos and Guadalupe rivers, the western boundary of the outer town.

The area east of Water Street was divided into fifteen ranges, each running north-to-south, with fifty-eight lots in each range. These lots measured 433 feet by 110 feet and were divided by streets seventy feet wide running only north-to-south.

Any mechanics were given town lots outright. The other town lots were sold at public auction and paid for in installments at six, twelve, and eighteen months. A buyer received a six percent discount for immediate payment. These lot receipts were used to build the church and for town needs.

There was a tax of one dollar per year on all inner town lots; outer town lots were tax-exempt.

The first structure in the inner town was the fort, completed in April 1827. It was built some sixty yards from the Guadalupe River on one of DeWitt's two "premium lots." The old fort was adjacent to Water Street and directly across from the jail plaza.

By March 1836, there were thirty-two structures in the inner town of Gonzales, twenty of them built prior to 1831. The first title to an inner town lot was recorded on December 7, 1833. Among the structures built prior to 1831 were Thomas R. Miller's store, the hat factory of Almeron Dickinson and George Kimble, the James Hinds home, the James Tumlison home, the Lewis D. Sewell home, the John Sowell home, the house of James B. Patrick, John Saddler's shop, the home of Umphries Branch, a structure called "Luna" owned by Benjamin Fuqua, the hotel of Winslow Turner, Adam Zumwalt's home and "kitchen," the Stephen Smith house, the home of George W. Davis, Best's home and smokehouse, and the Geron Hinds home.

Those structures built after 1831 included the John Castleman home, the Joseph Lawler home, the Thomas R. Miller home, the Eli Mitchell home, Stephen Smith's store, the store of Horace Eggleston, the home of William Arrington, the Joseph Martin home, Martin's mill, the home of Jacob C. Darst, the home of Dr. J.H.C. Miller, and James B. Patrick's new house.

By 1835, ninety-two of the 252 lots in the inner town were deeded; twenty-six of the deed lots had structures erected on them. All of the deed lots were west of the main plaza. At the time, only eighteen lots in the western portion of town were unsold. All of the northeastern and southeastern portions of town were still available for purchase.

The appraisal of lots was determined by their location. Valued highest were those blocks near the jail plaza; the lowest appraisals were in those blocks at the northern and southern end of town. Appraisals ranged from $17 for "Luna" and Turner's hotel to $7 for Branch's house.

A large majority of the lots sold in the outer town were west of Water Street; of 450 lots there, 123 were sold, most of them along the banks of the San Marcos River to the west and the Guadalupe to the south. In the area of the outer town east of Water Street, only twenty-two of 940 lots were sold, most of them directly east of the inner town.

Once Green DeWitt's *empresario* contract expired in April 1831, he showed no further interest in either leading or developing Gonzales. He became just another citizen and never held any elected political office.

In all, 189 land titles were issued in the DeWitt colony. Green was eligible for the "premium land" reflecting that number, but he received only the amount for bringing in one hundred families. At the time of his death in 1835, he was still owed the prorated portion of premium land.

The *empresario's* assumed profits never materialized. His premium lands were speculative and of no immediate value. Their value lay in the future and since they were carefully selected, DeWitt left a handsome landed estate to his children. Otherwise, Green DeWitt died a poor man. He clearly lacked the salesmanship, organizational abilities, zeal, and fervor of Stephen F. Austin. J.C. Clopper observed that "dissipation and neglectful indolence have destroyed his energies."

In 1831, his wife, Sarah Seely DeWitt, petitioned the government for an outright gift of land in her own maiden name. Typically, land was given to people who had preformed some rewarding service for the state or to poor individuals who had suffered much hardship. In her petition Sarah noted that her family had suffered much due to Indian incursions and supply shortages. She also stated that her husband "finds himself much embarrassed in his affairs on account of the enterprise that he has undertaken, and because of other circumstances which have placed the family in an unfortunate situation." In hopes of preserving a secure estate for herself and the children, Sarah asked for the league of land on which she then lived.

In endorsing his wife's petition, Green commented that he had sold her considerable amount of property and invested the money in his colonial schemes when they married. Since he had no way of reimbursing her at the time, DeWitt hoped that the government would cede her the land for her security.

On April 15, 1831, the league of land was granted Sarah personally "for herself and her heirs forever." Sarah Seely League is directly opposite Gonzales on the right bank of the Guadalupe River.[2]

From October 1828, until November 1832, the DeWitt colony was subject to the jurisdiction of the *ayuntamiento* of San Felipe de Austin and its civil and criminal code. During this time it was known as the District of Gonzales. Fielding Porter, *comisario* of police there, held office until June 1830, when he was murdered by Hirman Friley. After being escorted to San Felipe by Capt. Henry S. Brown, Friley was put in chains. On August 24, he escaped with the help of his friend, Noah Smithwick, who smuggled him a file and weapon. Friley was later killed attempting to escape from his hiding place in the hills. As punishment for aiding the prisoner in his escape, Smithwick was banished from Texas and did not return until 1835.

In August 1830, the Gonzales district elected another *comisario*, James B. Patrick, who defeated Silas Fuqua by a vote of 38 to 18. After completing Porter's term, Patrick was reelected in the general election that December.

According to Mexican law, once a municipality had more than 200 residents, it was required to elect an *ayuntamiento* composed of one *alcalde* (mayor), two *regidores* (councilmen), and a *sindico procurador* (city attorney) for one-year terms.

In November 1832, Commissioner Navarro appointed the first official municipal government of Gonzales. He selected Ezekiel Williams as *alcalde*, Winslow Turner as first *regidore*, Silas Fuqua as second *regidore*, and Stephen Smith as *sindico procurador*. They served until the lawful election in December when James B. Patrick, Silas Fuqua, Charles Lockhart, and Almond Cottle were chosen for these posts, respectively.

The first Gonzales *ayuntamiento* began sessions in January 1833. One of its first acts limited an individual to owning two inner town lots and four outer town lots.

During the February session, the *ayuntamiento* authorized the construction of a ferry across the Guadalupe River since there was no suitable fording place near town. The council contracted with Stephen Smith and John McCoy to build such a ferry at a cost of $95.75. Once the project was completed in July 1833, the *ayuntamiento* enacted the following rate schedule for users: $1.50 for a loaded wagon; $1.00 for an unloaded wagon; 12¢ for a man on horseback.

The Gonzales council also required that all able-bodied males must work a maximum of six days per year maintaining the two main roads. Such men would be fined $1.00 for each day of road work missed up to a maximum fine of $6.00 per year.

On May 28, 1833, John Francis Buetti was employed as translator and to "teach a Spanish school for six months at a salary of $220." Buetti was released of his duties at his own request on July 10.

In December 1833, the following officials were elected; James C. Davis, *alcalde;* Charles Lockhart, first *regidore;* Eli Mitchell, second *regidore;* Thomas R. Miller, *sindico procurador*. The next month Miller's home was rented for $18.00 a year as a municipal office.

By 1834 Horace Eggleston, Thomas R. Miller, and Stephen Smith were engaged as retail merchants in Gonzales. James B. Patrick was involved in wholesale trade. A credit economy was evolving; the *ayuntamiento* had set a 10% ceiling on interest rates.

The council in 1834 passed an ordinance prohibiting the shooting of guns or pistols within the boundaries of the inner town. The running of horses through town streets was likewise prohibited. Violators were subject to a fine of $25.00.

In hopes of stimulating investment, this session of the council repealed any limit on owning lots in the outer town; the investor could own as many lots as he was willing to improve.

In early summer of 1834, the first real "ball" in Gonzales was held at the new Miller Hotel. Colonists came from forty miles around to dance to the music of fiddlers John Tinsley and Washington Cottle. Mrs. Mulkego Williams and Miss Samanthia Burnes opened at the head of the Virginia Reel, which began the dance in the twenty-by-forty-foot hotel dining room lighted with candles. Cakes made of eggs, butter, and sugar were served with black coffee. The dance lasted until eight the next morning.

In December 1834, a new *ayuntamiento* was elected with Andrew Ponton chosen as *alcalde* and Joseph D. Clements as second *regidore*, two officials whose actions were to trigger the Texas Revolution.

From 1833 on, the DeWitt colony proved to be the least troublesome and most conciliatory toward the Mexican government. When Antonio López de Santa Anna led a revolt against the military regime of Gen. Anastacio Bustamante in December 1832, the Gonzales *ayuntamiento* issued a statement indicating reasons for their neutrality even as other such bodies declared for Santa Anna.

When reform-minded colonists held a convention at San Felipe on October 1, 1832, the Gonzales council was represented by Henry S. Brown and Claiborne Stinnet. After Mexican authorities informed them that their actions were illegal and asked to what extent they had participated, the Gonzales *ayuntamiento* replied in apologetic and disavowing terms.

When a similar convention was held at San Felipe in April 1833, the Gonzales council was represented by the same two delegates. This gathering went so far as to draft a state constitution for Texas. Some two weeks after they adjourned, Gonzales *alcalde* James B. Patrick informed the *jefepolitico* that the DeWitt colony favored separate statehood for Texas. When Patrick received a letter of censure in May 1833, the Gonzales council again attempted to explain away and apologize for their statehood sentiments.

A showdown was triggered in March and April of 1835, when the Monclova legislature passed a series of land laws allowing the unscrupulous sale of thousands of acres of Texas land to a small number of Anglo-American speculators. After a second such great land sale, Santa Anna annulled the legislation by decree and sent Gen. Martin Perfecto de Cos to Monclova to enforce his decision. Once the last land law was passed on April 7, the state legislature disbanded, and the government was captured attempting to flee to San Antonio. Among the few who remained in Monclova was Green DeWitt, who stayed to fight in the impending civil war. He soon contracted cholera, died on May 18, 1835, and was buried in an unmarked grave.

After Santa Anna dissolved the legislature of Coahuila-Texas, the DeWitt colony selected a committee of safety headquartered at Gonzales. The committee consisted of James B. Patrick, William Arrington, John Fisher, George W. Davis, Andrew Ponton, Bartlett McClure, and James Hodges.

When William B. Travis captured the Mexican post at Anahuac in late June 1835, he was denounced by the Gonzales *ayuntamiento.* Upon the urging of Edward Gritten, a special representative of Col. Domingo de Ugartechea, the body also proclaimed its loyalty to the Mexican government.

Dr. J. H. C. Miller of Gonzales even suggested the arrest of those responsible for the Anahuac clash. Dr. Miller, a strong loyalist, wanted all agitators removed and blamed the "war and speculating parties" for encouraging hostilities. Although Miller finally professed loyalty to the Republic of Texas in 1836, this man whom John Henry Brown referred to as a "Tory," "traitor," and "spy" was soon forced to flee Texas because of his earlier beliefs.

On September 26, 1835, delegates were elected to represent the Gonzales municipality in the general consultation to be held on October 15. Those elected were James Hodges, Joseph D. Clements, Benjamin Fuqua, Thomas R. Miller, and William S. Fisher. On October 4, William W. Arrington and George W. Davis were also elected to attend.

After the Anahuac disturbance, Colonel Ugartechea decided to disarm the Gonzales colonists, recover their six-pound cannon, and return it to San Antonio. This decision set the stage for the Battle of Gonzales.

In late September 1835, Cpl. Casimiro De Leon and a five-man company were sent to recover this obsolete weapon. Unknown to him, the Gonzales colonists had voted to keep the cannon and had buried it in the peach orchard of George W. Davis. Many local residents had moved their families to safety, and there were only eighteen men in Gonzales at the time. *Alcalde* Andrew Ponton thus sent Matthew "Old Paint" Caldwell to get help from Anglo-American settlements to the east, even as Corporal De Leon patiently waited across the Guadalupe for the cannon to be delivered. (Today there are two state markers at the site where the "Old Eighteen" refused to surrender the cannon to the Mexican soldiers. Both markers are located just off State Highway 183 at the south end of the Guadalupe River bridge as you enter Gonzales.)

On September 26, 1835, Ponton informed Colonel Ugartechea that he would surrender the cannon only when ordered to do so by the *jefepolitico* of the Department of Brazos, James B. Miller, who would never give such an order. Ponton also claimed to be under the impression that the cannon had been given to the colony in perpetuity for protection from Indian raids.

Ugartechea responded by sending Lt. Francisco Castaneda and one hundred Mexican cavalrymen to retrieve the cannon by force, if necessary, and not to be put off with excuses. Castaneda was also ordered to arrest Ponton and to punish those who resisted.

Late in the afternoon on September 28, twelve colonists crossed the Guadalupe and surprised De Leon and his men. The small Mexican detachment surrendered, were disarmed, and taken as prisoners to Gonzales. One of the Mexicans escaped while retrieving their horses and told Castaneda of their situation. Within a half mile of Gonzales, another soldier who had been released told Castaneda that an estimated 200 Anglo reinforcements had poured into town in the past two days.

By this time the colonists had deployed along the left bank of the Guadalupe and removed the ferry and all boats to their side of the river. Castaneda then wisely withdrew from his exposed position on the river bank. He then asked for an interview with the *alcalde* and was told that Ponton would return the next morning.

The next day, September 30, Lieutenant Castaneda appeared at the river crossing for the scheduled meeting with Ponton. He was told by *regidore* Joseph Clements that Ponton still had not returned, and that Clements would discuss the matter. The Mexican leader returned later in the day and asked Clements to surrender the cannon. The *regidore* replied that only through force would the cannon be given up and ended his prepared statement as follows: "We are weak and few in number, nevertheless, we are contending for what we believe to be just principles."

In communicating with Ugartechea on September 29, Castaneda said he appeared to be outnumbered and was ordered not to engage if such was the case. Castaneda decided to remain, however, and informed Ugartechea on September 30 that he would move up the river to look for a fording place. That night his force encamped some 300 yards from the river at DeWitt Mound. The next day, October 1, Castaneda's men moved upriver some seven miles and encamped at Ezekiel Williams' ranch, where they devoured his unpicked watermelons.

On September 29 there were only eighteen men in Gonzales — the "Old Eighteen." By the following night there were 150 armed men in town. Assuming that Castaneda would attack once he found a place to ford the river, the colonists decided to take the initiative. They organized and elected John H. Moore, a resident of LaGrange, as colonel and commander of the group; J.W.E. Wallace was elected lieutenant colonel. Wallace had lived in Gonzales since 1831 but owned a league of land in Austin's colony.

The six-pound cannon was then unearthed by John Darst, one of the Sowells, and Richard Chisholm. After removing the spike from the touchhole and cleaning it, they mounted the weapon on the axle of Eli Mitchell's cotton wagon. Their ammunition consisted of pieces of chain, metal scraps, and cut-up horseshoes forged into iron balls.

On the evening of October 1, fifty mounted colonists crossed the river with the cannon, then waited for the remainder of the army to cross on foot. Once they were all assembled on the other side of the Guadalupe, the men heard a sermon by Rev. W.P. Smith, an itinerant Methodist preacher from Moore's settlement.

That night the force moved upriver looking for Castaneda and hoping to attack at daybreak. When they were near the Mexican camp, Moore formed his men for an attack with the cannon in the center, the unmounted troops on either side, and fifty mounted men in front of the cannon. A thin skirmish line sent ahead of the main force was fired on by a Mexican picket, who wounded one of the colonists. Moore then relocated his cavalry at the right of the battle line.

Shortly after 5:00 a.m. on October 2, a dense fog lifted to reveal the two sides only 300 yards apart with the Mexicans on higher ground. When Colonel Moore's men opened fire, Castaneda retreated out of range and suggested a parley with Moore. When the two leaders met on an open prairie, Moore stated that his men were fighting in self-defense and to uphold the Mexican Constitution of 1824. Castaneda replied that he, too, believed in republican principles and that he simply wanted the cannon. At that point Moore asked Castaneda to either surrender and join the colonists or fight. Castaneda ended the discussion by saying he must obey his orders.

Both leaders returned to their ranks, but before Castaneda could order a retreat, the colonists fired the cannon once, killing one of the enemy. The Mexican detachment then scurried back toward San Antonio. During the excitement, one of Moore's men suffered a nosebleed when he fell off his rearing horse. Thus ended the Battle of Gonzales, which was actually fought near present Cost, Texas.[3]

By the next day, October 3, there were some 300 men in Gonzales. This force included Col. John H. Moore and his company from LaGrange, James W. Fannin and the Brazos Guard, Coleman with his Bastrop company, and a smaller unit from the Colorado district under Capt. Thomas Alley. Others present included William B. Travis, Ben Milam, John A. Wharton, and William H. Jack. Noah Smithwick, who arrived the day after the battle, observed that "we were all ready to fight."

Using John Sowell's blacksmith shop at Gonzales, gunsmith Smithwick described putting the arms in order:

> . . . We brushed the old cannon (an iron six-pounder), scoured it out, and mounted it on old wooden trucks — transverse sections of trees with holes in the center, into which were inserted wooden axles — and christened it "the flying artillery," . . . .We had no ammunition for our "artillery," so we cut slugs of bar iron and hammered them into balls; ugly looking missiles they were I assure you, . . .

After a war board was organized, they requested that Stephen F. Austin come to Gonzales and assume command of this first Texas army. By October 11, however, the men were demanding that they elect their leader, although a majority could not agree on any one commander. An agreement was then reached among the ranks to select Austin, who was in feeble condition due to his long imprisonment in Mexico City. Austin made a rousing speech in which he said, "I will wear myself out by inches rather than submit to Santa Anna's arbitrary rule. . . .Retreat is now impossible; we must go forward to victory." He was also promoted by John A. Wharton, who said that Austin could best unite the people and give them better standing abroad.

According to Creed Taylor, one of those present, a committee of six men was selected on October 6 to design a flag for Austin's army. It was made by Sarah Seely DeWitt and her daughter, Naomi Matthews. This "Old Cannon" flag, made from Naomi's wedding dress, was six feet long, three feet wide, and stitched of coarse white cotton cloth. In the center was a picture of the little cannon painted in black. A single black star was sewn above the cannon; beneath the cannon were the words: "Come and Take It."

On the morning of October 12, the Texan volunteer army of 600 broke camp and started for San Antonio under their new battle flag. Lt. Almeron Dickinson commanded the six-pound cannon, which was mounted on a carriage pulled by two yokes of Texas Longhorns.

The force was armed with Bowie knives and long single-barreled, muzzle-loading flintlock rifles. A company of lancers was also formed when some of the men converted old files into lances, then mounted them on poles cut in the river bottom.

On October 13, the dry axles began to smoke and the cannon carriage broke down. At that point the cannon was abandoned and buried on the west bank of Sandies Creek near the Old San Antonio Road (now State Highway 21). Both the carriage and the "Come and Take It" flag were burned, creating the appearance of an Indian campfire.[4]

Soon after the Siege of Bexar began on October 24, Commander Austin received two letters dated November 4 from L. Smither, who had been left in charge at Gonzales. The desperate situation in which Susanna Dickinson found herself is alluded to in both notes. In the first one, Smither said:

> . . . the companes that is coming on when in this place has broken open almost Evry house in this place and stole 100 dollars or thir about of Miller and treated the wimon of this place worse than all the comanshee nation could have done and draged me out of the house of Mrs. Dickerson ho thiy I have no doubt they would have kild if I had not bean there. . .

In the second letter Smither noted:

> . . . and finding the mob in town Mrs. Dickerson ho had been driven from her house cald on me to go and stay in her house to protect her person and property
>
> after goind to Bead thiy Enterd the house twice by bursting Evry door and window and coming in crowds and dragd me into the Streats and beat my head to a poltice and sould have kild me in the most torturing manner for no caws on earth but that I was in the house I used Evey means to pasefy them but the wild savage would have adherd with more humility. . . the wild savages would be preferable to the Insults of such Canebols. . .

After Ben Milam and 300 volunteers stormed San Antonio on December 4, the Siege of Bexar ended five days later when General Cos surrendered the Alamo, 1,600 Mexican troops, and twenty cannon to Gen. Edward Burleson and the Texian army. At this point most of the volunteer troops, who had signed up for only two months, assumed the war was over and returned to their farms.

On February 1, 1836, the Gonzales municipality elected two delegates to attend the convention at Washington-on-the-Brazos. The election results were as follows: Matthew Caldwell, 44 votes; John Fisher, 43 votes; Byrd Lockhart, 21 votes; Joseph D. Clements, 20 votes; Pleasant Bull, 7 votes.

Matthew Caldwell was born in Kentucky on March 8, 1798. The bachelor came to Texas from Missouri and was issued title to one league of land in DeWitt's colony in present Lavaca County on February 20, 1831.

John Fisher was born in Richmond, Virginia, on January 18, 1800. He migrated to Texas from Virginia in April 1832 and settled at Gonzales. His brother, William S. Fisher, led a company at the Battle of San Jacinto and was commander of the ill-fated Mier Expedition.

Both Caldwell and Fisher were seated at the convention on March 1, 1836. They were present the next day when the Texas Declaration of Independence was adopted. On March 2, Caldwell was appointed as courier to carry expresses to the Texas army. He left that day and did not return before the convention adjourned on March 17. At that time Fisher joined the "Runaway Scrape" and was seen at the Neches River headed for the United States on April 20.[5]

On February 23, 1836, General Santa Anna arrived at San Antonio and began a thirteen-day siege of the Alamo and the 150 men commanded by Lt. Col. William B. Travis. That very day one of

Travis' first requests for men and supplies was taken by Capt. Albert Martin to his hometown of Gonzales. *Alcalde* Andrew Ponton was also requested to immediately inform San Felipe de Austin of the situation.

Travis sent out four dramatic appeals for aid during the siege, and the *only* effective response came from the men of Gonzales. They had earlier organized a volunteer home guard unit, "The Gonzales Ranging Company of Mounted Volunteers," and had elected George Kimball, formerly a hatter from New York, as captain and commander. The original force consisted of twenty-two men; by the time they reached the outer limits of the DeWitt colony, ten more joined the group.

As the company went by the home of Sarah Seely DeWitt, her fourteen-year-old son, Columbus, insisted on joining the group, saying he could ride and shoot as well as any man. The worried mother gave Captain Kimball some type of signal, then told the lad to go fetch his horse some distance away. Once Columbus left, the company speedily departed.

Included in the Gonzales company were forty-two-year-old Isaac Millsaps (who left a blind wife and seven children behind) and three sixteen-year-old boys — William P. King, Galba Fuqua, and John E. Gaston, who was the stepson of George W. Davis.

When the company stopped at John Gladden King's stage stand, the robust man volunteered to join the group. Just as they were leaving, King's tall son, William P., thinking of his mother Millie and his nine brothers and sisters, caught the reins of Martin's horse and asked to take his father's place. After a brief argument Martin turned to Millie King and asked which of the two she could afford to lose. Although her husband protested when Millie turned to William, John Gladden King was detailed to remain at the stage stand, guard the food supply, and help those who followed to the relief of the Alamo.

Led by Captains Martin and Kimball and guided by John W. Smith of San Antonio, the "Immortal Thirty-two" broke through the surprised Mexican line and entered a door of the northeast corner of the Alamo at 3:30 A.M. on Tuesday, March 1, 1836.[6]

At the time, there were already eight other DeWitt colonists who had been in the Alamo since the beginning of the siege. They were Daniel Bourne, George Brown, Almeron Dickinson, Andrew Duvalt, John Harris, William Lightfoot, Dr. Amos Pollard, and Marcus L. Sewell.

The Gonzales arrivals were immediately assigned to positions along the north and east walls. Billy King, the only man to enter the Alamo without a gun, was assigned to Sgt. William Ward's cannon. Captains Martin and Kimball took command of their sections of the walls, and the rest of their men assumed the roles of riflemen.

On March 3, 1836, Pvt. Isaac Millsaps wrote the following letter to his family:

> My dear ones
> . . . All of our boys are well & Capt. Martin is in good spirits. . . . Col. Bowie is down sick and had to be in bed I saw him yesterday & he is still ready to fight. . . He tells all that help will be here soon and it makes us feel good. We have beef & corn to eat but no coffee, bag I had fell off on the way here so it was all spilt. I have not seen Travis but 2 times since here he told us all this morning that Fanning was going to be here early with many men and there would be a good fight. He stays on the wall some but mostly to his room I hope help comes soon cause we can't fight them all. Some say he is going to talk some tonight & group us better for defence. If we fail here get to the river with the children all Texas will be before the enemy we get so little news here we know nothing. There is no discontent in our boys some are tired from loss of sleep and rest. The mexicans are shooting every few minutes but most of the shots fall inside & do no harm. I don't know what else to say they are calling for all letters, kiss the dear children for me and believe as I do that all will be well & God protects us all. If any men come through there tell them to hurry with powder for it is short I hope you get this & know I love you all.
>
> Isaac

Several Gonzales residents played significant individual roles in the defense of the Alamo. Dr. Amos Pollard, one of the five physicians in the old mission, was placed in charge of the hospital, the second floor of the former convent located just north of and adjacent to the chapel.

Almeron Dickinson, captain of artillery, was one of ninety men who stayed on in occupied San Antonio after General Cos surrendered. With a crew of eleven, he was in personal command of the three twelve-pound cannon mounted on a platform in the rear of the roofless Alamo chapel.

During the thirteen-day siege, Almeron's wife, Susanna Dickinson, helped Dr. Pollard by nursing the sick and wounded. She was also an excellent cook and helped the Mexican women prepare beef, corn, beans, and tortillas in the kitchen on the first floor of the old convent.

About 10:00 the last night before the Mexican assault, Colonel Travis made a hurried visit to the chapel and sought out fifteen-month-old Angelina Dickinson. Travis had arrived at the Alamo in early February with a betrothal gift from his sweetheart, Rebecca Cummings. The gift was a hammered gold ring set with a black cat's--eye stone. Travis removed the gold ring, threaded it with a piece of string, placed it around Angelina's neck, hugged her, and said, "I won't have any more use for this, honey. Keep it to remember me." He obviously expected the women and children to be spared and was confident that Santa Anna would not harm a baby girl.

The three-part assault on the Alamo began at 5:00 a.m. in biting predawn cold on Sunday, March 6, 1836. The chapel was the last point taken by the Mexicans about 6:30 a.m. Amid the din of the battle, Susanna Dickinson and her baby girl took refuge in a dark little sacristy in the northern rear of the chapel. Her husband, Almeron, along with Jim Bonham and their small crew, were operating three cannon from the platform above her.

As the Mexicans poured into the Alamo plaza, Galba Fuqua ran into the chapel looking for Mrs. Dickinson. His jaw had been shattered by enemy fire, but Galba tried desperately to tell Susanna something, most likely a final message for his parents. When she said she could not understand him, the boy made a futile attempt to hold his shattered, bleeding jaws in place with his hands. As Susanna again shook her head negatively, the lad nodded, gave her a final pathetic glance, and returned to the walls to die.

Once the Mexicans were in the plaza compound, Captain Dickinson rushed into the sacristy and said, "Great God, Sue! The Mexicans are inside our walls! All is lost! If they spare you, love our child!" After kissing his wife he drew his sword and returned to his battle station. He either died by his cannon or at the foot of the east chapel wall when shot trying to leap to his escape.

All 189 male defenders of the Alamo perished. Susanna Dickinson was the only Anglo adult among the twenty-one women and children who survived the assault. As she was led from the chapel by Gen. Manuel F. Castrillon, she was hit in the calf of her right leg by a stray Mexican bullet.

The next day, March 7, Santa Anna received the survivors at his headquarters. While Susanna's calf wound was dressed, Santa Anna began to pet and admire little Angelina incessantly. Suddenly, he offered to adopt her, send the little girl to Mexico City, and raise her as his own child. Angelina would have all that money could buy, including the best schools and clothes, and her mother could come along!

Susanna desperately objected to the idea with help from Col. Juan Almonte, who persuaded a reluctant Santa Anna to forget the proposition. In a tone of resigned disgust, he suddenly announced that Mrs. Dickinson and her baby, with the black servant Ben as escort, would be sent to Gonzales with a message for Gen. Sam Houston. In the letter Santa Anna vowed to punish the ungrateful criminals but to protect the innocent not implicated in the rebellion.

When the pathetic little party left San Antonio, Mrs. Dickinson was on horseback, babe in arms, accompanied by Ben riding a horse beside her. A few miles beyond the Salado, Travis' black body servant, Joe, joined them after fleeing the city on foot.

By noon on March 13, this forlorn foursome was within twenty miles of Gonzales when they saw three horsemen fast approaching: scouts sent out by Houston. The general had reached Gonzales on the evening of March 11 to take command of the 374 volunteers gathered there. He had immediately heard details of the fall of the Alamo from two friendly Mexicans, Anselmo Borgara and Andres Barcena, who lived on *ranchos* near San Antonio. In order to prevent a panic, the wily Houston had them jailed as spies; nevertheless, twenty soldiers left camp that very night to care for their families.

On March 13, General Houston sent out scouts Deaf Smith, Henry Wax Karnes, and R.E. Handy to learn the exact Alamo situation, then report back within three days. When they met Mrs. Dickinson, Karnes rushed the news back to Houston while Smith and Handy stayed behind to accompany the survivors. With fatherly tenderness Deaf cradled little Angelina the rest of the way even as he learned from her mother that *all* of his old Gonzales friends were dead.

After arriving at Gonzales about 8:00 that night, Susanna sobbed out her story "of the butchering and burning, with some of the most stirring details" to General Houston, who held her hand and sobbed. As R.E. Handy remembered the scene, "for four and twenty hours after the news reached us, not a sound was heard save the wild shrieks of women and heart rending screams of their fatherless children. . ."[7]

After reading Santa Anna's letter and being told by Susanna

that a Mexican army of 2,000 was already at the Cibolo and headed his way, Houston ordered an immediate retreat eastward and the burning of Gonzales so it would be of no value to Santa Anna's forces. By 8:30 p.m. his troops were breaking camp; by 11:00 p.m. the families were all out of town. Once Gonzales was evacuated, a rear guard detachment of ten led by Captain Sharp began setting the town on fire. They were divided into two groups and began to burn buildings at opposite ends of town. The structures burned easily, and within minutes the town was an inferno. By dawn all of Gonzales was in ashes except for Adam Zumwalt's kitchen and Andrew Ponton's smokehouse, both of which were heavily damaged.

On the second day of his retreat, General Houston stopped at Bartlett McClure's log house on Peach Creek. McClure and his wife, Sarah Ann Ashby, had come to Texas from Kentucky in 1831 and settled ten miles east of Gonzales. Bartlett had been sent to East Texas to recruit "Redlanders" to fight, and Sarah was at her home with twenty-seven wives of Alamo defenders when they learned of their husbands' deaths. The large live oak in Sarah's front yard (the Sam Houston Oak) was the general's headquarters for a brief time.

Before the women fled, Sarah Ann penned messages in English and Spanish asking the Mexicans not to burn her house. Santa Anna and his army later camped on Peach Creek, and he stayed in the McClure house part of the time. When he departed his troops drove off or killed all the livestock, filled the wells with bricks from the kitchen floor, and burned everything except the dwelling house.

After the Battle of San Jacinto, the McClures came home and started building a fine two-story house on the original site in 1837. Modeled after Sarah Ann's father's home in Kentucky, it was completed in 1839. McClure, the first chief justice of Gonzales County, died on April 7, 1841, and was buried in the family cemetery near the house.[8]

After the Texian victory at San Jacinto, many Gonzales residents returned to rebuild their homes. Since there were no benchmarks in the burned-out area, many made camp on public property. When they were later asked to move, several families relocated up the Guadalupe River and settled in the area of Walnut Springs.

The site was founded in 1838 by thirty-four shareholders, all of them members of Matthew Caldwell's company of Gonzales Rangers. Ben McCulloch surveyed the townsite, then called Walnut

Springs. In 1839 the town name was changed to Seguin in honor of Juan Seguin, and it became the county seat of Guadalupe County.

Ben McCulloch was born on November 11, 1811, in Rutherford County, Tennessee. Without benefit of formal schooling, he became a well-educated man through extensive reading.

Ben and his younger brother, Henry, left Tennessee to follow David Crockett to Texas. However, a bout with measles delayed Ben's journey to the Alamo. After joining General Houston and the Texas army, he distinguished himself in the Battle of San Jacinto as commander of one of the six-pound cannons, the "Twin Sisters."

After 1836 McCulloch worked in Gonzales as a surveyor under Charles Lockhart. He was also a land speculator for a decade and represented Gonzales County in the First Legislature of the state of Texas.

Gonzales County was created by the Republic of Texas on December 14, 1837, with Gonzales as the county seat. The county covered the same area as the DeWitt colony and included portions of the present counties of Guadalupe, Caldwell, Comal, Lavaca, Fayette, DeWitt, Victoria, and Jackson.

The first Gonzales County court was organized on December 14, 1837. The first county officials included Bartlett McClure as chief justice, Ezekiel Williams as clerk, and Alfred Kelso as sheriff.

Soon thereafter the first courthouse was constructed in the Church Square, block 32. This one-room clapboard building was also used as a church, school, auditorium, and Masonic hall.

On September 3, 1838, the first district court organized with Judge James W. Robinson presiding, George W. Davis as clerk, and J.D. Clements as foreman of the first grand jury.

The first Gonzales post office opened on January 25, 1839, with Ezekiel Williams as postmaster. In March the city of Gonzales was incorporated, and W.W.T. Smith was elected as first mayor in 1840.

On March 19, 1839, Christopher C. DeWitt was granted permission by the county to establish a ferry "across the Guadalupe River at the Old Crossing." He operated this ferry until 1868.

At different times two town public squares served as the center of the Gonzales business district. One was the square bordered by St. Louis, St. James, St. Lawrence, and St. Joseph streets. Originally designated as Municipal Square in 1831, it is now Texas Heroes Square. The other square was bordered by St. Lawrence, St. Joseph, St.

George, and St. Paul streets. First designated as Jail Square in 1831, it was later changed to Market Square, then Confederate Square.

After arriving with her family in Gonzales in 1840, Mrs. John DuBose observed that there were seven or eight very good stores in town.

In 1845 Frederick David Meyer opened a cabinet shop in Gonzales. The Winslow Turner Hotel was also built on the south side of the 200 block of St. John Street. One of the first drugstores in town was the firm of E.L. Beaumont and Company, druggist and chemist. A soda fountain was added in 1854.

In 1852 Judge W.V. Collins built the Collins House, the first brick hotel in Gonzales, on the site of Adam Zumwalt's log home. It was also referred to as the Gayosa House, the name of a pretentious hotel in Nashville. Judge Collins sold his hotel to Nickelson and Company in 1854. Three years later, Captain Keyser purchased the place and renamed it the Keyser House. He registered the names of guests in ornate handwriting from 1857 until 1886. (The hotel registers are displayed in the Gonzales Memorial Museum.) At that time the Keyser House was torn down to make room for the Plaza Hotel, which was destroyed by fire in 1966.

In 1853 John William August Kleine, Sr., a German immigrant, opened the Kleine Furniture Store on the northeast corner of St. James and St. Matthew streets. Kleine, an expert cabinetmaker, built furniture and coffins from native trees.

John Cox opened another furniture store in 1853. J. Guichard's store sold fancy dry goods, hardware, French liquors, fruit preserves, cigars, and groceries.

By 1854 Gonzales had eleven large dry goods and provision stores, two drugstores, two furniture stores, one silversmith shop, two hotels, several boardinghouses, four blacksmiths, two livery stables, three or four carpenter shops, two tailor shops, two paint shops, two bakeries, a printing office, and a newspaper.

On January 31, 1854, John Mooney of Gonzales was authorized by state law to build a toll bridge across the San Marcos River a mile and a half above Gonzales. The bridge was completed by Mooney and Peck on March 15, 1856.

The oldest structure in Gonzales is the Horace Eggleston House, one of the first homes erected after the town was rebuilt. Eggleston, a native of Ontario County, New York, married Sarah

Ann Ponton on May 3, 1835, and they had six children. The well-to-do merchant and attorney had fought in the Battle of San Jacinto.

After purchasing the site for his home in 1845— lots 1 to 6 in block 15 of the inner town — Eggleston built the house in 1848. It originally faced the Guadalupe River on St. Michael Street. This "dog-run" cabin was built from some eighty logs. The heavy timbers were handsawed in a pit by using a "whipsaw." Deep notches were cut in the corners, then dovetailed to provide almost airtight joints. Spaces between the logs were filled with mud, then plastered over with clay.

The cabin had two large rooms with a wide, open hall ("dog run") between them. For protection against intruders, there was no outside door. Two doors opened onto the dog run on either side, and sturdy dogs kept watch throughout the night and day.

Doors and windows were cut out after all the logs were in place. Window panes were made of paper and coated with hog lard or bear grease. The house also had a brick fireplace.

Horace Eggleston died on March 10, 1855. His house was used for a time as a hotel for travelers.[9]

The Fly House is on the site of a home built by Andrew Ponton, the second *alcalde* of DeWitt colony. Ponton's residence occupied block 12, lot 1, and was burned prior to the Runaway Scrape except for the smokehouse. After San Jacinto, Andrew rebuilt a substantial house of walnut timber on the original site. The remains of his old chimney up to the hearth stone can be seen under the house.[10]

After the Texas Revolution, Gonzales men continued a noble tradition of military service. In January 1837, a law provided for a Ranger company of fifty-six men to protect the Gonzales County frontier. President Sam Houston selected Joel W. Robison as first lieutenant and Nathan Mitchell as second lieutenant.

Evidently, Indians were still an ever-present danger in the area. On December 9, 1838, a band of Comanches carried off four children of Mitchel Putnam, who lived two miles below Gonzales on the Guadalupe River. Rhoda (age seventeen), James (age ten), Elizabeth (age six), and Juda (age two) were gathering pecans in the woods at the time of the raid. At the same time the Comanches captured Matilda Lockhart (age thirteen), the daughter of Putnam's neighbor, Andrew.[11] A few months later, James and Juda were returned to their parents. Elizabeth was kept for two years before her father traded a gray mule for her. Rhoda took an Indian husband and stayed with the tribe for twenty-seven years before being returned to her family.

On January 15, 1839, President Lamar named Matthew Caldwell captain of a Ranger company for the defense of Goliad. On March 23, Caldwell was appointed a company captain in the First Regiment of Infantry.

In the Battle of Plum Creek (August 1840), a force of 200 volunteer militia led by Maj. Gen. Felix Huston, Col. Edward Burleson, and Capt. Matthew Caldwell intercepted some 600 Comanches and Kiowas retreating to the high plains with 1,500 stolen horses and mules. The fifteen-mile running battle began five miles southeast of present Lockhart and continued to present Kyle. Eighty-six Indians were killed with only two militia dead, but the marauders managed to get away with most of their loot.

Gonzales volunteers at Plum Creek included Captain Caldwell and some of his Rangers, Capt. John James Tumlinson and his company, James Bird, Ben McCulloch, C.C. DeWitt, Alonzo B. Sweitzer, Andrew Liel, Kit Achlin Gipson, Charles Braches, Dr. Caleb S. Brown (surgeon), Thomas W. Short, and David S.H. Darst.

In June 1841, "Old Paint" Caldwell served as captain of Company D in the ill-fated Santa Fe Expedition. Upon his release from Perote Prison in Mexico, he hastened to the relief of San Antonio after the city was captured by Brig. Gen. Adrian Woll and 1,300 Mexican troops on September 10, 1842. The mayor of San Antonio, John W. Smith, escaped and sent a note to Gonzales asking for help.

On September 12, Caldwell and eighty-five men arrived at Seguin, where he was elected to command the volunteer force of 210 men. Texas Ranger Capt. John Coffee "Jack" Hays was chosen to lead a scouting company of forty-two of the best mounted men.

By midnight on September 17, Caldwell's force was camped on the east bank of Salado Creek, some six miles northeast of San Antonio. Protected by a natural embankment and dense timber, his men could shoot into an open prairie to the east and northeast. "Old Paint" decided to make his stand in this location and sent Hays' company into town to lure the enemy into his trap.

Shortly after 9:00 a.m. on September 18, Hays and seven other Rangers approached the Alamo at a gallop from the east; shouting insults and cutting capers, they challenged the Mexicans to come out and fight. When Captain Perez and 150 cavalrymen gave chase, Hays' men retreated toward Caldwell's position and engaged in a long-range skirmish with the Mexican cavalry.

About 1:00 P.M., General Woll arrived with 400 infantry reinforcements, 160 more dragoons, and two artillery pieces. After Woll formed his men into two battle lines — infantry and cavalry — on the prairie, Caldwell sent out only fifteen to twenty men at a time to skirmish with the enemy for the next few hours.

It was growing late when Woll finally ordered his infantry to make a frontal assault on the Texian position in the creek bottom. As they charged across the open prairie, protected marksmen dropped Mexicans by the score, most being hit in the head or breast. One of Caldwell's men remarked that "it was such an easy-going affair" and "seemed like child's play." Toward sunset Woll reassembled his battered troops and ordered a retreat to San Antonio.

During the daylong Battle of Salado, Captain Caldwell lost only one man. Stephen Jett was killed by Indians who tried to steal his horse. Sixty Mexican bodies were left on the battlefield, while forty-four dead and 150 wounded troops were carried away. The next morning General Woll ordered a mass funeral in San Antonio rather than the planned grand victory *fandango.* On September 20, the defeated Mexican invasion army evacuated the city.

Matthew Caldwell was married twice, first to Mrs. H. Morrison in Washington County on May 17, 1837. After her death he married Mrs. Lily Lawley. Caldwell had three children: Martha married Ishham D. Davis; Ann married Johnson Baker Ellison; Curtis died as a boy.

Matthew Caldwell died at home in Gonzales on December 28, 1842, and was buried two days later with a military funeral in the Gonzales City Cemetery. Caldwell County was created and named for him on March 6, 1848. The State of Texas erected a five-foot gray granite marker at his grave in 1930.

Among those taking part in the Mier Expedition and the subsequent "lottery of death" was R.H. Dunham of Gonzales, who drew one of the seventeen black (or death) beans at Salado, Mexico, in late March 1843. Dunham was among 305 Texans who attacked Mier, Mexico, on December 25-26, 1842. After surrendering, they escaped into the mountains for six weeks before being recaptured at Salado. One-tenth of them were ordered to be shot. In the manner of a lottery, 159 white beans and seventeen black beans were poured into a clay pitcher. Then the Texan prisoners, chained together in pairs, were ordered to reach up into the pitcher and draw beans in alphabetical order.

After drawing one of the black beans, young Dunham wrote

the following letter to his mother, displayed today in the Gonzales Memorial Museum:

> Dear Mother:
>
> I write to you under the most awful feelings that a man ever addressed a mother for in half an hour my hour will be finished on earth for I am doomed to die by the hands of the Mexicans for our late attempt to escape the (order) of Santa Anna. That every tenth man should be shot. We drew lots, I was one of the unfortunate. I cannot say anything more. I die I hop with firmness farewell may God bless you and may He in this my last hour forgive and pardon all my sins.
>
> Farewell, your affectionate Son,
> R. H. Dunham

During the Mexican War, the most prominent Gonzales leader was Ben McCulloch. His first company of Texas militia was mustered into federal service on June 13, 1846, and discharged on August 18 the same year. McCulloch's company of Texas Rangers was assigned as the chief spy company under Gen. Zachary Taylor. The military intelligence they provided Taylor proved invaluable in the Battle of Buena Vista and may have saved the general from a disastrous surprise attack. Ben's second company of Texas Mounted Volunteers (Spies) was mustered in on January 31, 1847, and discharged on June 14 and July 31, 1847. His name became a household word as a result of Samuel Reid's book, *The Scouting Expedition of McCulloch's Texas Rangers.*

In 1849 Ben went west with the Forty-niners but found little gold in California. After serving as sheriff of Sacramento County from 1850 until 1852, he returned to Texas and was appointed United States marshal by President Franklin Pierce in 1853.

McCulloch was an avid reader of military strategy and tactics, but his lack of formal military training kept him from his ultimate ambition — commanding a U.S. cavalry regiment. A product of the frontier military tradition of natural leadership, he saw the West Point monopoly of command in the 1850s as a privileged military caste that endangered republican ideals.

Ben was bitterly disappointed when Secretary of War Jefferson Davis denied him command of one of two new cavalry regiments raised in 1855. He was likewise passed over in 1861 when a West Pointer, Earl Van Dorn, was assigned to command the Department of Texas.

From 1840 until his death in 1877, Thomas J. Pilgrim was the foremost religious and educational leader in Gonzales. He was born in Middlesex County, Connecticut, on December 4, 1805, and graduated from the Hamilton Theological and Literary Institute in New York. A licensed Baptist preacher and schoolteacher, Pilgrim came to Texas as one of the thirty-five settlers in Elias Wightman's colony. The group landed at Matagorda on the schooner *Little Zoe* in January 1829.

Pilgrim walked eighty miles to San Felipe, where he served as interpreter and translator of Spanish documents for Austin's colony and started the Austin Academy with forty students. In the spring of 1829, he organized the first Sunday school in Texas with thirty-two pupils. Within a few weeks Mexican authorities forced him to close the school.

Between 1831 and 1836, Pilgrim conducted school in the Columbia area. In 1838 he went into the mercantile business with Morgan R. Smith at Columbia. He also married Lucy Ives that year and received a land grant in Gonzales County. (The community of Pilgrim, located sixteen miles southwest of Gonzales, is on the land patented to him.)

After Lucy's death Thomas married Sarah Jane Bennett on April 13, 1841. Sarah was the daughter of Valentine Bennett, one of the "Old Eighteen." Five of their twelve children lived to adulthood in Gonzales. As the family grew, Pilgrim built a two-story house on the corner of St. Matthew and St. James streets.

In May 1847 Pilgrim organized the first Sunday school in Gonzales. He was also president of this Union Sunday School. In 1854 he reported an average attendance of thirty-two boys, forty-two girls, and a total of 304 instructed since the school began. In 1857 a committee was appointed to persuade more children to attend, and Thomas and Sarah Jane were assigned to the southwest quarter of town. For over thirty years, Pilgrim was actively involved in the Union Sunday School movement. (In February 1881 the school was finally divided when the Methodists organized their own Bible study.)

Thomas Pilgrim served as president of the board of trustees of Gonzales College and was a member of the board of visitors of Baylor University during the 1852-53 school year. He was also county treasurer and served as a justice of the peace for three terms. Pilgrim died on October 30, 1877, and was buried in the Gonzales City Cemetery as was wife Sarah Jane, who died on February 1,

1883. Their youngest child, Carey Judson, was owner and editor of the *Gonzales Inquirer*.

Another prominent newcomer, Dr. George Washington Barnett, settled in the Gonzales area in 1846. After practicing medicine in Tennessee and Mississippi, Dr. Barnett brought his wife, Eliza Patton, and their six children to Washington municipality in January 1834, where they settled on a farm near present Brenham.

Dr. Barnett took part in the capture of San Antonio in December 1835. He was one of four delegates from Washington municipality who signed the Texas Declaration of Independence. George then joined his family in the Runaway Scrape, going as far as Beaumont before they heard the news of San Jacinto.

For service in the Texas army from October 8 to December 22, 1835, Barnett received a bounty certificate for 320 acres in Gonzales County on December 4, 1837. For taking part in the storming and capture of Bexar, he received a donation certificate for 640 acres in Gonzales County on May 22, 1838.

Dr. Barnett served in the Senate of the Republic of Texas, representing Washington County from September 25, 1837, until January 16, 1843. Starting with the Third Congress, he also represented Montgomery County and then Brazos County in the Seventh Congress.

In 1846 Barnett moved to his land in Gonzales County and settled near Wrightsboro. While hunting deer fifteen miles west of Gonzales, he was killed by a band of marauding Lipan Apaches on October 8, 1848. He was buried in an unknown grave in the Gonzales City Cemetery. (In 1936 a centennial monument was erected in his honor.)

In 1849 the city of Gonzales built and presented to the county a two-story courthouse building located in the center of the middle public square. In February 1852, the county commissioners ordered Thomas Pilgrim to obtain benches, tables, and glass windows for the courthouse.

Construction on the third county courthouse began in February 1857. Charles Payne of Travis County was the architect and Benson and Bledsoe of Guadalupe County were the contractors. The cornerstone for the sandstone building was laid on July 4, 1857, in the center of the cross forming the public squares.

The courthouse, which also served as a community center, was not actually completed until after the Civil War. As of April 1870,

$30,000 had been spent for construction of the unfinished structure. The ill-fated building burned on December 3, 1893.

Gonzales College, the first institution in Texas to confer the A.B. degree on women, was chartered on April 15, 1852, as a nondenominational, privately owned school. The stone for the two-story building, located at 820 St. Louis Street, was hauled from a Peach Creek quarry ten miles from town. Capt. John Mooney built the structure at a cost of $7,250. Attached to the building was a 500-gallon rock cistern. Cast-iron seats and desks were later added.

The first college session of ten months opened on April 4, 1853, with fifty students; that number increased to 120 by midterm. Rev. John Freeman Hillyer, a Georgia native, was the first president of Gonzales College. Mrs. Mary Hill and Dr. Coleman were in charge of the female department, music, and ornamental branches.

In his first annual report to the stockholders in 1854, trustee president Thomas J. Pilgrim noted that the cost of the building and all equipment — $10,000 — had been paid for.

In 1853, the city council funded a brick music building on the college lot. Due to increased enrollment, a second two-story building known as the Male College was erected out of native stone in 1855. At that time the original structure was renamed the Female College. During the Civil War the Male College was razed and the stones used to build Fort Waul. Gonzales College then became co-educational.

The course of study included English, higher branches of mathematics, science, Latin, Greek, French, Spanish, German, philosophy, history, painting in oils, music, bookkeeping, commercial law, surveying, astronomy, meteorology, embroidery, and woodwork. The music department offered instruction in piano, melodeon, and guitar.

Tuition per course for each five-month term was as follows: $10 for reading, writing and spelling; $15 for arithmetic, English grammar, geography, and composition; $20 for Greek, Latin, French, German, Spanish, higher mathematics, and guitar lessons; $25 for piano or melodeon.

Final exams for graduating students were held at the end of each year, followed by public recitations before a committee of twenty local gentlemen.

There were two five-month terms in the ten-month session, with July and August as vacation periods and one week for Christmas holidays.

An eight-page weekly paper, *The Schoolgirls Bouquet,* was published by the student body. The college could also boast of a valuable library collection and reference books.

In 1857, Melvin H. Allis joined Gonzales College as a professor of mathematics. Allis, a native of New York, received an M.A. from Rochester University.

In the spring of 1862, all of the professors, including President Brooks and Principal Allis, and some of the older students left the college to enlist in the Confederate army. For the duration of the war, Mrs. Brooks and the professors' wives operated the college.

Allis enlisted in Hood's Texas Brigade, was captured, and held in Rock Island prison for eighteen months. While imprisoned he wrote several books which he later used in his teaching.

The *Gonzales Inquirer*, one of the first newspapers west of the Colorado River, was founded in 1853 by D.S.H. Darst, an original DeWitt colonist, and S.W. Smith of Alexandria, Louisiana. Soon after the first issue appeared on January 4, 1853, Darst lost interest in the newspaper and sold his stock to Smith, who served as editor of the *Inquirer*. Other personnel included Mrs. Smith as assistant and proofreader, John Dowden as printer, James Grundy as apprentice, and John S. Conway as printer's devil.

Mr. Smith used an old Washington hand press and shipped his materials by wagon train from the ports of Lavaca and Indianola. For many years the *Inquirer* was a four-page, seven-column edition. Advertisers from New Orleans and New York City purchased space in the paper. During the Civil War and Reconstruction period, editions were printed on flowered wallpaper or wrapping paper.

The *Inquirer's* first home was on the second story of the building on St. George Street facing Texas Heroes Square. Smith later built a small brick office on what became the lawn of Mayor Robert H. Walker. He finally settled in a brick building on St. Paul Street, the current location of the newspaper.

Churches were established in Gonzales before the Civil War by the Methodists, Baptists, Presbyterians, and Episcopalians. The Methodists were the first denomination to hold services in Gonzales. The Methodist Gonzales Society dates from 1835, when John Wesley Kenny preached on the Guadalupe River near town. Five years later the Victoria circuit was organized with Rev. J.P. Sneed in charge. When the circuit was divided in 1845, Rev. DeVilbiss was assigned the Gonzales circuit and organized a church at a meeting under an oak tree on the town square.

On October 4, 1851, trustees of the Methodist Episcopal Church South asked the county commissioners for permission to build a church house on the west half of block 24 in the inner town. The new church sustained $100 in fire damages in April 1854.

The second Methodist church was completed on October 23, 1874, at a cost of $3,708.73. This two-story structure had a bell tower and was known as "The Old Red Brick Church." The second floor served as a meeting place for the Masonic Lodge Royal Arch Chapter, which jointly owned the building until they sold their interest in 1897.

On November 23, 1899, James Shapley of Houston made the low bid of $6,456 to build a new Methodist church. During construction the congregation met in the county courthouse. The new building, which was dedicated on October 31, 1900, featured Gonzales buff brick and ornamental stained glass windows. (An annex to the north was erected at a cost of $3,500 in 1928. The sanctuary was remodeled in 1948 at a cost of $40,000, thereby increasing the seating capacity from 250 to 400.)

The first Baptist church in Gonzales was organized in 1840 by Rev. Z.N. Morrell, author of *Flowers and Fruits in the Wilderness* and a famous circuit-riding preacher. During one of his first Gonzales sermons, Indians stole his last horse and scalped a man nearby. As a result his meetings were armed gatherings. This first Baptist church was disbanded in 1844.

On July 31, 1847, the First Baptist Church was organized with nine charter members, including Thomas J. and Sarah J. Pilgrim. Rev. Richard Ellis was first pastor, and Mr. Pilgrim served as church clerk. A month later Mitchel P. Ponton, Horace and Sarah Jane Eggleston, and "Dilsey," a black servant of B. Duncan, joined the church. The first to join on profession of faith was Nathan Burkett, who was baptized at the ford in the Guadalupe River. Services were held in the Masonic Hall.

In 1851 the church secured a ninety-nine-year lease for the southern half of Church Square. At that time Thomas Pilgrim and two others started a fund drive for a frame building and raised $1,000 in two months. In August 1854, the Missionary Baptist Church of Christ was dedicated by Pastor James H. Stribling.

In March 1879, a stylish picket fence was built around both the Baptist and Methodist churches. That October the Baptists completed a one-story frame parsonage to the rear of the church at a cost of $750.

In June 1886, a new Baptist church was dedicated. By 1903, there were also two missions in Gonzales, the West End Mission and the East Avenue Mission, which later became East Side Baptist Church in the 1900 block of St. Louis Street.

In 1902, G.N. Dilworth and Hugh Lewis agreed to guarantee one-half of the cost of a new brick building if the congregation furnished the balance. While the church was constructed between 1905 and 1908, meetings were held in the courthouse. The new structure featured a semicircular auditorium and cost $18,000. In 1914 its name was changed to the First Baptist Church.

(Two large Sunday school classrooms were added to the church in 1913. An additional Sunday school unit was built in 1926. A two-story education building was built north of the main building in the 1930s.)

On February 29, 1852, the Gonzales Presbyterian Church was organized at the home of Mrs. J.G. Logue with Rev. T. Case presiding. The next year Rev. James McCrae became pastor of the "Old School Presbyterian Church," which had twenty-six members in 1860. For years the church met in the courthouse or at the Baptist church.

In 1871, Rev. W.M. Kilpatrick started a fund-raising campaign. At that time the city council leased a church site on Military Square and St. Louis Street. The new church, which was dedicated on May 23, 1875, was constructed of hand-hewn oak sills with walls of Florida pine. With Rev. W.M. Hall as pastor, the new First Presbyterian Church experienced its greatest growth with eighty-nine members by 1880.

In 1924, a new brick building was erected, featuring a new Estey pipe organ and beautiful stained glass windows as memorials. The pastor at this time was Rev. J.E. James, Doctor of Divinity.

As early as 1855, the Gonzales Episcopal Church of the Messiah was listed as a parish in union with the Diocese of Texas. Rev. R.S. Dunn was assigned to the church, which had seven communicants — four of them physicians — in 1856. Services were usually held in the Methodist church. By 1860, there were twenty-three communicants and a Sunday school.

In October 1879, the Episcopal church was granted use of lots 2,3,4 and 5 in block 46. Actual construction started at 721 St. Louis

Street in 1880, and the new church building — the oldest in Gonzales — was consecrated on April 27, 1881. The structure is wooden with a coupled stone foundation. The roof is supported by handwrought structural iron beams, rare for the area. The handcarved pews, altar, and imported pointed arch stained glass windows around the nave of the church date from 1880. The pulpit and altar rail are of handcarved rare Guadalupe walnut.

The building interior is the same as when built. The present sacristy, organ loft, and bell tower were added later. The stone tower houses the original bell, given to the church by the Woman's Society of Trinity Church, Baltimore, Maryland, and placed in the tower in January 1883. This bell, the largest between Houston and San Antonio, weighs 600 pounds with 200 pounds of attachments.

By May 1882, the new Episcopal church had over fifty communicants. Members of the vestry were James T. Mathieu, Dr. J.C. Jones, E. Dudley, John Darst, W.H. Atkinson, Ed Titcomb, and George Swift.

The parish rectory was completed at a cost of $1,000 for Rev. N.B. Fuller in May 1886. A new rectory was built and paid for in 1914, one "as handsome and commodious as can be found in the state."

(In 1928, the church was changed in its outward appearance and new furnishings were added. The renovation included a new stone tower at the new entrance of the church.)

On the eve of the Civil War, there were twenty-one military posts in Texas and 2,700 Federal troops. The Committee on Public Safety, acting under the authority of the secession convention, boldly demanded that Maj. Gen. D.E. Twiggs surrender all these troops and evacuate all Federal forts in Texas. On February 18, 1861, Twiggs complied in a ceremony at the Main Plaza in San Antonio. In what has been called the first battle of the Civil War, Ben McCulloch and a group of volunteers forced the surrender of the Federal garrison there.

In May 1861, McCulloch was commissioned a brigadier general in the Confederate army and given command of the Army of the West. He was assigned to protect the Indian Territory and to stop any invasions from Kansas. Under his command Confederate troops won the Battle of Wilson's Creek (Oak Hill) on August 10, 1861.

Serving under Gen. Earl Van Dorn, McCulloch commanded the Arkansas, Louisiana, and Texas forces in the Battle of Pea Ridge (Elk Horn Tavern). On March 7, 1862, the second day of the battle, Ben was killed by a volley of shot from sharpshooters. His body was taken to Austin and buried with military honors in the State Cemetery.

On February 23, 1861, the citizens of Gonzales County voted for secession from the United States by a margin of 802 to 80. During the Civil War, a total of twenty-two volunteer companies were organized in the county, including home guard units.

On May 11, 1861, Company A of the Fourth Texas Regiment was organized in Gonzales. The eighty-two officers and men were led by Capt. J.C.G. Key, 1st. Lt. Stephen H. Darden, and 2nd. Lt. A.J. McKean.

The "Gonzales Rifles" company was organized in town on May 25, 1861. Led by Capt. Isham G. Jones, this unit later became Company I, Eighth Regiment, Texas Cavalry of Terry's Texas Rangers.

On April 15, 1861, Company I of First Regiment, McCulloch's Volunteer Texas Cavalry, was organized. Capt. Travis H. Ashby led these seventy-seven officers and men. Before leaving town the company was presented with a handsome flag by the young women of Gonzales. The presentation was made by Miss Lou Scoggins, a member of the graduating class of Gonzales College.

Between October 3, 1861, and April 9, 1862, Capt. Alonzo T. Bass formed Company C of the Sixth Infantry Regiment of Texas Volunteers. Of the seventy-five officers and men, sixty-seven were from Gonzales County.

Company B of 25th Cavalry Brigade, Texas State Troops, was organized on August 6, 1863. The sixty-nine officers and men were led by Capt. W.H. Kelly.

On May 25, 1861, the "Gonzales Rebels" company was organized by Capt. L.M. Rayburn. This unit became Company E, Eighth Regiment, Texas Cavalry of Terry's Texas Rangers.

Capt. William D. Goff organized the "Wilson Rifles" company on June 8, 1861.

On June 13, 1862, the Spy Company of Gonzales was organized. This outfit of eighty-three officers and men was led by Capt. John R. Smith and was attached to the Waul Legion of Volunteers.

In the summer of 1861, Capt. Mark L. Evans organized a Gonzales company which became Company C, Eighth Regiment, Texas Cavalry of Terry's Texas Rangers.

On April 3, 1862, Capt. T.J. Cutchings organized Company B, Heavy Artillery of Cook's Battalion.

A company of cavalry for Texas State Troops was organized on

March 15, 1864. This unit of seventy-one officers and men was led by Capt. S.J. Denman.[12]

One unit deserving of special attention is the "Gonzales Invincibles," a company organized by Capt. George Washington Lafayette Fly on July 8, 1861. This outfit became Company I, Second Texas Regiment, Volunteer Infantry. Their leader, G.W.L. Fly, was born in Mississippi on June 2, 1835, and moved with his family to Oyster Creek in Brazoria County, Texas, in 1853. There his father, William, owned a plantation worked by 100 slaves.

When William Fly died in 1855, his widow and son, G. W. L., moved to Big Hill Prairie fourteen miles east of Gonzales. George returned to Mississippi in April 1857, to marry Callie Bell. One of their three children was William Madden Fly.

During the Civil War, Captain Fly fought at Shiloh and Corinth, was twice taken prisoner, and was promoted to major in January 1863. When Callie Fly received word that he had been killed in battle, she dressed in mourning for six weeks before receiving a long-delayed letter from her husband. The joyful wife took her three children and traveled by horse and buggy to Vicksburg, Mississippi, to see him. They were accompanied only by a black boy as driver and a black girl as nurse.

In 1865, Major Fly was named commander of the Port of Galveston. The next year he opened Stonewall Institute, a boarding school, at Big Hill Prairie. After the school closed in 1870, Fly moved to Gonzales to practice law. From September 1873 until July 1875, he was president of Gonzales College. In 1880, Major Fly was elected to one term in the Texas legislature. He moved his law practice to Victoria in 1886 and died there on January 27, 1905. Both he and his wife are buried there.

Another prominent Confederate leader from Gonzales was Gen. Thomas Nelville Waul, who arrived in 1851 and purchased a plantation near town on the Guadalupe River. A retired Gonzales lawyer and spellbinding orator, Waul traveled about in a "magnificent ambulance, drawn by four large, fine black mules and a special driver" as he recruited fighting men in the spring of 1862. When this "artful and eloquent" man spoke at the Gonzales courthouse, the crowd went wild; even children pleaded to join the Confederate army.

In the summer of 1862, he organized the famed Waul's Legion at Camp Waul near Brenham. General Waul's 2,000 men included twelve companies of infantry and six cavalry companies. After the war he lived for a time in Gonzales.

In late 1863, the Confederate government ordered that a fort be built in Gonzales to protect against an inland invasion if the port of Indianola was attacked. Fort Waul was designed by Col. Albert Lea, the Confederate chief army engineer for Texas, who located the fort on Waldrip Hill just north of Gonzales.

Fort Waul was started by 200 men in early 1864. By July the fort magazine and granaries were completed. The fort measured 750 feet by 250 feet. Inside was a blockhouse measuring 250 feet by 50 feet. It was constructed from stone from the Male Department building of Gonzales College, which had earlier been damaged by a storm and then torn down.[13]

Gonzales women, such as George Littlefield's widowed mother, Mildred, also did their part to support the war effort. While all her boys — four sons and two sons-in-law — were in the Confederate army, Mildred Littlefield and her two daughters ran three plantations. She gave away wagonloads of corn to soldiers' wives, which was measured out by the barrel. When the Texas coast was blockaded, Mrs. Littlefield produced homespun cloth for her own family and slaves. Fort Waul was dug in part by her slaves.

The end of the Civil War brought even greater economic disruptions and shortages in the Gonzales area. A case in point is an experience of young Jim Towns, who endured "the greatest disappointment of his life" at that time. In 1865, his mother, who lived in a log cabin on the Guadalupe River, sent Jim into Gonzales with an ox cart load of roasting ears, hoping to trade them for something to eat or a sack of salt. Towns spent a day driving around town trying to sell or trade off the roasting ears. Since there was not a dollar's worth of money or a spoonful of salt in Gonzales, Jim finally swapped a few dozen roasting ears to a traveling photographer for a sad-looking tintype picture of himself. (Jim Towns later became an open range cattleman in the Gonzales area.)

After the war Professor Melvin Allis came home and became president of Gonzales College, serving in that capacity until 1873. In 1866 he married Thankful Hannah McClure, a former student, who graduated from college in 1862 and taught there until 1874. The couple had no children of their own but did adopt two daughters.[14]

In September 1873, Maj. G. W. L. Fly, an experienced teacher, became president of Gonzales College and served until July 1875.

At that time the Masonic and Odd Fellows lodges of Gonzales took over sponsorship of the school, which was actually conducted by the trustees of School District No. 1 under the name of Gonzales Male and Female College.

In 1885 the city of Gonzales took over the school. In 1890 the property of Gonzales College was sold to W.M. Atkinson, a graduate, who remodeled the building as his private residence. (The Atkinsons retained ownership until the 1940s, when the late Henry Reese II purchased and remodeled the house. As of 1993, the home was owned by Mrs. Frank Wilson.)

During the Reconstruction period (1865-1870), Gonzales was spared from federal military occupation except for one tragic interval. On February 29, 1868, the *Gonzales Inquirer* reported that a squad of fifteen to twenty Union soldiers commanded by Sergeant Dwyer had been encamped on the town's public square for several months. Initially, they seemed to behave quietly. Two weeks before the news article appeared, however, the soldiers began to frequent grog shops and saloons and to quarrel with and bully local residents.

On February 21, 1868, two Union soldiers attacked two young men, who were forced to shoulder a heavy billet of wood around the square. The soldiers then beat up three other men: one for smiling, another who refused to unbutton his vest, and the third who did not offer them a drink.

This outrageous behavior prompted the mayor of Gonzales to file two complaints with Union Major Whittemore stationed in Seguin. After being ordered to leave Gonzales, the soldiers entered the Keyser Hotel the next night and roused Dr. Isaac W. Cunningham of Belmont from his sleep. They beat him severely, dragged him out into the street, and shot him dead. When the mayor sent a third complaint, the Union soldiers were finally moved out of Gonzales two days later.

After the war, Gonzales was home to Dr. John Curtis Jones, a pioneer in Texas medicine. Jones was born in Lawrence County, Alabama, on March 10, 1837. Upon receiving a master of arts degree from LaGrange College, he traveled to Scotland where he obtained an M.D. degree in obstetrics from the University of Edinburgh. Dr. Jones then took a surgical course in Dublin and practiced in London and Paris.

In 1861 he was called home by Confederate President Jefferson Davis and assigned to duty in the Army of Northern Virginia as surgeon of the Fourth Texas Regiment of Hood's Brigade. It was

Dr. Jones who attended Gen. John Bell Hood when he lost his leg at the Battle of Chickamauga in 1863.

At the end of the war, Dr. Jones rode to Texas and settled in Gonzales, where he practiced medicine until his death. In 1867 he married Mary Kennon Crisp, the daughter of a Colorado County planter, and they had three sons and two daughters.

Dr. Jones brought the first hypodermic needle to the United States, and it is displayed today in the Gonzales Memorial Museum. He was both county physician and health officer of Gonzales County. A member of the Texas State Medical Association, he served as vice-president and chairman of the section on surgery.

Dr. Jones performed the operation of lithotomy upon his own father. He was among the first physicians in Texas to successfully open the abdomen for the relief of intestinal obstructions and for the treatment of wounds.

In 1872 construction started on his $8,000 two-story home at the corner of Hamilton and St. Vincent streets. The home is Victorian Italianate in style, as evidenced by rounded, full-length, shuttered windows, the roof and porch column brackets (many since removed), the original cupola (destroyed in a 1910 hurricane), and the use of a glass paneled front door. The L-shaped structure has wings only one room wide to maximize ventilation and interior light.

The interior of the house features exquisite woodwork. Dr. Jones brought a German woodcarver to Texas to handcarve the elegant staircase and mantels made of local walnut. He lived with the family for two years while working on the interior woodwork.

The focal point of the entry hall is a free-standing curved circular staircase. It leads to the Bishop's Room on the second floor, which was reserved exclusively for the use of visiting Episcopalian Bishop Elliot.

The parquet floor in the entry hall and parlor is hand-fitted of six different hardwoods: red oak, white oak, maple, ash, walnut, and ebony. Wainscoting and paneling of now-extinct Mississippi curly pine is dominant throughout the dining room, living room, entry and parlor. The ceiling in the entrance hall and parlor is hammered steel, finished on the site.

In the dining room is a chandelier identified as a late 1800s fifteen candelabra Maria Teresa, originally from Mexico City. It contains some seventy large triangular prisms, 154 flat prisms, and over 400 rosettes.

Dr. Jones died on January 25, 1904. His descendants owned the house until 1952, when the J.C. Scott family purchased the dilapidated structure. In the next eight years, they painstakingly restored and refurbished the property. What had been a city eyesore was transformed into a resplendent, livable 3,700-square-foot jewel of a home. The Scotts lived in the house until 1960. Since that time there have been three other owners. The Dr. John C. Jones House is now open to the public on weekends and to bus tours by appointment.

From early 1871 until June 1874, John Wesley Hardin, the greatest gunman in Western history, used Gonzales County as a sanctuary. His autobiography lists forty shooting victims. After killing three state policemen, Hardin stopped to visit his four Clements cousins, who were open range cattlemen south of Smiley. After staying for a time at their ranch on Elm Creek, Wes was persuaded that he could beat the law by taking a herd of 1,200 Longhorns up the Chisholm Trail to Abilene, Kansas. Trail boss Hardin started north on March 1, 1871. He killed ten men on this trail drive, bringing the total to twenty-three victims before his eighteenth birthday.

John Wesley married sixteen-year-old Jane Bowen of Coon Hollow in March 1872, and the couple settled in a three-room house at Fred Duderstadt's ranch near Nopal in Sandies country. Their first child, Molly, was born in Gonzales on February 6, 1873. John Wesley, Jr., and Callie were born in 1875 and 1877, respectively, after their father fled Texas.

The Gonzales County Jail was completed at a cost of $5,800 in 1854. It was located on block 4 of Market Square, later redesignated as Jail Square, and was the scene of two sensational events in the 1870s.

After killing a black state policeman at Pilgrim's place, Hardin was brought there to await trial. On October 10, 1872, Mannen Clements smuggled him a hacksaw file to cut the jail bars. Guards on duty told Wes when to work, and he escaped by being pulled through the stubs of the cut bars by a horse.

In 1878, Jane Hardin's brother, Brown Bowen, was arrested at Pollard, Alabama, and brought back to Texas to face murder charges. Six years earlier, he had shot Tom Halderman in the back at the Billings store in Smiley. When Brown was found guilty, his father Neal asked son-in-law Hardin to take the blame since he was liked in Gonzales County and could "come clean there."

Wes had been tracked down in Pensacola, Florida, for killing Deputy Sheriff Charles Webb of Brown County. Even though he was also in custody at the time, Hardin said he had no choice but to refuse Bowen's request. Brown Bowen went to the gallows on May 17, 1878, as a Gonzales crowd of 4,000 looked on.

Many Gonzales cattlemen trailed their Longhorn herds up the Chisholm Trail in the postwar years. The most prominent of these cowmen were George Norwood Dilworth and his brother James, George W. Littlefield, and Bob and Dunn Houston.

George Norwood Dilworth was a prominent cattleman, rancher, and banker during this period. When George was thirteen, his widowed mother Elizabeth brought him and younger brother James Colwell to Gonzales in January 1850. Mrs. Dilworth purchased a farm six miles northwest of town on the San Marcos River.

In 1854 George Dilworth started his career as a trail driver by taking a herd of horses from Tampico, Mexico, to Chicago. He and brother James also operated his mother's cotton farm. On February 16, 1858, George married Martha Ellen Huff.

During the Civil War, George served a year in the Confederate army at Galveston before hiring a substitute. He then began to haul cotton to Matamoros and returned with loads of salt, accumulating specie on each trip.

Bachelor James C. "Doc" Dilworth was a lieutenant in Terry's Texas Rangers and was severely wounded in Tennessee. On August 9, 1869, he married Sarah Ellen Broyles, who nursed him back to health in her home during the war.

In 1865 the Dilworth brothers became partners of Hugh Lewis in the firm of Lewis & Dilworth, dealers in groceries, iron, and plantation goods. They were later joined by George W. Littlefield.

In 1866 George and James founded the firm of G.N. & J.C. Dilworth, Bankers and Brokers, the first banking institution in Gonzales County. The partners operated out of a two-story brick building on the corner of St. George and St. Joseph streets. The Dilworth Bank adjoined the W.H. Boothe and Company store south of Plaza Square.

In 1868 prominent attorneys James F. Miller and W.B. Sayers organized the second bank in Gonzales. The Miller-Sayers Bank was located in an upstairs room of the two-story building on the corner of St. Lawrence and St. Joseph streets.

In 1866 the Dilworth brothers and C.C. "Doc" Burnett drove a herd of cattle to Salt Lake City, marking the beginning of trail driving in Gonzales County. Both Dilworths continued to drive cattle north during the trail drive era.

In 1871 George Dilworth and Levi Moses Kokernot became partners on trail drives. At various times George formed land and cattle partnerships with R.A. and J.D. Houston and with J.H. Parramore. His brother James was a partner of George W. Littlefield in cattle drives until Dilworth's death in May 1877.

The Dilworth brothers purchased a portable steam sawmill and a steam gristmill in 1867. When they began to operate independently in 1872, the bank continued as Dilworth & Anderson until the mercantile partnership of Lewis & Dilworth took it over. When that partnership ended in 1881, the bank was renamed the Banking House of G.N. Dilworth.

In 1885 George built a handsome, two-story stone bank building at 319 St. Lawrence Street, a structure forty-three feet wide and eighty feet deep. (This building was later occupied by the law offices of Perkins, Dreyer, and Rather.) In 1903 he brought his sons, R.S. and C.E. Dilworth, into the banking partnership.

George Dilworth also worked tirelessly to bring a rail connection to Gonzales. As a result the town of Dilworth on the San Antonio and Aransas Pass Railroad was named in his honor in 1885, when the line was extended from Shiner to Lockhart.

George and Martha Dilworth were devout members of the First Baptist Church and were major contributors to the present church building.

George Dilworth died at San Antonio on January 4, 1911, and was buried in the Gonzales Masonic Cemetery, as was his widow, who died on April 22, 1913.

Another local cattleman, George W. Littlefield, became a millionaire and major benefactor of the University of Texas. Littlefield was born in Panola County, Mississippi, on June 21, 1842. A year earlier his father, Fleming, married widow Mildred Satterwhite White in spite of her family's vigorous objections. After years of bad blood, Fleming Littlefield fled to Texas in the fall of 1850 after shooting a hired gun sent by the Satterwhites to kill him. His family followed him to Texas in early 1851, when George was nine.

Littlefield purchased 1,760 acres of rich bottom land on the Guadalupe River fifteen miles northwest of Gonzales. He and partner Samuel J. Mays also opened a store in town. After Fleming died of pneumonia in January 1853, his widow Mildred purchased a plantation on the Belmont Road five miles out of Gonzales. The new Littlefield home place included a main house and slave quarters made of brick.

George Littlefield attended Baylor University at Independence from February 1857 until October 1858, when he left school to dispose of the Mississippi property of his half-brother, Charles E. White. He was only seventeen when he brought a slave caravan and $4,500 in gold back to Texas.

In August 1861, Littlefield volunteered as a second sergeant in Isham Jones's Company I, Eighth Texas Cavalry, Terry's Texas Rangers. Body servant Nathan went off to war with George, who participated in the battles of Shiloh, Chickamauga, and Lookout Mountain and was promoted to brevet major for exceptional bravery.

While on a recruiting leave, Littlefield married Alice Payne Tiller of Houston in January 1863. Both of their children died in infancy.

In late December 1863, the major suffered a severe shrapnel wound to his left hip at Mossy Creek in eastern Tennessee. Old Nath carried his master from the field and nursed him during five months confined to bed. George was on crutches when he was discharged and sent home to Gonzales in late September 1864.

The next month Littlefield took charge of the family plantation and took up the job of cotton farming. Beginning in 1868, three successive crops were destroyed by either worms or flooding in the river bottoms. His wife, Alice, later recalled that they lived on $150 a year in 1869.

At this time Littlefield began to see the wild cattle roaming his range as his economic salvation. In the spring of 1871, he took ten cowboys and a cook and drove 1,100 head up the Chisholm Trail to Abilene, Kansas. There he sold his herd to a Mr. Savage at $40–$50 a head. After returning to Gonzales by rail and stagecoach, he paid off all his debts, bought a house and lot, and moved into town that year.

Littlefield then entered into a cattle partnership with J.C. "Doc" Dilworth, which lasted from 1872 to 1876. Dunn Houston drove a Littlefield herd in 1872. His brother Bob later joined the major in range and trail speculations. Within five years of that first cattle drive, Littlefield herds were in the Dakotas, Kansas, Nebraska, and Colorado.

George trailed up to 30,000 head of cattle annually until 1884, when he began to ship his herds by rail. He did all the marketing himself and relied on trail boss Charles C. McCarty on the range. Littlefield had only one business rule: "When everyone is wanting to sell, I buy; when everyone is wanting to buy, I sell."

The need for good winter grass ranges led the major to establish four ranches, two in the Texas Panhandle and two in New Mexico. The first, the LIT Ranch, was started in the Canadian River Valley near Tascosa, Texas, in the summer of 1877. Four years later a Scottish syndicate from Edinburgh paid Littlefield $253,000 for 12,000 branded LIT cattle and his simple range rights.

In the spring of 1882, his favorite nephew, Phelps White, founded the LFD Ranch at Bosque Grande on the Pecos River in New Mexico. The next year George organized the Littlefield Cattle Company there and left White in charge. (Phelps White became the richest man in the Pecos Valley. By 1920 his interest in the cattle company was worth $2 million.)

The terrible drought of 1886 forced Littlefield to abandon the Pecos range and relocate to the southeast in the Four Lakes country along the New Mexican-Texas border. This plains country was full of fresh buffalo grass, which he watered with windmills and wells spaced ten miles apart. By 1888 the Four Lakes Ranch embraced 15,000 acres and 35,000 head of cattle. The actual Four Lakes Range was one and a half million acres. (In 1915 the Littlefield Cattle Company sold the ranch to C.J. Ballard for $5 an acre.)

In 1901 the major purchased the Yellow House Ranch. Located in four Panhandle counties, this southernmost division of the XIT Ranch covered 235,858 acres.

Over the years Littlefield also acquired the Mill Creek Ranch in Mason County and the Little Elm Creek Ranch in Kimble County.

Beginning with range Longhorns, he bred up to the best type of Hereford, branding from five to six thousand calves each year. Ironically, he once remarked that "the only practical knowledge I have gained in ranching is that a cow will have a calf."

Littlefield moved from Gonzales to Austin in 1883 and organized the American National Bank there in 1890. The bank began with a capital stock of $100,000 and operated for twenty-one years in a corner of the Driskill Hotel.

The major then moved his banking operations into the nine-story Littlefield Building at Congress Avenue and Sixth Street. This structure was equipped with two sixteen-passenger elevators.

Littlefield kept from $800,000 to $1 million in his personal bank account. His office desk in the rear of the bank was always piled high with papers. On Sundays his foremen would visit the bank to go over ranch accounts in detail. His faithful body servant, Old Nath, always accompanied Littlefield to work, either walking behind him or giving him a buggy ride.

In 1911 Governor O.B. Colquitt appointed Littlefield to the board of regents of the University of Texas. His palatial, turreted red mansion adjoined the university on the north and became a part of the campus after his wife's death. (The Littlefield home is off Guadalupe Street between 24th and 25th streets.)

George Littlefield died in Austin on November 10, 1920. After his body lay in state in the university's Wrenn Library, he was buried in the family plot in Oakwood Cemetery. His wife Alice and servant Old Nath were later buried on either side of the famed cowman.[15]

Robert Augustin "Bob" Houston also drove many herds up the Chisholm Trail from Gonzales. He and brothers James Dunn and William Buckner were all cattlemen and substantial landowners.

Bob Houston married Sallie J. Broadus on January 12, 1870. All of their eight children were born in Gonzales. The family lived in a large frame two-story house on the northeast corner of St. Paul and St. Francis streets. The likable Bob had a mirthful nature and was known for pulling stunts purely for fun.

In 1878 Houston joined Lewis and Dilworth in trailing 4,000 Longhorns north. On the trail he noticed that many houses and barns had weathervanes depicting the animals raised on the property. This inspired him to place a large, gold-plated Longhorn steer branded "T-41" atop his own mansion.

After finding that such a weathervane could not be built in Kansas City, Bob commissioned a New York firm to create a steer and ship the project in pieces to Gonzales. There a local tinner, W.C. Franks, brazed the sections together, pounded the owner's brand into the metal on both sides, and mounted the gold steer on Houston's new home. This unique weathervane was three and a half feet high, four and a half feet long, and weighed 130 pounds.

After Houston's death in February 1895, his home became a boardinghouse called the Arlington Hotel. His prize Longhorn weathervane later sat atop the Randle-Rather building, the city hall, and finally the remodeled Gonzales fire station.

Bob's younger brother, James Dunn Houston, was a partner of

George W. Littlefield in the cattle business. On one trail drive, Dunn's herd of 3,150 wild steers smelled water, turned back, ran twenty miles, and recrossed the Red River. While trying to herd the crazed animals back to the north side, Dunn swallowed too much of the alkali water and became violently ill with cramps. Jim Towns, one of his drovers, poured a half-full bottle of paregoric down Houston's throat. He soon fell asleep and was fine the next day.

By the mid-1890s, Dunn and Bob Houston owned more than 22,000 acres with 12,000 head of stock in Gonzales and Wilson counties. Dunn also owned and operated a large ranch on the Pecos River. At the time of his death, he was a major stockholder in the Lockwood National Bank of San Antonio.

Between 1895 and 1899, Dunn Houston built a red brick Victorian landmark at 619 St. Lawrence Street. Known today as the Lewis-Houston House, this grand home has fifteen main rooms, five bathrooms, several halls and walkways, and an indoor conservatory. Each of the main rooms has an individually designed fireplace. The foyer is still graced by two canvas wall murals purchased in New Orleans when the home was being built. The light fixtures in the family dining room, banquet dining room, living room and foyer hang from carved medallions. The oak hardwood floors on the first story still have the original inlaid pattern.

In 1900 Houston sold his mansion to George Norwood Dilworth and his wife, Martha Ellen. Five years later Margaret Dilworth Lewis, the widow of J.P. Lewis, came home to live with her parents. Her two children, Susan and Jim, grew up in the house. After the death of her parents in 1911 and 1913, Margaret inherited the mansion and lived there until her death in 1950.

In 1953 her daughter, Susan Lewis Peck, sold the house to the Texas Rehabilitation Hospital to be used as a doctor's residence. Ultimately, the home was purchased by Vernon E. and Sue Person in June 1967. (After the death of her husband, Mrs. Person lived in the Lewis-Houston House and operated an antique shop there.)

Cattlemen were not the only businessmen to prosper in the period after Reconstruction. In the 1870s, John William Kleine built Kleine's Hall on the northwest corner of Plaza Square. The first floor displayed his furniture, and the second story served as a popular social center.

After 1874 the nearest railroad to Gonzales was the Galveston, Harrisburg, and San Antonio line passing through Harwood, twelve miles away. In 1882 a branch line was built to Gonzales. On August 9 the first train arrived at the depot in the 800 block of Hamilton Street. A second rail connection came in 1888 when the San Antonio and Aransas Pass Railroad built through Gonzales.

In 1882 Gonzales claimed twenty-three mercantile stores, two hotels, two livery stables, two tin shops, three blacksmiths, four bar rooms, one photo gallery, and a barber shop.

Beginning in 1879, the firm of Peck and Fly was one of the major businesses in Gonzales. William Madden Fly was born at Big Hill Prairie on December 26, 1857. After receiving his first schooling at Stonewall Institute, William continued his education in Gonzales when Major Fly moved the family into town in 1870.

At age fourteen young Fly went to work as a "printer's devil." In late 1871 his finger was badly mashed and William sought first aid at the Tate and Badger Drug Store, where he was persuaded to become a clerk. He advanced to registered pharmacist before the store went out of business in 1879.

At that time Fly and Ben Peck, Sr., opened the firm of Peck and Fly, stocking groceries, hardware, sporting goods, and pharmaceuticals. William's principal job, however, was that of cotton broker.

Trail outfits loaded out at Peck and Fly's store. They purchased enormous amounts of supplies on credit there and always paid the bill.

In 1890 Peck and Fly spent $10,000 constructing a two-story red brick building on St. Joseph Street facing Public Square. Two years later they added a third story, the only such building in town at the time.

When Ben Peck died in 1913, he was replaced by Fly's son-in-law, Warren Taylor. The Peck and Fly store remained in business until the mid-1940s.

William Fly married Clara Belding in 1883, and they had two daughters. He served several terms in the state legislature and was a 33rd degree Mason, serving as Grand Master of the Grand Lodge of Texas. He died in 1944 and was buried beside his wife in the Gonzales Masonic Cemetery.

Another Gonzales institution, the *Inquirer*, consolidated with the *Gonzales Index* under one name, the *Inquirer-Index*, in February 1876. Within a year the *Inquirer* reclaimed its original name, with S.W. Smith again becoming editor until the end of 1877.

From the summer of 1876 until January 1878, the firm of Smith and Beach (Dr. D.L. Beach) operated the paper before selling half interest to Carey J. Pilgrim. The firm of Beach and Pilgrim operated the paper for three years until Dr. Beach retired. Carey Pilgrim, a noted writer, then became owner and editor of the *Inquirer*. Before his retirement in 1885, Pilgrim increased the paper's circulation and gave it statewide prominence.

In 1883 Pilgrim built a home at 707 St. George Street for his bride, the former Mary Fleda Boothe. The two were married in December 1882, in the First Baptist Church. Their home was built on land that was a wedding gift from her parents, who lived next door. Their daughter, Carey Boothe Pilgrim, was born there on October 18, 1883.

The one-story house features a long center hall with two rooms on either side. The rooms have double fireplaces and floors made of wide pine boards. The beautiful parlor mantel is of a carved white marble, and a large walnut-framed mirror hangs over it.

Carey J. Pilgrim died of pneumonia in El Paso on June 25, 1887, and was buried in the Boothe family plot in the Gonzales City Cemetery. His widow, Mary Fleda, later married George Barnett and died on April 24, 1927. (The Pilgrim home remains virtually unchanged and has been occupied by family members since it was built. It is known today as the Chenault Home.)

Pilgrim's apprentice of four years, Henry Reese, Jr., served as junior partner for a year before taking over the *Inquirer* in 1885. The newspaper was to be owned by the Reese family until 1991.

There have been several other newspapers in Gonzales over the years, including *The South-Western Index* (1869-1878), *The Gonzales Gazette* (1886-1890), which became the *Gonzales Enterprise*, *The Drag Net* (1895), *The Gonzales Reform* (1905), which was a German newspaper, *The Gonzales Globe* (1905), and *The Gonzales County News* (1939-1942).

In 1885 T.N. Matthews built another historic home at 829 Mitchell Street. It was constructed of Florida long-leafed pine shipped by water to Indianola and hauled by ox teams to Gonzales. The house featured double doors with decorated glass at the top on both the first and second floors.

In 1890 James Bailey Wells, Sr., purchased the Matthews home. His wife was the daughter of James Hodges, Jr., who led an expedition which arrived at Gonzales in 1828. Hodges was also a representative to the Consultation of 1835.

The historic house is now known as the J.B. Wells Home. The furnishings include a walnut bed with a carved headboard and a trundle bed underneath, a New Orleans lamp stand, a hall tree made from an old organ, and a love seat constructed from walnut chairs.

The J.B. Wells Home is now used for meetings of the Gonzales Chapter, Daughters of the Republic of Texas. The original barns and servants quarters are still on the grounds.

In 1884 a grand jury recommended to the commissioners court that a new jail be built. Plans were approved on May 30, 1885, for a structure to be located on Principal Square just north of and adjacent to the courthouse. The architect for the new county jail was Eugene T. Heiner, and the contractors were Henry Kane and Snead & Company Iron Works. Built at a cost of $21,660.20, the three-story brick jail was completed and approved by the commissioners court on February 5, 1887. The Southern Structural Steel Company did extensive repair to the jail in 1905 at a cost of $900.

The front door of the jail leads to an entrance hall and the sheriff's office. To the left are the family quarters of the sheriff, consisting of three rooms, a kitchen and a bath. To the right is a hall; the first room on the right was used as the jailer's bedroom. The corner room was a cell used by women and children. At the end of the hall and extending to the left is an all-metal dungeon.

The stairway leads to the second and third floors and into a large room known as the "runabout" cell. The room is thirty-by-thirty feet, two stories high, and was used by those inmates who were not hardened criminals.

There are also three death cells on the second floor. They are made of iron strips two inches wide and a quarter-inch thick, welded together to resemble the strands of a flyswatter.

A permanent scaffold was built in the second-story corridor in 1891. Only six steps were necessary to descend to the gallows platform from the third story. The gallows were torn down in 1953 or 1954. The present gallows are a reproduction.

To the right and left of the death cells are doors leading to the regular cells in the east and west wings. There are stoves in the corner cell walls. The northwest cell contains the original commode and lavatory.

The third floor cells are identical to those on the second floor.

Some of them were used for keeping lunatics, women, and youthful offenders.

In the event of riot, the county jail could hold between 150 and 200 prisoners. [16]

Another milestone in public safety was reached in 1884, when the Gonzales city council accepted a bid for the installation of eleven fire hydrants and two hundred feet of fire hose.

On June 26, 1886, a disastrous fire resulted in the destruction of six buildings, including the Thomas Hotel.

The first fire company was organized in Gonzales in late October 1892. Four years later the first uniformed company — "Old Reliable Hose Company No. 1" — was operating with one two-wheeled cart and a hand-drawn hook and ladder truck.

In 1879 the Reverend Father Mancy was sent to Gonzales to attempt to establish a Catholic church. Efforts were continued by Father J. Kossbiel, who was offered the free use of Kleine's Hall for celebrating Mass in 1881. That October Father Kossbiel began a list of subscriptions for building St. Joseph's Church. The campaign was continued by Father Garesche, and carpenters started work on the church in April 1883. They completed the task in February 1884, and the blessing of the 760-pound church bell was celebrated on May 13, 1886. The shepherd of the flock, Father Garesche, died on December 8, 1910.

A second Catholic church was built and dedicated on July 9, 1911. It was named St. James, and the old St. Joseph Church was moved to the corner of St. Lawrence and St. John streets to serve the Mexican-American congregation.

On May 12, 1894, amid cries of fraud and kickbacks, the new Populist-controlled commissioners court authorized the issuance of $70,000 in bonds to build a new courthouse. On July 13, Otto P. Kroeger of San Antonio was awarded the contract to build the facility. J. Riely Gordon, the renowned courthouse architect, designed the three-story Romanesque Revival structure. Gordon designed thirteen courthouses in Texas, including those in Victoria, Bexar and Ellis counties, the latter of which is one of the most familiar architectural landmarks in the state.

The cornerstone of the new Gonzales courthouse was laid by the commissioners on April 23, 1895, and construction was completed in 1896.

The building base is constructed of precast concrete made to resemble stone. The red brick came from St. Louis, and the white limestone was hauled from the Maurin quarry located ten to twelve miles east of Gonzales. The structure is built in the form of a Greek cross, and the four semicircular entrance bays fill in the four corners of the cross. The main entrances have open Roman arcades at the first level. The courthouse has a square central stairwell adorned with ornamental ironwork which rises from the basement to the third floor. Sammis mosaic floor tile covers the county and district courtrooms, as well as the hallways.

A central square clock tower rises above the red tile hip roof and is flanked by four open cupolas. Each side of the tower has three narrow Gothic windows and a clock on each of the four sides. The clock was acquired from Seth Thomas Company at a cost of $990 and was installed in March 1896. (The clock fell silent for many years due to age and wear. In 1990 Mr. Henry Christian of Gonzales spent over $11,000 giving the clock a complete overhaul and rebuilding. Since that time the historic timepiece has kept accurate time and tolled the hour to the town business district.)

The bid of George D. Barnard & Company was accepted to furnish all wooden furniture at a cost of $3,457.83. There is no way of confirming that any of the existing furniture is original. For example, the theater-type pews in the second floor courtroom are not original but came from an old church.

Originally, the courthouse had a basement and three floors. Until the late 1960s, the basement had a dirt floor and was used for storage. After being paved, part of it was utilized as a men's restroom and the remainder was adapted for use by the county clerk's office.

The large west room on the first floor was originally a county courtroom. It was later the county tax office and then used for record storage.

The courtroom on the second floor has not been changed. One unusual feature is the balcony above the judge's bench. A circular staircase behind the judge leads from the basement to the dome above the courtroom and includes a connecting door to the small balcony. Over the years there have been many sinister explanations for the balcony and stairs.

The third floor — now the fourth floor — originally included a south room as a dormitory for jurors. The east room was a jury room, and a small restroom joined the two rooms. The north room had no designated use. A decade ago, the grand jury room was remodeled.

Amazingly, this magnificent structure cost the county only $64,450 when it was constructed.

The Gonzales County Courthouse is located at 414 St. Joseph Street. It is listed in the National Register of Historic Places and is also a Texas Historic Landmark.

In late March 1894, John Wesley Hardin moved his three children to Gonzales and opened a law office in the Peck and Fly Building. He had just been released from the state penitentiary after serving sixteen years and five months for killing Deputy Sheriff Charles Webb.

After five rebellious years in prison, Wes became a model prisoner in 1883. He began to read the Bible and theological books, became superintendent of the Sunday school, headed the debate team, and started studying law in 1889. While her husband was involved in a self-improvement program, Jane Hardin worked herself to death running a farm on the Duderstadt Ranch and died at age thirty-six on November 6, 1892. She was buried in Asher Cemetery near Old Davy and the Mound Creek settlement.

Although the reformed gunman neither gambled nor drank and attended the Methodist church each Sunday, Hardin had few legal clients in Gonzales. The girls were soon sent back to the Duderstadt Ranch, leaving only John Wesley, Jr., with his father.

Hardin's dream of a new life began to fade when he unwisely jumped into local politics. In 1894 there was a heated race for sheriff of Gonzales County with W.E. Jones the Democratic nominee and Deputy Sheriff Bob Coleman the Populist candidate. Hardin became the key issue in the campaign after he wrote a newspaper article in the *Drag Net* claiming that the corrupt Jones in 1872 had allowed him to escape the Gonzales jail, had protected him from arrest, and was thus unfit to be a law officer. Wes even made his law office Coleman's campaign headquarters, and the war of words became so heated that John Wesley, Jr., was taken back to the Duderstadt Ranch for his own safety. Hardin announced that he would leave town if Coleman was defeated, and when Jones won the November election by only six votes, he kept his word. While packing his bags, Hardin was inspired to write the story of his life after finding a large stack of old letters that Jane had saved for him.[17]

Two of the finest old homes in Gonzales were built in the 1890s: the Charles T. Rather House and the Kennard-Bowden House.

Rather, a local cotton planter and baker, built a house at 828 St.

Louis Street in 1892. Located on part of the old Gonzales College campus, this home is constructed of Louisiana cypress, Bastrop pine, and Gonzales white brick. The brick foundation is two feet thick, extends four feet into the ground, and supports ten-by-ten cypress beams.

The interior features solid brass doorknobs, documented wallpaper, oriental floor rugs, and pine paneling. Each of the four fireplaces originally had facings of English tile. The mantels are of white oak and cherry. A flower and fan motif is visible in the glazed sections of the double front and back hall doors and in carvings on the walnut newel posts of the broad stairway.

(As of 1993, the Rather House was owned by Lee Sloan.)

In 1895 Mr. and Mrs. James Blake Kennard built a home at 621 St. Louis Street. Kennard, a local lumberman, married Anna Braches, the granddaughter of Charles Braches, in the early 1890s. Friends throughout the United States shipped Kennard select pieces of wood as material for his new home. Built in the Queen Anne style, it is among the few such remaining residences in Texas.

The two-story central portico has Romanesque arches at the first level and an open colonnaded gallery at the second story. A tall, bold tower stands to one side of the porch with wraparound porches on the opposite side. The windows are of French beveled glass and Tiffany leaded glass. The shingle and clapboard siding is painted green. Floors in the Kennard-Bowden House are inlaid wood.

(As of 1993, the house was owned by the Bowdens.)

A Gonzales landmark, the Randle-Rather Building was constructed in 1896 and 1897 in the 400 block of St. George Street. Built by James Polk Randle, owner of a dry goods store, and Charles T. Rather, a farmer and banker, this three-story Roman Revival structure was made of natural clay local brick.

The original main entrances were open Roman arcades at the first level, then later enclosed for more building space. The center front features balconies on the second and third levels. Rising above the third-floor balcony is a square, fourth-level tower with Roman arched windows.

The first floor housed the Gonzales National Bank, which later became Farmer's National Bank. The second floor was designed to house various businesses, including physicians and surgeons J.W. Nixon and W.J. Hildebrand, the St. Louis Millinery Parlor, and upholsterer and mattress maker J.B. Conrad.

The third floor was devoted to the K.D. Club. The initials stood for "keep dry," a warning that someone noticed on a large empty cardboard carton. This social club included young, affluent, and prominent Gonzales gentlemen. The group sponsored formal balls attended by guests from San Antonio, Cuero, and Victoria. The highlight of the social season was the Christmas Ball, with women attired in fine silk and satins and the men in frock-tailed coats.

On June 1, 1897, the firm of Reese and Beach published the first issue of the *Daily Inquirer*, a four-page, five-column edition. Before his death, Beach sold his interest to Emmett Smith of Itasca. The partnership lasted until 1916, when Reese purchased Smith's interest in the newspaper. Since that time the *Inquirer* has been a Reese family institution.

When Henry Reese, Jr., died in 1923, his wife Annie Laura became publisher with Sidney Smith serving as editor. Three years later Henry Reese III took over active management of the paper. He also served as president of the South Texas Press Association and was instrumental in the founding of the Gonzales Warm Springs Foundation, serving as secretary-treasurer until his death.

Reese and his younger brother, Edward, who joined the *Inquirer* staff six years after Henry, published many special editions of the paper, including the 100th anniversary edition issued in 1953. This 130-page edition required months of planning and work. Although Henry became ill in the early stages of the project, he managed to finish his dream. After Henry's death on August 25, 1955, Edward Reese became managing editor of the *Inquirer.*

The *Gonzales Inquirer* and its counterpart, Reese Print Shop, are probably the oldest continuously operated businesses in the town. They were separated after the *Inquirer* was bought out by Guadalupe Valley Publishing Company in 1991.

On May 26, 1904, the First Lutheran Church of Gonzales was organized on the second floor of the Brenner Drug Store. Two months later the members agreed to rent the German Methodist church for $25 a year. Rev. William Dziewas from Shiner served as first pastor. By May 1914, the church had thirty members. A Sunday school was organized three years later.

In July 1921, the city offered the Lutherans the Nettie Willett School and one-half square of land on North Avenue for $1,000. The offer was accepted, the school was remodeled, and the first worship services were held there on August 11, 1921.

Two churches, the First Lutheran Church of Gonzales and the Christ Lutheran Church of Monthalia, were united in one parish and served by the same pastor, who held services in Gonzales on the first and third Sundays of each month.

In 1924 the church was renamed the First Evangelical Lutheran Church. (A new church building was dedicated on July 7, 1942, at a cost of $3,000. The project also included 395 days of labor pledged by church members. In 1947 the congregation purchased a pipe organ at a cost of $2,900.)

On November 21, 1899, the poultry industry began in the Gonzales area when a Mr. Boyer and J.R. Pennington shipped eighteen barrels of dressed turkeys to California. The 300 turkeys were packed in ice and shipped by railway express. (Gonzales now ranks as the top producing county in eggs, chickens, and turkeys.)

At the turn of the century, a renowned prisoner was held in the new Gonzales jail. Gregorio Cortez was a small, wiry father of four who became a folk hero after killing two sheriffs and making an incredible flight to the Rio Grande.

In 1901 Cortez and his brother Romaldo were renting farm land ten miles west of Kenedy. On June 12, W.T. "Brack" Morris, the sheriff of Karnes County, and a deputy approached Gregorio's house looking for a horse thief who had been trailed from Atascosa County to Kenedy. It seems that a local man named Villareal had just acquired a mare by trade from Gregorio, and Sheriff Morris wanted to question Cortez about the matter. When the sheriff appeared at his house, Gregorio had a .44 revolver in his belt and his brother, Romaldo, was unarmed.

Deputy Boone Choate asked in shaky Spanish if Gregorio had recently traded a horse, and he honestly replied, "No." The deputy then thought he heard Cortez say, "No white man can arrest me." What the suspect probably said was, "You can't arrest me for nothing." When the sheriff drew his gun, Romaldo lunged at him and was shot in the mouth. Morris then whirled to face Gregorio but shot hastily and missed. Cortez then shot the sheriff three times with his revolver. One wound in the right arm severed an artery, causing Morris to slowly bleed to death.

After leaving his wounded brother in Kenedy, Gregorio started north on foot, covered eighty miles in forty hours, and hid at the home of Martin Robledo, who lived at Ottine in Gonzales County. Sheriff Robert M. Glover, a good friend of Morris, had in the meantime pressured either Gregorio's mother or wife into telling him where the fugitive was headed. As a result Glover's posse of eight men reached Ottine shortly after Cortez arrived at Robledo's house.

The lawmen were possibly drunk when they decided to rush the house. As the mounted Sheriff Glover approached the southeast corner of the front porch, he and Cortez began to exchange fire. Both men continued to blaze away until the sheriff fell dead from his horse.

Now the most wanted man in Texas, Cortez headed for Laredo using sorrel and brown mares to ride over 400 miles. During a ten-day chase, he was pursued by posses numbering up to 300 men. At noon on June 20, the exhausted Cortez walked into Cotulla. Two days later, on his twenty-sixth birthday, he was betrayed by a Mexican informer and arrested by Texas Ranger Capt. J.H. Rogers at a sheep camp only thirty miles from the Rio Grande.

On July 24, 1901, Cortez stood trial at Gonzales for the murder of County Constable Henry Schnabel, who had actually been killed by one of his fellow possemen in the shootout at Ottine. Nevertheless, Gregorio was found guilty of second-degree murder and given fifty years in prison.

On August 9, 1901, Romaldo Cortez died in the Karnes City jail. Two days later Gonzales County Sheriff F.M. Fly thwarted an attempt by a mob of over 300 — most of them from Karnes County — who tried to take Gregorio from the jail and lynch him.

On January 15, 1902, the Texas Court of Criminal Appeals reversed the Gonzales verdict.

In the meantime, on October 7–11, 1901, Cortez was tried at Karnes City for the murder of Sheriff Morris. Although he was found guilty and sentenced to death, the Court of Criminal Appeals reversed the verdict eight months later on grounds of prejudice.

After the case was first moved to Goliad and then Wharton counties, Cortez was tried again at Corpus Christi, April 25-30, 1904. This time he was found not guilty of murdering Sheriff Morris. The jury of Anglo-American farmers agreed with the claim of the defense that Cortez had shot the sheriff in self-defense and in defense of his brother.

Meanwhile, Cortez was found guilty of murdering Sheriff Glover in a trial at Columbus, mainly because the defense built its case around the contention that Cortez had not fired the shots that had killed the sheriff. After being given a life sentence, Gregorio entered the Huntsville penitentiary on January 1, 1905. [18]

In 1910 two historical monuments were unveiled in Gonzales: the Confederate Monument and the Texas Heroes Monument. In 1902 Mrs. A.T. Barber, president of the United Daughters of the Confederacy, Chapter No. 545, initiated a fund drive for monuments to those from Gonzales County who fought for the Confederacy. On July 21, 1909, the cornerstone for the monument was laid. The sculptor was German-born Frank Teich, who came to Texas in 1883 and had studios in San Antonio and Llano. His monument had a base of gray Texas granite. The Confederate soldier atop it was made of Carrara marble and faced north.

When the Confederate Monument was unveiled on April 10, 1910, excursion trains helped boost the crowd to between 4,000 and 5,000. During the ceremony County Commissioner J.D. Gates was honored for being the first enlisted man to volunteer for Confederate service from Gonzales County.

The Texas Heroes Monument was unveiled on October 20, 1910. Funded by the Texas legislature at a cost of $5,200, the monument was sculpted by Pompeo Coppini, an Italian native who came to Texas in 1901 to work with Frank Teich. His monument has a red Llano granite pedestal on which is mounted a bronze figure of a bareheaded Texas frontiersman. The figure is gripping a rifle in his right hand, with his left arm tense and hand clenched.

A bronze bas-relief adorns the south face of the granite pedestal. Coppini's design depicts eight defiant, alert men surrounding a small cannon. On the lower section of the bas-relief is the legend, "Come and Take It."

The Texas Heroes Monument was a project of the Gonzales chapter of the Daughters of the Republic of Texas and their president, Mrs. J.W. Hildebrand. Her father, Judge Fly, addressed the gathering at the ceremony, and Mrs. Hildebrand pulled the cord to unveil the monument.

In 1914 Gonzales cattle baron Walter H. Kokernot built a huge home for his wife Virginia, daughter, and four sons at 228 St. Andrew Street. Built in the Greek, Four-Square architectural style, the main house had three stories, nine fireplaces, thirty rooms, and sixty stair-steps from the basement to the penthouse. The house also included a two-car garage and stables for three horses.

The wealthy Kokernots often entertained friends in the downstairs reception hall, living room, dining room, and conservatory. Their daughter Josephine was married in the home.

In the 1940s the Kokernots moved to their ranch near Alpine and sold the house to a cousin. At that time the mansion was converted to apartments and renamed the St. James Inn. To finance the renovations, the green glazed tile roof was sold. Later the veranda was removed and several fireplaces were closed.

The Gonzales Memorial Museum is a Texas Centennial historical memorial, a gift from the State of Texas commemorating the "Immortal Thirty-two" from Gonzales who died at the Alamo. The museum, amphitheater, and reflection pool were built in 1936 for the Texas Centennial by the federal Works Projects Administration. The murals inside were painted by James Buchanan Winn.

The fascinating history of "The Lexington of Texas" is exhibited in the Gonzales Memorial Museum. Built of Texas shell stone and trimmed in Cordova cream limestone, the museum is located at 414 Smith Street.

Among the prize displays is the authenticated "Come and Take It" cannon, owned by Dr. Patrick J. Wagner of Shiner. The museum also houses a replica of the cannon created in his blacksmith shop by the late R.C. Schauer of Cost, who lived only a short distance from the site of the battle. Fashioned from drill stem pipe and hammered with a thin bronze plate, the cannon was first fired by Schauer and his seven-year-old grandson on November 5, 1935.

The first exhibit in the north wing of the museum is titled "DeWitt's Colony" and includes pictures of Green, Sarah, and son Christopher Columbus DeWitt.

Across the rotunda is the south wing of the museum, where surface finds of Indians and articles of those who arrived after the pioneer settlers are displayed.

Among the more rare items on display is a hypodermic syringe brought from France to Texas by Dr. J.C. Jones (1837-1904.) This syringe is one of the first of its kind ever made. [19]

A project of the Thomas Shelton Chapter, Daughters of the American Revolution, the museum is governed by a six-member museum board.

(The Gonzales Memorial Museum is open six days a week: Tuesday through Saturday from 10:00 A.M. until noon and from 1:00 P.M. until 5:00 P.M.; Sunday from 1:00 P.M. until 5:00 P.M. The museum is closed on Monday.)

In 1956 the first "Come and Take It Days" Celebration was

held in Gonzales. It was organized by George Nixon Shuler and the local chapter of the Gonzales Junior Chamber of Commerce, the Jaycees. Shuler, the son of a local native, began planning for the gala annual weekend event in 1955. When interviewed as to his motive for such an affair, Shuler said,

> I was raised in Gonzales. I became amazed by the lack of interest here in the town's vast historical background. . . . But up until this year (1956), nothing had been attempted on a large scale to exploit our historical background to give us all a sense of pride in living in Gonzales and a common cause for celebration. . . .

In 1955 Shuler approached the Chamber of Commerce and the Retail Merchants Association about sponsoring such a celebration, but neither group expressed interest in the project. His opportunity came in July 1956, when C.H. Nelson, Jr., president of the newly organized Jaycees, showed enthusiasm for Shuler's idea and named him chairman of a committee to investigate the possibility. After the chamber directors endorsed the celebration, nineteen local civic clubs attended the organizational meeting. At that time Shuler was appointed as chairman of the Come and Take It Association, and the celebration idea caught fire.

The first "Come and Take It Days" Celebration began on September 26, 1956. The countywide contest for "Queen of the Texas Frontier" was held in the Memorial Building, and the crown was won by a young woman from Nixon, Alice Faulkner, who later married Jackie Dunn of Stockdale.

An essay contest concerning the history of Gonzales resulted in winning entries by Opal Lee Clark of Cheapside and John Wayne Cook of Cost.

During the festivities Janice Dickinson (later Mrs. Buddy Lester,) a descendant of Almeron and Susanna Dickinson, lay a wreath at the foot of the Texas Minuteman Statue on Texas Heroes Square.

A ceremony was also held at the site of the Battle of Gonzales fought near Cost. Miller Harwood gave the address, and Ross Boothe, Jr., and Charles Chenault, Jr., placed a flag at the Cost monument.

The celebration also featured the largest and best parade ever seen in Gonzales and a visit by a granddaughter of Sarah Seely DeWitt.

In recent years the "Come and Take It Days" has grown into a three-day weekend celebration with food booths, beer garden, crafts and commercial booths, a parade, carnival, and street dances. The event is held during the first weekend in October on the two historic squares in downtown Gonzales. A reenactment of the October 2 battle is held on Saturday afternoon at the Pioneer Village Living History Center, which is located one block north of Highway 90A on Highway 183. On Sunday there is a memorial service to honor men from the Gonzales area who served in the Texian Army during the Texas Revolution.

Pioneer Village is a collection of eight restored nineteenth-century homes, a working blacksmith shop, and a broom factory. The Center is a twelve-acre tract that includes an 1830s log cabin, an 1840s log home, an 1856 cypress-sided home, an 1870s church, an 1892 two-story Victorian house and museum, smokehouse, barn and blacksmith shop. On some Sundays the 1870 Hamon Church still holds services, and ghosts of former congregations whisper as visitors sit in a pew.

At the Pioneer Village Living History Center, a costumed director and local curators recreate the Gonzales of 1835 by conducting period demonstrations, seminars, and tours "in costume" and "in character." Pioneer Village hosts thousands of schoolchildren from throughout the state all during the year.

The Center also offers battle reenactments throughout the year. Among the special events are the Republic of Texas Days on April 3, the Gay Nineties Celebration the second weekend in June, Come and Take It Days on October 2, the Fall Festival on Thanksgiving weekend, and the Christmas Pilgrimage in December.

The Center is open Wednesday through Saturday from 10:00 A.M. until 4:00 P.M. and on Sunday 1:00 P.M. until 5:00 P.M. Different admissions are charged for adults, senior citizens, and students.

Other attractions in Gonzales include tours of the Old Jail Museum and the Memorial Museum, Courthouse Trade Days on the last Saturday from April through November, the Spring Garden Show in April, a car show, and performances of live dinner theater at the Crystal Theater, built in 1917 and located at 511 St. Lawrence Street. It was formerly the New Playhouse, where silent films were shown accompanied by a pit orchestra.

The Gonzales County Historical Commission sponsors a "Driving Tour of Historical Gonzales." Their brochure provides a self-guided driving tour with sixty-four stops of historic interest. The Gonzales Chamber of Commerce and Agriculture sponsors a "Walking Tour of Historical Gonzales." Their pamphlet lists thirty-one locations within walking distance of the chamber office. Visitors on either tour will encounter simple Texas cabins, prairie-styled homes, fanciful Victorian cottages, Greek Revival mansions, and grand public and private buildings.

Since just prior to World War II, the poultry business has dominated the Gonzales area. Millions of fine broilers have taken the place of the prairie chickens of Green DeWitt's era. Today broiler production in the area ranks tops in the state.

Gonzales is still a major cattle-producing area, evidenced in the many feed lots, shipping areas, and cattle auctions. (As of 1993, there were between 78,000 and 80,000 breeding age cows in the county.) Today, however, huge herds of whiteface Herefords have supplanted the wild Longhorn cattle of George Littlefield's day.

The local economy is still largely based on agriculture, but the tourist trade is growing each year. Fortunately, most of the historical landmarks of Gonzales remain today. "The Cradle of Texas Independence" is justifiably proud of her founder's role in early Texas history. Since the mid-1950s, the residents of Gonzales have admirably presented that proud and fascinating heritage to countless visitors.

Green DeWitt, Empresario of the DeWitt Colony.
— Photo courtesy Gonzales Memorial Museum, Gonzales, Texas

Sarah Seely DeWitt, the Mother of Gonzales.
— Photo courtesy Gonzales Memorial Museum, Gonzales, Texas

Andrew Ponton, an early alcalde *of Gonzales.*

Col. John H. Moore, Texian leader in the Battle of Gonzales.

— Photos courtesy Gonzales Memorial Museum, Gonzales, Texas

George W. Davis, who buried the "Come and Take It" cannon in his peach orchard.
— Photo courtesy Hugh Shelton, First Shot Photographics, Gonzales, Texas

Susanna Dickinson, the only Anglo adult survivor at the Alamo.
— Photo courtesy The Center for American History, The University of Texas at Austin

George W. Littlefield, cattleman and banker.
— Photo courtesy The Center for American History, The University of Texas at Austin

McClure-Braches House, where the widows of the Alamo defenders gathered.
— Photo courtesy Hugh Shelton, First Shot Photographics, Gonzales,

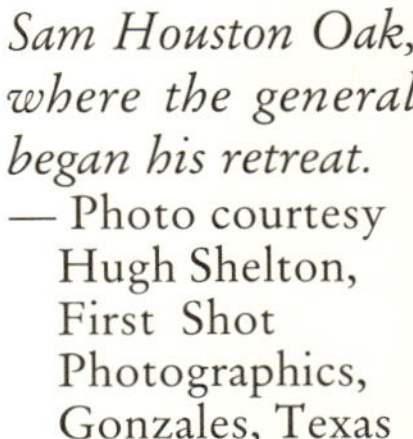

Sam Houston Oak, where the general began his retreat.
— Photo courtesy Hugh Shelton, First Shot Photographics, Gonzales, Texas

McClure-Braches House and Sam Houston Oak.
—Photo courtesy Gonzales Memorial Museum Gonzales, Texas

Thomas J. Pilgrim, pioneer educator and religious leader.
— Photo courtesy The Center for American History, The University of Texas at Austin

The Pilgrim House, built by Carey J. Pilgrim in 1883.
— Photo courtesy J. C. Hoke, Wharton, Texas

The Eggleston House, built in 1848, the oldest structure in Gonzales.
— Photo courtesy J. C. Hoke, Wharton, Texas

The Old Gonzales College — 1853, 820 St. Louis St.
— Photo courtesy J. C. Hoke, Wharton, Texas

The Episcopal Church — 1881, 721 St. Louis St.
— Photo courtesy J. C. Hoke, Wharton, Texas

The Fly House, now the Buffington Funeral Home.
— Photo courtesy J. C. Hoke, Wharton, Texas

T-41 Weathervane on Gonzales Fire Station.
—Photo courtesy J. C. Hoke, Wharton, Texas

Fort Waul state marker, near intersection of S. H. 90A and S. H. 183.
— Photo courtesy J. C. Hoke, Wharton, Texas

Fort Waul interior grounds.
— Photo courtesy J. C. Hoke, Wharton, Texas

Texas Heroes Monument
— Photo courtesy J. C. Hoke, Wharton, Texas

Confederate Monument
— Photo courtesy J. C. Hoke, Wharton, Texas

"The Old Eighteen" state markers, just off S. H. 183 at the south end of the Guadalupe River bridge.
— Photo courtesy J. C. Hoke, Wharton, Texas

Old Gonzales County Jail.
— Photo courtesy J. C. Hoke, Wharton, Texas

Replica of gallows, Old Gonzales County Jail.
— Photo courtesy J. C. Hoke, Wharton, Texas

Gonzales Courthouse during construction.
— Photo courtesy Hugh Shelton, First Shot Photographics, Gonzales, Texas

Gonzales County Courthouse.
— Photo courtesy J. C. Hoke, Wharton, Texas

The Randle-Rather Building, built in 1897, 400 block of St. George St.
— Photo courtesy J. C. Hoke, Wharton, Texas

The Peck and Fly Building, built in 1890, St. Joseph St. facing Public Square.
— Photo courtesy J. C. Hoke, Wharton, Texas

The Lewis-Houston House, built in 1899, 619 St. Lawrence St.
— Photo courtesy J. C. Hoke, Wharton, Texas

The Kennard House, built in 1895, 621 St. Louis St.
— Photo courtesy J. C. Hoke, Wharton, Texas

The Charles T. Rather House, built in 1892, 828 St. Louis St.
— Photo courtesy J. C. Hoke, Wharton, Texas

The John Curtis Jones House (1872), corner of Hamilton and St. Vincent.
— Photo courtesy J. C. Hoke, Wharton, Texas

The "Come and Take It" Cannon.

— Photo courtesy J. C. Hoke, Wharton, Texas

Gonzales Memorial Museum.

— Photo courtesy J. C. Hoke, Wharton, Texas.

Map of Gonzales.

— Photo courtesy Visitors' and Newcomers' Guide, Gonzales Chamber of Commerce and Agriculture, Gonzales, Texas

II

Columbus: A Walk Into a Proud Past

Situated along the banks of the Colorado River amid huge magnolia and oak trees, Columbus appears to be a typically quiet, small town. Motorists racing by on Interstate 10 are oblivious of the many tourist attractions in one of the oldest Anglo towns in Texas. A closer look reveals a wealth of historical treasures restored and preserved by energetic citizens who display their town's proud past to help assure its future.

Columbus has fifty-seven historical markers within the city limits, including a National Historic District clustered around an 1891 showcase, the Colorado County Courthouse. The little town is filled with vintage houses and buildings, including the 1856 Tait town house and the 1886 Stafford Opera House. Ironically, a town whose landmarks reflect culture and civility was a killing field at the turn of the century because of two bloody family feuds.

According to conventional wisdom, Columbus was established in 1823, making it the oldest continually settled Anglo-American community in Texas. The town was supposedly built on the site of an Indian village called Montezuma and is said to have sprung from Beeson's Crossing. However, the available evidence indicates that none of this is true.

Based on the most recent scholarship, Montezuma, the earliest place named in the area, was located seven miles south of present

Columbus at the junction of the Colorado River and the Atascosito Road. Stephen F. Austin considered establishing a town in the vicinity of present Columbus in August 1823. Columbus sprang from Dewees' Crossing upriver from Beeson's. This new town was first named in 1835 and born two years later.[1]

In late December 1821, four of Austin's "Old 300" colonists — Jesse Burnam, Robert and Joseph Kuykendall, and Daniel Gilleland — began the first Anglo settlement on the Colorado River. Burnam's Crossing was some distance north of present Columbus.

By early 1822, Benjamin Beeson was operating a ferry some three or four miles downriver from present Columbus. In a census of March 4, 1823, Beeson gave his age as thirty-seven and listed his occupation as farmer. His wife, Betsy, was age thirty and the couple had six children. Benjamin received his league of land on August 3, 1824. In addition to his ferry, he built a gin, grist mill, and saw mill. Betsy Beeson kept a boardinghouse for travelers.

Beeson died less than one year after the Texas Revolution. On March 1, 1837, his estate was inventoried and appraised at a total of $15,292. His league of land with improvements and a gin was valued at $7,000. He had three male, three female, and six child slaves appraised at $4,950, about one-third of his total estate.

Adjoining Beeson's grant to the north on the west bank of the Colorado was the land of Elizabeth Tumlinson. Present-day Columbus is located on her grant. She was the widow of John Tumlinson, who was killed by Indians near the Guadalupe River in the summer of 1823. Elizabeth received her league and labor of land on August 16, 1824.

William Bluford Dewees, the "father of Columbus" and one of Austin's "Old 300" colonists, was born in Kentucky on September 8, 1799. After being raised by a Baptist minister, his first exposure to a sinful world came at Natchez when William saw his first steamboat and observed "men, women and children mingling together in every species of vice and dissipation."

Dewees lived in Arkansas for a year, then traveled to Nacogdoches, where he heard of Moses Austin's colony in Texas. After returning to Pecan Point, Arkansas, he joined the enterprise and reached the Brazos River with three or four families on January 1, 1822.

In the fall of 1822, Dewees reached the Colorado River at the crossing of the old LaBahia road. Hearing a barking dog, he noticed a small log cabin on the opposite bank of the river. Aylett C. "Strap"

Buckner and Peter Powell had built this cabin near present La-Grange in 1819. The two old adventurers told Dewees about a few families twelve miles below them on the east bank of the Colorado. When William reached Burnam's Crossing, he found his old friend, Jesse Burnam.

On August 3, 1824, Dewees and James Cook, both single men, received title to a league of land in present Colorado County. In the census of 1826, William was listed as a blacksmith. Later that year he went to Mexico on a trading trip. Upon his return he lived in San Antonio for three years.

In February 1829, Dewees returned to the Colorado and built a new cabin on the west bank of the river ten miles above the Atascosito road. On April 18, 1831, he received title to one-half league west of and adjacent to the Tumlinson grant.[2]

After Mexican governor Jose Trespalacios divided Austin's colony into two districts, Baron de Bastrop convened the Colorado settlers on November 20, 1822. They elected John Tumlinson as *alcalde* of the Colorado District, Robert Kuykendall as captain, and Mose Morrison as lieutenant.

On August 9, 1823, Baron de Bastrop met with James Cummins at Sylvanus Castleman's home on Cummins Creek just north of present Columbus. Cummins was instructed to assemble the concerned colonists at Castleman's place to explain that Austin was to have "complete authority to organize the colonial establishment which the Mexican government has granted him in his province. . ." A week later fourteen men met at Robert Kuykendall's home and unanimously elected James Cummins as *alcalde* of the Colorado District.

Cummins was granted six leagues and one labor of land on July 7, 1824. He received a land bonus because he built a saw and grist mill. His home on Cummins Creek served as a community center on the Colorado until his death in 1849.

The settlers' first encounter with the fearsome Karankawas came on February 23, 1823, when three young men — H.W. Law, John Alley, and John C. Clark — went down the Colorado by canoe to obtain corn. The Karankawas had come up country and camped at the mouth of Skull Creek about fifteen miles below the settlement. As the three returned with their canoe loaded with corn, they were ambushed at the mouth of Skull Creek. Law and Alley were killed by arrows; Clark jumped into the river and swam to the bank. Although he suffered seven severe arrow wounds, Clark managed to escape by crawling into a heavy cane brake.

Late that evening Robert Brotherton rode to the same "kronk" camp, assuming they were friendly. When he dismounted they wrestled his gun from him and shot Robert in the backbone as he fled. The arrow wound did little damage, and he managed to reach the settlement a few hours later.

The next morning a company of fourteen men, including Dewees, found the Karankawas camped in a thicket just before dawn as the Indians were preparing breakfast. When they heard talking, the alarmed Indians rushed out and the white men opened fire. Nineteen Karankawas were killed, and two of the wounded escaped into the open prairie.

After the battle Dewees attempted to scalp a dead Indian with long, beautiful plaits of hair. He passed up the opportunity for a battle trophy because "the skin of his head was so thick, and the sight so ghastly, that the very thoughts of it almost makes the blood curdle in my veins."

By the time Austin returned from Mexico City in April 1823, there were twenty-five families near Beeson's Crossing. These settlers included Abram, Rawson, Thomas and William Alley, Caleb R. Bostick, David Bright, Robert Brotherton, James Cummins, W.B. Dewees, Thomas Kuykendall, James McNair, James Nelson, Gabriel Straw Synder, Nathaniel Whiting, and Elizabeth, James, and John Tumlinson.[3]

In August 1823, Austin, Baron de Bastrop, surveyor Rawson Alley, and some slaves surveyed 170 acres on the Colorado River eight miles above the Atascosito crossing. This site in the vicinity of present Columbus was to be the capital of the municipality of Colorado and the headquarters of Austin's colony.

W.B. Dewees visited with Austin a few days while lots were being laid off for a town. The *empresario* later changed his mind and chose a similar spot on the Brazos since most of his colonists were on that river. This capital was called San Felipe de Austin, a name suggested by the Mexican governor in San Antonio.

In a letter written on December 1, 1823, Dewees told of great suffering and shortage of provisions caused by dry weather, poor crops, and game leaving the country. Single men had remained to protect the settlement and hunt for food in companies for fear of Indians. Despite an all-day hunt, they often could not find deer or turkey. Hungry children would wait for the return of the hunters at night and eagerly run to meet them. According to Dewees, they would either be wild with delight or would cry bitterly. The women bore their sufferings without complaining, trying to appear cheerful and happy, and took up guns to assist in standing guard. Luckily, the Tonkawas were friendly to the settlers, supplying them with dressed deer skins for clothing.

After his mother wrote William asking him to come home, he replied in a letter dated January 1, 1824:

> . . . . Now, mother, you and my sisters are in Kentucky, where you have plenty to eat, and no person to disturb you at night. Now, if you will contrast your condition with the poor helpless women and children in this wilderness, you would not ask me to come home. Mother, I am determined to be honest and brave. . . .
>
> I will, as soon as circumstances permit, come home to see you. But we boys cannot withstand the entreaties of the women and children not to leave them; for they say if we leave them, their husbands can not kill game and protect them from the savages. . . . Mother, I believe every woman and child we can save from the savages will add one jewel in our crown when we leave this world. . . .

In November 1824, a wounded, bleeding Mexican struggled into the settlement. He had been driving a large herd of horses and mules to Louisiana with a Señor Corasco, a prominent horse trader, when they were attacked by robbers at a nearby creek. All the drivers were murdered except the wounded Mexican. (The scene of the massacre was later named Corasco Creek.)

Seven men from Beeson's Crossing, including Dewees, trailed the robbers to the Brazos and killed all but one as they were preparing to swim the river. Austin had advised his colonists to follow thieves and bring back the stolen property but not the thieves since a whipping only exasperated them. Acting on this directive, the Anglos cut off the head of one of the robbers and stuck it on a pole as a warning to other marauders.

In 1824 Milton Cook opened a tavern at Beeson's. His visitors included Ben Milam, Lorenzo de Zavala, William Barret Travis, Jim Bowie, Davy Crockett, and Sam Houston. Another not-so-welcome guest was the British doctor John Charles Beales, a naturalized Mexican citizen and agent. After announcing that he was authorized to establish another settlement on the Colorado, Dr. Beales had several tense confrontations with local settlers at Cook's tavern. Evidently, he really coveted the land for England but failed to dislodge the colonists at Beeson's.

In 1826 local residents held the first Fourth of July celebration in Texas by holding a dance and buffalo hunt on the Colorado. Four settlers traveled sixty miles from Gonzales to join in the festivities. While they were gone, James Kerr's tiny settlement was destroyed by raiding Comanches and Wichitas on July 2.

In November 1831, Dewees wrote:

> . . . It is nothing uncommon for us to inquire of a man why he ran away from the States but few persons feel insulted by such a question. They generally answer for some crime or other which they have committed. . . .
>
> There is no such thing as attending church, since no religion except the Roman Catholic is tolerated, and we have no priests among us. Indeed, I have not heard a sermon since I left Kentucky, except at a camp-meeting in Arkansas.

The following businesses were known to exist at Beeson's Crossing between 1823 and 1835: Benjamin Beeson operated a ferry, gin, grist mill, and saw mill; his wife Elizabeth kept an inn or boardinghouse; William Demetrius Lacy established a tanyard and saddle shop; James Nelson was a tanner and currier; Caleb R. Bostick was a carpenter; James McNair was a clothier; William B. Dewees was a gunsmith and blacksmith; James Cook was postmaster; Milton Cook ran a tavern; John McCrosky was a tanner and currier.

On October 2, 1835, the first shots of the Texas Revolution were fired in the Battle of Gonzales. This "Come and Take It" battle occurred when 168 Texians confronted and refused to return a six-pound cannon to 150 Mexican cavalrymen. The little cannon had been loaned to Gonzales residents in 1831 for defense against the Indians.

Among those who participated in the Battle of Gonzales was a company from the Colorado under the command of J.W.E. Wallace. This unit also took part in the Siege of Bexar, which began on October 24, 1835.

On January 11, 1836, the general council of the provisional state government organized the Colorado Municipality and authorized the sending of two delegates to a convention at Washington-on-the-Brazos to be held on March 1, 1836. The Colorado delegates who signed the Texas Declaration of Independence were W.D. Lacy and William Menefee.[4]

After hearing the news of the fall of the Alamo, Gen. Sam Houston began a six-week retreat eastward from Gonzales at midnight on March 13, 1836. When he camped on the east bank of the Lavaca River, Houston sent an aide to Beeson's seeking men, supplies, munitions, and artillery. This assistance was to be sent to Burnam's Ferry on the Colorado. After ferrying some 1,000 civilians and his army across the river on the morning of March 18, General Houston made a sharp right turn south along the east bank toward Beeson's Crossing.

Houston's army reached Beeson's late on March 19 and stayed there until March 26. During this time his force grew to some 800 men. Houston deployed a small unit of his troops under Col. Sidney Sherman at a shoal known as Dewees' Crossing. He encamped his main army under Col. Edward Burleson seven miles south around the river bend at Beeson's.

During this time Mexican Gen. Joaquin Ramirez y Sesma was camped with 725 men on the opposite bank two miles above Houston's location. (Today there is a state historical marker there at Glidden Mill on State Highway 90. Sesma's camp is now in a residential area of Columbus.)

On the night of March 24, General Houston called for W.B. Dewees and asked for his opinion about the chance of success if the Texan army crossed the river at the ford and attacked the Sesma camp. Dewees was dismissed after saying the chances were very favorable.

That night Dewees and two other men crossed the Colorado to spy out the Mexican camp. At daybreak they climbed a tree and noticed an unusual parade with music and booming cannons in the encampment. Upon returning to Houston's tent, Dewees learned that a man named Carr (James Kerr) had arrived from Victoria bringing news that Santa Anna was marching from there to reinforce Sesma. The parade witnessed by Dewees was in fact the celebration of the arrival of Santa Anna.

On March 26, General Houston addressed his troops, telling them that James Walker Fannin and his army of U.S. volunteers had surrendered to Mexican Gen. Jose Urrea near Goliad. Since he now commanded the only Anglo army in Texas and did not expect reinforcements, he dared not risk attacking the reinforced Mexican camp across the river. When he finished his speech, Houston ordered the burning of all homes and buildings and an immediate retreat to the Brazos.

This decision to give up the heavily populated area between the Colorado and Brazos triggered a wave of desertions and the panic civilian flight known as the "Runaway Scrape."

At this time there were seventy-five families camped on the Colorado, including that of Dewees, who left the army and joined the civilians in retreat. While camped at Spring Creek, twenty-five miles east of San Felipe, William and others went to Harrisburg to bring up two cannon, the "Twin Sisters," for Houston's army encamped at Leonard Groce's Bernardo plantation. General Houston then ordered Dewees to take a company of men and guard the women and children between Spring Creek and the Trinity River.

When Dewees' train of some seventy-five wagons reached the San Jacinto River, they found it swollen to the top of the banks. There was no ferry, and the rapid stream made the use of rafts too dangerous. According to William it was two inventive Yankees who solved the problem of crossing the river. They first cut two very tall pine trees, peeled off the bark, then laid the two logs across the river close enough to position wagon wheels on them. The men then pulled the loaded wagons across the swollen river with a rope, completing the task in half a day.

On April 22, 1836, the morning after the battle, Dewees received news of the San Jacinto victory while encamped twenty miles away with 150 to 200 families. He immediately started for home and arrived with three families on the east bank of the Colorado on May 10.

In one of his letters, William described the scene as follows:

> Here all was gloom and desolation. Our once happy homes were now in ashes! The cattle had been driven off and there was naught to welcome us back again to the homes which we had left but a few weeks before. All was stillness round. . . . A shudder ran through our frames on beholding the change. . . .

Since he did not know where the Mexican army was, Dewees rode down to the Atascosito Crossing. There he hid in the timber and observed General Filisola's army crossing the river on their way out of Texas. William then rode back to his family and built rafts for crossing the Colorado. After doing so, the small group lived in camps until they could build houses. At this time Dewees had only a half bushel of corn and a dream — a new town at Dewees' Crossing.

The earliest known use of the name "Columbus" was on December 30, 1835, when it appeared in a petition for the creation of a new municipality. The document stated that the petitioners had "Laid out a Town on the Calerado at an Eligible place which Town they have styled the Town of Columbus" for use as a seat of justice for the new municipality.

In a letter dated December 25, 1835, William Dewees mentioned that a new city had been laid out but "no building has as yet been commenced, on account of the unsettled state of the country." In choosing a name for the new town, Dewees was probably influenced by Washington Irving's book, *A History of the Life and Voyages of Christopher Columbus* (1828), which made the explorer a major hero in Dewees' mind.

On March 17, 1836, the Republic of Texas created Colorado County. Later in the year Columbus was chosen as the county seat. Colorado County was created along with Lavaca, Fayette, Wharton, and Lee counties from the original municipality of Colorado.

In 1837 William Menefee and Stephen Townsend were elected as chief justice and sheriff, respectively, of Colorado County. The country was divided into three districts — upper, middle, and lower — with two justices of the peace and a constable in each. William Dewees served as justice of the peace in the middle district from 1837 until 1839.

In April 1837, District Judge Robert McAlpin "Three-Legged Willie" Williamson convened the first district court session ever held in Colorado County. According to local legend the session was held under a century-old live oak. (The remains of the District Court Oak still stand adjacent to the courthouse square in Columbus.) However, the earliest reports of the session state that it was held in an old log building near the river, probably the schoolhouse known to have been near the river as early as 1833.

Judge Williamson earned a legendary reputation as a great trial lawyer, a courageous district judge, and a politician with a marvelous sense of humor. He was among the most humane judges of his day, and he tended to assess sentences as light as the law allowed.

In another early case tried in Columbus by Judge James W. Robinson, the hapless W.H. Bibbs was found guilty of grand larceny (probably cattle theft) and threw himself upon the mercy of the court. Judge Robinson decreed that the prisoner should receive thirty-nine lashes on his bare back, be branded on the right hand with the letter "T" (for thief), and pay the cost of suit or remain in custody. Once the judge was informed that the sum of $500 could not be found west of the Colorado, he remitted that portion of the sentence, and the bloodied, scarred culprit was released from custody.

Columbus was established in the league of land originally granted Elizabeth Tumlinson on August 16, 1824. After her death, the six children inherited the land, which was divided into six numbered parts. On December 19, 1833, the children or their representatives drew lots for the numbered land. On September 6, 1834, John J. Tumlinson, who drew lot 2, sold half of his part to Dewees for $112. On this land William established the new town of Columbus some months later.

On January 23, 1837, the first sale of Columbus lots occurred when John W. Holman purchased lot 1 of block 13, lot 4 of block 8, and lot 4 of block 12 for $200 from Dewees. On May 22, William sold an undivided half interest in most of the remaining town lots to J.W.E. Wallace for $1,480.

Columbus took off as a real estate venture in the spring of 1837, when three advertisements for the sale of town lots appeared in the *Telegraph and Texas Register*. In the third ad dated June 3, 1837, proprietors Dewees and Wallace asserted that Columbus was being built on the same site that Austin had surveyed in 1823. The town was at the bend of the river known as Dewees' Shoals or Ford. Around the bend of the river by its meander is ten miles; across it by land, it is but 700 yards.

According to the advertisement, town lots were being sold in Columbus on July 2 at prices ranging from $150 to $500. Sixteen buildings had been erected with fourteen more under contract. The proprietors had presented blocks 2, 3 and 17 to the county with the proceeds to be used for building a courthouse, jail, and other public edifices. They also announced that Mr. Arnold of Lexington, Kentucky, had opened an academy with thirty-four pupils.

Andrew F. Muir's book, *Texas in 1837*, is based on the notes of an unknown traveler who made the following observation:

> .... Columbus, a small town, consisting of two public houses, two small stores, and half dozen shanties stand upon the west side of the Colorado River.... Corn and cotton were both growing in the neighborhood.... The situation of this place is decidedly more desirable than any I had yet seen for a town, as unites a healthy atmosphere with agricultural and commercial advantages. It will undoubtedly be the head of navigation for many years, as the falls on the river just above the town cannot be avoided with-

> out an immense expenditure of labor and money. . . . The people of this settlement had more the appearance of industry than any I had yet seen, and. . . there would be little to complain of more than is common among men anywhere. . . . I saw a large number of springs, good water may be had almost anywhere by digging from fifteen to forty feet. . . .

In 1838 Dewees noted: "Emigrants are fast flocking into the country, money and provisions are plenty, and I see no reason why we should not be happy."

In 1840 William donated a block of land in Columbus for use as a school site. For years this block on Walnut Street was referred to as Seminary Square and has been in continuous use for school purposes from 1854 to the present. Both Colorado College and the white high school were located on this land.

After 600 Comanches carried out a raid to the Gulf Coast against Victoria and Linnville in August 1840, four volunteer companies were formed to intercept them as they retreated to the high plains with 1,500 stolen horses and mules. W.B. Dewees led the Columbus company along with contingents from Matagorda, LaGrange, and Bastrop.

In a letter dated December 17, 1840, Dewees described the Battle of Plum Creek as follows:

> . . . . The four companies concentrated here, and by dint of very hard riding succeeded in overtaking the enemy at Plum Creek. [The battle site is five miles southeast of present Lockhart.] Orders were instantly given to charge upon the foe. This was done as they were crossing the creek, which being very boggy, they found great difficulty in doing; and we were enabled to kill a great many of them, liberate the prisoners, and force them to give up their spoils before they were able to cross the creek. We still continued to follow them after they had crossed, constantly firing upon them. They did not attempt to fight but little, but seemed bent on escaping from us. We kept up the pursuit till their force scattered. . . . The number of Camanches killed we never ascertained, but it was quite large: of our own men not one was killed. . . . [Eighty-six Indians and two Texians were killed. The volunteer force of 200 was led by Maj. Gen. Felix Huston. Both sides could claim victory since the Comanche goal was to avoid a fight and get home with their loot.]

William Bollaert, an English traveler in Texas in 1843, described Columbus as follows:

> .... Barter is the present system of trade. Cotton for sugar and coffee, and bacon for boots... corn for calomel, quinine and whiskey, beef for brandy, etc. Thus a Columbus trader's books would be an interesting MS. for the British Museum.

The German scientist Dr. Ferdinand Roemer traveled in Texas from November 1845 to May 1847. He noted that

> .... Columbus presents a friendly aspect. The frame houses, numbering eighteen or twenty provided with wide porches stood charmingly in the shade of the old live oaks. Neither were the inevitable requisites of the Texas town lacking, for I counted three stores, two taverns and a smithy.

Dr. Roemer also observed no new buildings under construction and much excitement over a horse race with single bets up to $500.

In 1837 merchants and planters from Columbus, LaGrange, and Matagorda decided to make the Colorado River navigable for steamboats. Their immediate concern was the removal of "the raft," a massive driftwood obstruction on the river whose head was twelve miles above Matagorda. On December 14, 1837, they persuaded the Texas Congress to pass a special law incorporating the Colorado Navigation Company.

The company had its main office in Matagorda and was empowered to issue capital stock of $125,000 in shares of $100 each "for the purpose of clearing a channel susceptible of navigation by steamboats or other craft for the Colorado River." The company was required to open a channel permitting steamboats to pass fifty miles upstream within four years or forfeit its charter. Once the fifty-mile channel was completed, the company could levy tolls on craft using the river.

In Columbus three commissioners were authorized to receive subscriptions for stock: J. W. E. Wallace, Robert Brotherton, and Stephen Townsend. Although the company hired a civil engineer to survey the raft in 1839, no further action was taken due to lack of funds.

On April 14, 1838, the keelboat *David Crockett* arrived at the head of the raft after a five-day trip downriver from Bastrop. From that time on, Matagorda teamsters met boats there and shuttled cotton bales and other freight into town, where the cargo was loaded onto other boats.

In November 1841, Mr. Winburn's keelboat reached the head of the raft from Columbus in four and one-half days, bringing down cotton grown on Capt. John Duncan's plantation. A second trip was completed by December 18. W.B. Dewees and partners Ward and Ingram then loaded the keelboat with a splendid assortment of goods for the up country and Columbus.

On June 1, 1842, delegates from counties along the lower Colorado met in Columbus to discuss the raft problem. A five-man committee reported that $30,000 would be required to remove the raft. They recommended that the money be raised by subscription through county committees and that the work start once $10,000 was raised. After two years this effort also ceased.

On January 18, 1844, the Texas Congress rechartered the Colorado Navigation Company with minor changes. In June of that year, Samuel Ward of LaGrange agreed to build a steamboat for the company at the head of the raft. Ward purchased the engine and equipment in Pittsburgh and his steamboat, the *Kate Ward*, named in honor of his sister, arrived at Austin on March 8, 1846. The sidewheeler was 115 feet long, twenty-four feet in the beam, and had two engines of seventy horsepower each. She drew only eighteen inches of water unloaded and could carry 600 bales of cotton. During high water in 1848, the *Kate Ward* escaped around the raft and reached Matagorda Bay.

The Colorado Navigation Company was rechartered for a third and final time on September 5, 1850. With $17,000 raised in stock sales, engineer W.T. Ward utilized the *Kate Ward* as a snag-boat to clear a channel from the mouth of the Colorado through the seven-mile-long raft in December 1852. By that time, however, the company had been forced to suspend operations because none of the six counties involved had paid their subscriptions.

The most successful approach to the raft problem was undertaken by the U.S. Army Corps of Engineers. Between November 1853 and March 1854, the Corps dug a bypass channel around the raft and through a series of lakes. For the first time, a steamer from Matagorda could ply directly to Columbus and LaGrange through safe, navigable waters.

The years between 1854 and 1860 marked the best period of navigation on the Colorado. During this time the paddlewheelers

Betty Powell, Lareno, Flying Jenny, and *Moccasin Belle* made regular trips up the Colorado as far as Bastrop.

On May 1, 1871, the last recorded steamer, *Providence*, made an excursion trip from Columbus to Dripping Springs on the Colorado. Leaving Columbus at 8:00 A.M., the boat arrived about noon and the small party went ashore to gather dewberries and admire the scenery. At 4:00 that evening, the *Providence* returned to her landing at Columbus.

By July 1839, a stageline connected Columbus with Houston. Brown and Tarbo, owners of the Texas U.S. Mail Line of Stages between Houston and San Antonio, began to pass through Columbus on February 22, 1847. Their line introduced the new broad carriage wheel that would not bog down in the soft prairies.

Mail contractors E.M.B. Sawyer and B. Risher ran numerous early stage routes out of Eagle Lake. One of their stages left Eagle Lake at 10:00 A.M., went through Columbus, and arrived in San Antonio at 3:00 P.M. the next day. Another route departed from Eagle Lake at 10:00 A.M., stopped at Columbus, and arrived in Austin the second day at noon. Both lines ran every other day.

After C.K. Hall joined the firm in 1860, the three partners controlled sixteen of the thirty-one passenger and mail lines in the state, employed over 300 men, and used over 1,000 mules and horses in their Texas and Louisiana operations.

In 1861 Sawyer, Risher and Hall ran a line of four horse stages from Eagle Lake to the railhead of the Buffalo Bayou, Brazos, and Colorado Railroad at Alleyton. The line then continued to San Antonio via Columbus, Halletsville, Gonzales, and Seguin.

During the Civil War, the Confederate States Mail Line operated in conjunction with passenger stages and was run by Giddings & Meiers. There was brisk trade and traffic between the BBB&C railhead at Alleyton and the critical cotton shipping points of Brownsville and Matamoros. Thus weekly stage service ran through Columbus.

After the war, Columbus was the western railhead for the Galveston, Harrisburg and San Antonio Railroad. As a result Risher and Hall ran a stageline six days a week, Sundays excepted, from Columbus to San Antonio. All of the stages left Columbus in the evening on the arrival of the Harrisburg trains. Another line ran from Columbus to LaGrange three times a week: Monday, Wednesday, and Friday. All of these schedules were both passenger and mail lines.

By 1871 ownership of the line was divided, with Sawyer having four routes under his name. Risher and Hall retained seven lines, including Columbus to LaGrange, Columbus to San Antonio, and Victoria to Austin through Columbus. Two of the lines operated daily; the other five maintained tri-weekly schedules.

In 1873 S.T. Scott and Company's U.S. Mail Stage Lines left Columbus tri-weekly at 5:00 P.M. for LaGrange on the arrival of the BBB&C train. The line left Columbus daily at 5:00 P.M. for San Antonio on the arrival of the GH&SA train.

Within a few years railroad competition caused the stagelines to cease operations due to loss of riders.

Newspapers in Columbus date from 1839, when the *Columbus Sentinel and Herald* was published, followed by the *Columbus Herald* in 1840. Neither paper lasted more than a year.

On Saturday, September 5, 1857, the first edition of *The Colorado Citizen* was published by brothers James Davis, Benjamin Marshall, and A. Hicks Baker, who came to Columbus from Lockhart, where they had published the *Southern Watchman*. By 1861 the publication date of the *Citizen* had been changed to Friday.

In 1861 Ben Baker joined the Confederate army, followed by brothers Hicks and Jim in 1862. Their newspaper was suspended for the duration of the war. Hicks was killed in the Civil War, and Jim's health was broken.

At war's end Ben and Jim Baker returned to Columbus and resumed publication of the *Citizen* on Thursday, June 8, 1865. The masthead listed the editors as "J.D. Baker & Bro." When Jim left for health reasons, Ben could not afford his brother's interest, and the two sold the paper to Columbus attorney Fred Barnard. The last known issue of the *Colorado Citizen* appeared on May 5, 1866, and the new owner changed the name of the paper to *The Columbus Times.*

The *Times* was sold by 1869, when Barnard hired Ben Baker as "publisher" and started a second paper with the old name, *The Colorado Citizen.* The first edition came out on January 28, 1869. In early October 1871, Barnard sold the paper to Robert Levi Foard, Wells Thompson, and George Millan McCormick, partners in a local law firm. Barnard bought the paper back less than a year later and, sometime in 1873, sold it to Ben Baker, who was listed as editor in the May 28, 1874, edition.

The new *Citizen* had to suspend publication twice in the nineteenth century, first when Baker contracted the disease during the yellow fever epidemic of October 1873. The second suspension came when the *Citizen* office burned on February 5, 1880, with publication resuming on March 25.

In 1879 a small newsheet, *The Occasional*, was published in the office of the *Citizen*. Described as a "breezy, lively little sheet," this popular circular was the work of Gail Borden Johnson, son of Jesse Johnson and grandson of the dairy king, Gail Borden, Jr.

Ben Baker was also a civic leader, serving as alderman and three-term mayor of Columbus. He married Virginia "Jennie" Frances in 1874, and the couple had three children. Their home at 722 Jackson Street was built in 1869. (As of 1973, it was privately owned by Mr. and Mrs. Robert Huebel.)

After Baker's death on December 8, 1907, his family ran the *Citizen* until widow Virginia Baker sold it to Irvin Guy Stafford in April 1908.

Beginning in 1910, the *Colorado Citizen* went through a succession of owners, including Elias Barry, the Colorado Citizen Publishing Company, D.O. Bell, William Ralph Gray, Charles Mrazek, William Lewis Penderfraft, and Henry Hurr, who changed the paper's name to the *Colorado County Citizen* on January 6, 1927.

After being purchased by C.P. Kendall in April 1938, this paper was later owned by Elizabeth McLeary and Leigh McGee, the Belcher Publishing Company, and Nancy and Jerry Scarborough.

Other Columbus newspapers include the *Columbus Plaindealer* (1879), the second *Columbus Times* (1880-1881), the *Free Politician* (1882), *Die Deutsche Warte* (*The German Beacon* 1896), the *Columbus Light* (1898), the *Columbus Evening Tribune* (1899), the *Columbus Chronicle* (1908) and the *Columbus Banner Press* (1985-1986), which was renamed the *Banner Press Newspaper* in 1986.

A schoolhouse, one of the first in Austin's colony, was built on the site of present Columbus several years before 1833. That December a survey of heirs of the Tumlinson land grant located lot 2 on the west bank of the Colorado River, continuing downstream "to a spring which breaks out of the bank of the same — near the schoolhouse, where a stake is planted." Evidently, both the artesian well, located east of the present county jail, and the school were well-known landmarks at the time. This schoolhouse was burned along with all other houses by Gen. Sam Houston during his retreat.

After the Texas Revolution, W.B. Dewees wrote that a new

school was built in the same location to be near both water and firewood. In his *History of Columbus*, O.A. Zumwalt, a local druggist, historian and mayor, noted:

> . . . . The first school building in Columbus was a community project, and a result of cooperation between the people of the settlement who desired to educate their children; this desire causing them to unite and construct the building with their own labor and pay for it out of their own thrift.

According to Zumwalt, this "primitive schoolhouse" was in existence until a new school was constructed in 1854.

On June 3, 1837, an advertisement in the *Houston Telegraph and Texas Register* mentioned that Columbus had an academy of thirty-four pupils under the superintendency of Mr. Arnold of Lexington, Kentucky.

After 1837 Miss Frances Trask operated Independence Academy, a boarding school for young ladies, at Independence. The academy was attended by several young women from Colorado County, including Miss Katy Dunn, later the wife of Sam K. Seymour, Sr.

Rutersville College opened near LaGrange on February 1, 1840. Two Columbus residents, Mrs. Malzena Zumwalt and Mr. F.G. Mahon, attended the college in the 1840s.

In 1845 the advent of a ferry on the east side of the Colorado made private schools in Columbus more accessible. Prospective students could then cross the river by horseback or foot for twenty-five cents and twelve and a half cents, respectively.

The foremost champions of education in early Columbus were the Masons. Caledonia Lodge No. 68, AF&AM, first met on February 18, 1850. A charter was granted to the lodge that December and delivered on February 3, 1851. After meeting in a building rented from Metz & Payne, the Masons moved into the Sons of Temperance lodge rooms on December 2, 1850.

On November 1, 1852, a committee was appointed to solicit funds to build a lodge and begin a female seminary to be operated by the lodge. In February 1854, the Masons borrowed $600 at twelve percent interest to complete the funds needed, and the building was finished during the year.

The Masonic school for girls opened in Columbus at the corner of Walnut and Live Oak streets. The rectangular-shaped, two-story frame building faced west and was bordered by a fence. The school was variously referred to as the Masonic Female Academy, Seminary, or Institute. In later years the lower floor was rented and the upper floors became a meeting room.

On September 7, 1855, the *Colorado Citizen* ran a story about Professor Riley's Female Institute, which was to open in the Masonic Hall the first Monday in September. The school was for girls and young ladies only, with no boys admitted. Readers were well advised that

> only a limited group of girls out of the A,B,C's are to be admitted, thus giving him (Prof. Riley) ample time to devote to his more advanced students and not crowding his school with little shavers who are annoying to the other pupils. . . .

By 1860 the school was known as the Columbus Female Seminary. Professor Riley was still principal and was assisted by Misses Nannie and Carrie E. Martin. Alex Foots served as secretary of the board of trustees.

By 1861 the seminary had three instructors: Professor Riley was professor of ancient languages and natural science; Rev. J.J. Loomis was professor of mathematics, moral science, and belles lettres; Miss Mary Haswell was teacher of ornamental branches.

The origins of Colorado College can be traced to December 1, 1857, when Mr. and Mrs. L. M. Crawford donated land to the "German Lutheran Church" on the condition that the building on the lot be available to them as teachers for school purposes. Colorado College was probably the school started by the Crawfords on the lot they donated: block 75, lot 4, the block bounded by Spring, Fannin, Washington, and Back streets.

The evolution from the Masonic female seminary to Colorado College began in the fall of 1856, when some friends of education met in conference at the Lutheran church and appointed a committee of three to establish a first-class college. The three committee members — Rev. Gideon Scherer, Rev. J.J. Scherer, and George Metz — drew up a bill of incorporation and sought subscriptions.

On December 26, 1857, the state legislature granted a charter to Colorado College in Columbus. The next day the cornerstone of a new Colorado College building was placed by John Mackey of the Caledonia Lodge. It was built on the land given in 1840 by W.B. Dewees for educational use. (This is the block just west of the

Nesbitt Memorial Library.) Although the college remained on Walnut and Live Oak, it operated "under the auspices of the Lutheran Church" rather than Masonic sponsorship. The local Masonic lodge continued, however, to pay the tuition of many students.

The Colorado College building was a brick, three-story structure which could accommodate 300 students. It was topped by a white square wood cupola. Gideon Scherer took the lead in constructing the building. The bricks were made by his sons at the kiln of Dr. C.W. Tait's plantation. Dr. Tait served as chairman of the board of trustees for the college. Among the twenty-five trustees were Gideon, J.J., and Jacob Scherer, who made the largest contribution — $600 — to the college.

In April 1858, John J. Scherer became pastor of the Lutheran church. After serving for a year, he then became president of Colorado College and professor of ancient languages. The college continued to operate through the Civil War.

After the war, Colorado College was plagued by financial problems. While on a fund-raising tour in 1867, President Scherer married E. Kate Killinger of Virginia.

In addition to Professor Scherer, the college faculty included Rev. J.W. Tays, professor of English studies, and Mr. James Allen, professor of mathematics.

In March 1867, the college curriculum was advertised as follows: spelling, reading and writing — $2 per month; English, grammar, geography and arithmetic — $3 per month; history, algebra, composition rhetoric and philosophy — $4 per month; ancient language, German, and higher branches of mathematics — $5 per month. Students could board with private families for $10 to $12 per month.

In 1868 J.J. Scherer approached the Synod of Texas about purchasing the college and relieving it of debt, but there was no interest in the proposal. After Scherer resigned as president, Dr. Dan Bittle was elected as his successor. Bittle's grandiose plans for the college required additional funds, resulting in Scherer's appointment as financial agent. He was successful in raising a large sum of money, visiting from Virginia to Maine.

Reverend Scherer left Columbus permanently in 1871 and began working with the newly funded Marion Female College in Marion, Virginia. In his autobiography Scherer claimed to have taught from 1,500 to 2,000 students while president of Colorado College and expressed regret for not doing more to lead them to

Jesus Christ. He later made four return visits to Texas and was president emeritus of Marion Female College when he died on May 30, 1919.

On March 20, 1871, Colorado College was sold at a sheriff's auction to the English Lutheran Church. The church then gifted the building to Odd Fellows Lodge No. 51, IOOF, which repaired and reopened it that September.

From 1869 until 1871, Mr. R. Kleberg headed a German-English school which met in the old Female Academy building. In 1877 Capt. P.J. Oakes and his wife, Kate, conducted a Masonic Academy high school in the same building. In the mid-1870s, A. Prause headed another German-English school in the German Lutheran Church, and Professor Whitehead conducted a school of dance in the same period.

During the Reconstruction period, white students were either taught in private schools or sent off to boarding schools. In 1870 a planned public school in Columbus failed to open because no teachers could be found to teach black children. White teachers from the North were brought in but soon went home when they found a "generally unsocial atmosphere" among the local white population. Between 1871 and 1873, all public schoolteachers and students in Columbus were blacks.

In 1875 separate public schools opened again for whites and blacks with separate school boards for each until 1889. From then on, one mostly white board received state funds from the county judge and allocated money to the Negro schools.

In 1881 Colorado Academy was reactivated and reorganized by Professors P. Riley and Crisp. Meeting in the renovated old Colorado College building the academy opened with 160 students. Colorado Academy — later Columbus High School — was also attended by pupils from Eagle Lake, Alleyton, and Osage. On May 19, 1891, six girls and one boy had their graduation exercises at the Stafford Opera House.

By November 1891, the old Colorado College building was torn down and replaced by the new "City Public School Building" designed by famed architect Nicholas Clayton of Galveston. The yellow brick, two-story building had six rooms — each 24x30 feet — and a small cupola.

By 1892, Colorado Academy had become Columbus High School, with an enrollment of 240 students. Capt. James E. Binkley was the principal, Mrs. Kate W. Oakes was the first assistant, and there were three other female teachers by 1896. Soon the seventh and eighth grades had a weekly literary journal. By 1910, there was a high school baseball team. An eleventh grade was added by 1912. In 1923, a new high school building was under construction.

The first Lutheran minister in the Columbus area was Rev. Louis Cachland Ervendberg. Although he named a location in Germany as his birthplace, his own daughters believed he was of French origin and that his name was an assumed one.

In 1837 Maria Sophia Dorothea Louisa Muench arrived in Chicago from Germany and soon married Ervendberg, whose pastorate was at nearby Salt Creek. After the death of their first child, a son, the couple moved to Houston in September 1839. During the year that Ervendberg was pastor of the German First Protestant Church, he recorded only one entry in his register of church activity, a baptism dated January 18, 1840.

Forced to support himself by selling garden produce, Ervenberg moved to northern Colorado County for health and economic reasons in 1840. There he established a Free Protestant congregation without strict doctrinaire tenets at the German community of Blumenthal (German for "valley of flowers.") Three overlapping or successive place names — Cummins Creek, Westmunster, and Blumenthal — were in use before the present community name of Frelsburg gained prominence in the 1850s.

Reverend Ervendberg learned to farm and also had small congregations at Industry, Cat Spring, and Columbus. In 1843 he was elected justice of the peace in Precinct 3. In performing at least one secular wedding, he signed himself as "minister of the German protestant church in Texas."

The Colorado County portion of his register closes with a series of baptisms on November 18, 1844. The first of the four was witnessed by Prince Carl von Solms-Braunfels, who possibly hired Ervendberg that very day to become the pastor of the colony of German settlers called the Adelsverein. After joining the German immigrants on the shores of Lavaca Bay, he held a Christmas service there, then traveled with them to New Braunfels in April 1845. The Columbus church was disbanded when Reverend Ervendberg accepted this more lucrative and prestigious post.[5]

In 1852 Gideon Scherer took a ship from Virginia to Galveston, seeking both a better climate for his sickly wife and to found a Lutheran church. The next year he moved to Columbus, where he organized the first Lutheran congregation in Texas to use the English language.

In 1854 Gideon's brother, John Jacob, arrived in Columbus after another teacher beat him to a position at San Felipe. After finding employment at Oakland Academy in Prairie Point, J.J. later pastored the Columbus church for one year.

The Scherers' father, Jacob, arrived in Columbus at age sixty-nine in 1854, making the overland trip of 1,300 miles in three months.

In 1855 the Scherers' church was refused membership at the First Evangelical Lutheran Synod of Texas Convention because they could not subscribe to all Lutheran confessional statements. That spring the three Scherers helped build a church, the Luther Chapel, at a cost of $1,104.64 and $76 for bell and lamps. The church was built on two parcels of land transferred to Gideon Scherer by Margarett I. McKeon of Alexandria, Virginia. This church site was block 48, lots 1 and 2, the northeast corner of the block bordered by Spring, Washington, Live Oak, and Prairie streets.

In the spring of 1858, Gideon Scherer resigned his pastorate for health reasons. His brother, J.J., filled the vacancy that April and served for one year.

In 1859 Pastor Hy Bohnenberger was appointed as "missionary-at-large" for a far-flung circuit that included Indianola, Navidad, Columbus, Austin, and Fredericksburg.

Jacob Scherer's wife, Elizabeth, died on October 26, 1855. He died on March 2, 1860, and was buried by his wife in the City Cemetery. Their son, Gideon, died in 1861.

Pastor Arnold Jaeger arrived in Columbus in 1871, and a new Lutheran church was built the next year. When Reverend Jaeger died of yellow fever in 1873, the congregation dissolved.

In 1916 Pastor Paul Piepenbrok of Weimar organized a Lutheran church in Columbus, but it soon dissolved. During the next four years, local Lutherans were cared for by four pastors as a mission.

On December 7, 1919, St. Paul's Lutheran Church was organized. The Home Mission Board named Rev. T.R. Streng as first resident pastor in 1921. After the Ladies' Aid Society purchased a lot for a building in March 1922, that group donated $2,500 for a new church and construction began in June 1923.

Catholics in Columbus were ministered to by Father Peter Victor Gury, who was pastor at Frelsburg from 1854 until 1887. During this period he started the first theological seminary in Texas there.

In 1872 St. Matthias Catholic Church was built in Columbus on land donated by the Tait family. Father M. Orth was pastor of St. Matthias parish until March 1880. He was succeeded by Father J.S. Major, then Father J.J. Wicart in 1881. During the next decade there was no resident priest in Columbus.

St. Matthias parochial school was operated by three nuns from the Divine Providence order until it closed due to lack of pupils in 1901.

In the winter of 1908, Rev. T. Smyth-Vaudry became resident pastor at St. Matthias. He was followed by Rev. F.S. Strobel in 1913 and Rev. James Marsolier in 1920.

After fire destroyed part of the church, parishioners decided to build a new house of worship in April 1929. Leo M.J. Dielman of San Antonio was the architect and Arthur J. Willrodt of Columbus was the building contractor. Construction was helped along by a large donation from the Catholic Church Extension Society on the condition that the church be renamed St. Anthony Church, in honor of St. Anthony of Padua, the great wonder worker.

Between June and December 1848, Rev. Henry Niles Pierce, the missionary for Washington County, conducted the first service of the Protestant Episcopal Church for several families in Columbus.

In 1855 Rev. Hannibal Pratt arrived in Columbus and preached the fifth Episcopal sermon delivered there from the Lutheran pulpit. At age sixteen he had come from Tinmouth, Vermont, in 1844 to work with his uncle, Rev. Caleb Ives, pastor of Christ Episcopal Church in Matagorda. Reverend Pratt entered Trinity College in 1848 but left before graduating due to ill health and was ordained a deacon in 1854.

Pratt described the people of Columbus as having ignorant prejudice and knowing little about the Episcopal faith. He lived in Columbus with his mother and sisters. Traveling by stagecoach, he held two services a month in Columbus, one in LaGrange, and one in Richmond.

On April 14, 1856, St. John's Church of Columbus was admitted into the Diocese of Texas as the twenty-third parish. (It now ranks as eighth in the state in point of continuous existence.) One of the first and most active members was Mrs. Fannie Darden, who moved to Columbus in 1853. She was part of the first church organization, which consisted of three ladies in a sewing society.

In 1857 Reverend Pratt reported to the Committee for Missions that he had twenty candidates for baptism, black and white. His salary was raised from $250 to $500 that year.

Missionary Pratt was only thirty years old when he died of chronic indigestion and a "hic-cough" on December 11, 1858. Reportedly his last words were, "All is well. All is well. It is the Lord, let Him do as seemth Him good." Reverend Pratt was buried by the Masons.

Since St. John's Church had no building, Rev. J. N. Goshorn of Gonzales held services in the county courthouse. He was stationed in the vacant church on January 1, 1861, but also visited LaGrange once a month.

In May 1861, Reverend Goshorn organized a Sunday school with forty-five scholars and a full state of teachers who used literature ordered from New York. There was also a class of black children. In 1862 the pastor claimed thirty-five communicants and forty Sunday school scholars. Reverend Goshorn served at Columbus until early 1864, when he became rector pro-tem of Christ Church, Houston.

In 1866 Rev. J. Wilkins Tays wrote a letter published in the *Spirit of Missions.* He said that Columbus had a population of 1,500 and described the town as having a deserted appearance with fences down and overgrown streets and yards. At the time, Reverend Tays was serving Richmond, Columbus, and LaGrange. He lamented that the church meeting room in the courthouse was filthy by Sunday since shows, plays and dances were also held there until late on Saturday night. The congregation wanted to build a plain, unassuming building seating 300 and costing from $1,500 to $2,000, but Tays considered it impossible to raise more than half of that amount.

In May 1867, Reverend Tays moved to Indianola. That October his wife and one of his four children died during a yellow fever epidemic.

Between 1867 and 1874, St. John's Church had no resident pastor. At various times during this period, the bishop licensed lay readers Robert Robson, W.S. Delaney, and T.J.P. Tallman to lead the congregation.

On October 13, 1871, the southern half of the half block on Milam Street was deeded to Bishop Gregg for a church building. A construction fund was started and the first services in an unfinished church building were held on March 6, 1874. Rev. T.J. Morris began to hold monthly services there, and St. John's Episcopal Church was consecrated on April 3, 1879. Harry Youens made the font still in use, and Mrs. Fannie Darden served as church organist.

The first parish register, dated 1874, was started by Reverend Morris and lists nineteen families and forty-nine communicants, including Texas pioneer Dilue Rose Harris and her children. During this time Reverend Morris served five churches before moving to San Augustine in 1879.

During the 1880s, the Columbus congregation almost ceased to exist. There was no vestry and services were sometimes conducted by Miss Maggie Howard with only women in attendance.

On June 20, 1906, St. John's Church received money for a rectory provided in the will of Mrs. Fannie Darden. When the old church was damaged by a storm in February 1909, it was moved to a more central location on the lot after undergoing extensive repairs. In 1923 the house on the church property was remodeled into a parish hall, which became the center of social activities in Columbus.

The Columbus Methodist Church traces its beginning to June 1824, when Methodist preacher Henry Stephenson held services at Beeson's Crossing.

Texas was a missionary district of the Mississippi Conference until 1840. Missionary circuit riders Jesse Hord and J. Lewis preached in Columbus in 1839. In a letter to presiding elder Joseph P. Sneed in 1840, Reverend Hord noted:

> The Lord in mercy has given us a great religious excitement at almost every appointment on my circuit. . . . We have literally taken Columbus and other places. . . .

During this period Colorado County was in the Egypt Circuit, which covered 400 miles and sixteen appointments. Many of the great circuit preachers in Texas Methodism made diary entries noting experiences in or near Columbus, including John Wesley Kenney, H.S. Thrall (who wrote two histories of Methodism in Texas), John Wesley DeVilbiss, Joseph P. Sneed, Jesse Hord, Daniel Carl, and Wesley Smith.

In 1848 trustee Isam Tooke "sold" the Columbus congregation a one-dollar lot near the banks of the Colorado River. At this time

Rev. J.E. Kolbe was the pastor. Other trustees included Asa Townsend and W.B. Dewees.

Another church lot was added in 1849, and the first house of worship was constructed in 1853. The town was in the "Columbus Circuit" by 1857.

In October 1863 the twenty-fourth session of the Texas Conference met in Columbus for several days. The following resolutions were among those adopted:

> — that missionaries be appointed to minister among the armies of the Trans-Mississippi Department.
>
> — that every preacher make a special effort to secure funds in Confederate money or cotton.
>
> —that the first Friday in January next, be appointed as a day of fasting, humiliation and prayer for the deliverance of our country from the power of the foe, and for the success of the church in evangelizing and saving the people . . .

In 1873 a frame 40x60-foot church building was completed. Two years later half interest was sold to the Lutheran church, and the church building was shared by the two congregations until 1897.

In February 1897, Mrs. Sarah E. Stafford gave the church a piece of property at the corner of Washington and Milam streets, the site of the present sanctuary. The other half interest in the old church was sold to the Lutherans. In July 1897, the new First Methodist Church was completed at a cost of some $3,200. The pastor was Rev. S.F. Chambers, and the church was dedicated that October by Bishop J.G. Granberry.

A Baptist Sunday school was reported in Columbus in the late 1830s, but the First Baptist Church was not founded until 1855. Pastor P.B. Chandler and his thirteen members obtained membership in the Colorado Baptist Association that year. By 1859 there were thirty-eight white and three black church members. In that year the congregation built the "Concrete Church," the largest auditorium in town, on the corner of Washington and Live Oak streets.

Due to the disruption of the Civil War, there is an absence of church records until after 1867. From then until the late 1880s, the church maintained a Sunday school but often had no pastor. During this period the Lutherans, Methodists, and Presbyterians temporarily used the "Concrete Church."

In 1909-10, a new two-story church with four impressive columns was built on Walnut Street. In 1917 the old "Concrete Church" was sold to the Columbus Civic Club. The old bell was retained, however, and later used in the new church.

After World War I the congregation purchased a parsonage on Travis Street across from the church building.

During 1845 and 1846, the Colorado County commissioners court met in the home of W.B. Dewees. On October 12, 1846, commissioners Dewees and Asa Townsend were appointed to inquire as to the cost of building a courthouse in Columbus and to report their finding, which was done in a special session of the court on January 30, 1847.

As a result of this report, the county commissioners awarded N.H. Fisher a contract for $950 to build a courthouse. The wood frame, two-story structure was to be 33x20, with the courtroom 22x20 feet. On July 2, 1847, Fisher was awarded $66.50 for extra work done, and the courthouse was completed in 1849.

Because of inadequate space and the need for a jail, the commissioners court met on May 18, 1852, and accepted plans drafted by K.P. Boyce for a new courthouse and connecting jail. Both were completed in 1857. The two-story courthouse was constructed of concrete and sandstone rocks on the site of the present building. It was enclosed by a circular split rail fence.

During the Mexican War, Company E, First Regiment, Texas Mounted Rifles, was recruited at Columbus. The original officers included Claiborne C. Herbert, captain; Alfred Evans, first lieutenant; James Coffee, second lieutenant. There were ten noncommissioned officers and fifty-nine privates. Company E was mustered into federal service on June 7, 1846.

The eight companies in this regiment were led by Col. Jack Hays and were popularly known as Hays' Texas Rangers. The First Regiment served as scouts for Gen. Zachary Taylor in his advance from the Rio Grande to Monterrey. In September 1846, Hays' rangers captured two fortified hills and the Bishop's Palace, the key to the western defense of the city. They then led the house-to-house fight in capturing Monterrey. One of Captain Herbert's men, bugler W.I.D. Augusten, was killed on September 21, 1846, in the battle at Monterrey. Despised by General Taylor because they were too violent and lawless, the First Regiment was discharged on October 2, 1846.

C.C. Herbert returned to civilian life as one of the more successful farmers in Colorado County. In 1848 he sold a Mrs. Thatcher thirty-five slaves for $16,000 and purchased thirty slaves and all increase from Henry Hill of New Orleans for $14,000. The federal census of 1850 showed Herbert as owning real estate valued at $58,575. The census of 1860 showed him as owning $346,080 in real property and $58,000 in personal property.

Several other prominent individuals settled in Columbus during the 1840s. Among them was Col. Robert Robson, who moved there from Dumfries, Scotland, in 1839 and built a three-story concrete castle at the south end of the present North Bridge on State Highway 71. The castle was made of homemade lime and gravel and was surrounded by a moat with a drawbridge. Most of the rooms were 20x20 feet, and the ballroom was sixty feet long. Robson's castle was probably the first building in Texas with a roof garden and running water. Water pumped from the Colorado was stored in a tank on the roof, then piped throughout the castle.

Colonel Robson entertained planters from Matagorda to Bastrop on his fifty-acre estate, where he introduced the Huisatche tree from Mexico. Episcopal services were also held there by Dr. Lawrence Augustine Washington, the grandnephew of George Washington.

After the castle was undermined by a record-setting flood in July 1869, it was torn down in 1883, and a beef-packing plant was built on the site.

Robson also owned a plantation estate called the "Scotch Hermitage" in Montgomery County. English visitor William Bollaert spent considerable time there and was a traveling companion of Robson in late 1843 and early 1844. Bollaert referred to this estate as a "hunting lodge," but noted that his Scotch friend loudly protested against hunting or firing his gun on Sunday.

The wealthy Robson was also a stockholder in the Kennedy Colony. William Kennedy was the author of a book titled *Rise, Progress and Prospects of the Republic of Texas* (1841) and a longtime friend of Bollaert. Sam Houston promised Kennedy a 4,500,000 land grant southwest of San Antonio, but Kennedy turned back his grant to the Republic after being appointed British consul at Galveston.

The 1850 census listed Robson as living in Colorado County

and being age forty-six. He was also listed in the census of 1860 but not that of 1870.

In the late 1840s, Dr. Lawrence A. Washington brought his wife and four children from Virginia and settled fourteen miles south of Columbus near present Vox Populi. He had studied medicine in Philadelphia and inherited land and personal property left to his father by George Washington, including an extensive library and an eight-foot-tall mahogany clock. Dr. Washington lived on his farm near the mouth of Skull Creek for some twenty years. After losing his fortune and slaves after the Civil War, he drove some cattle to California before settling in Denison, Texas, where he died in 1883. Dr. Washington left his library and clock with Dr. John H. Bowers of Columbus.

Another prominent newcomer was Dr. Charles W. Tait, a native of Elbert County, Georgia, who was born on June 4, 1815. He was educated at William and Mary College, Tuscaloosa College, Pennsylvania College, and the Jefferson Medical College in Philadelphia. On the same day in 1837, he received two degrees, one in civil engineering and the other in medicine and surgery.

Dr. Tait served as a ship's surgeon in the U.S. Navy until 1844, when he returned home to Black's Bluff, Alabama, to take charge of the family plantation and over 100 slaves. When the plantation overseer presumed to propose marriage to his sister Lucy, Charles "put him in his place" by challenging the suitor to a duel and fatally wounding him. As a result of this incident, Dr. Tait moved to Texas several months later. During the Mexican War he served as a surgeon with Col. Jack Hays' First Regiment, Texas Mounted Rifles.

In 1847 Dr. Tait began Sylvania Plantation on 1,907 acres southeast of Columbus. It was initially worked by fifteen slaves imported from back home. The log story-and-a-half plantation house he built on McKenzie Creek that year is located nine miles southeast of Columbus. The two lower rooms still have the original divided, Dutch-type doors. The house had an open gallery running through the center, two chimneys, four fireplaces, and a children's room reached only by a stairway from the bedroom of their parents below. The original kitchen was set off from the northwest corner of the house. Just under the roof at the front are long, narrow windows, created by the omission of a log and intended for gun slits.[6]

On February 14, 1848, Dr. Tait married Louisa M. Williams of Bastrop and brought his bride to Sylvania, where all eight of their children were born.

In 1850 Tait entered the cattle business with forty-six head. During the next ten years, he also did surveying and engineering for both the Buffalo Bayou, Brazos and Colorado Railroad and the Columbus Tap Railroad and was paid for his services in land. He was elected to the Fifth and Sixth Texas Legislature in 1853 and 1855.

In the 1860 census, Dr. Tait had real property valued at $61,636, personal property worth $57,320 and owned sixty-three slaves. By 1861, Sylvania Plantation had grown to 5,458 acres.

Tait was a just and well-liked master. Among his general rules were: Never punish a Negro when in passion; never require of a Negro what is unreasonable; be sure the Negro knows for what offense he is punished; do not overwork — and thus injure — your hands.

Among his specific rules were: Always require the Negroes to eat breakfast before going to work; stop work at twelve noon and allow as long as one hour for dinner; no profane or obscene language is to be allowed among the Negroes; every Negro cabin is to be inspected every Sunday morning for cleanliness; every Negro is to appear in the field on Monday morning in clean clothes.

Five of the Tait children died, most in infancy, from malaria or yellow fever at Sylvania Plantation. As a result, Dr. Tait decided to escape the damp, unhealthy atmosphere and move to higher ground on his 240-acre "city farm" in Columbus.

The Tait Town House, located at 526 Wallace Street and built in late Greek Revival style, was started in 1856 and completed after the Civil War. Tait's slaves molded, baked, and laid the bricks for the chimneys and basement and cut the lumber with a power saw run by a motor rescued from the *Moccasin Belle,* which had run aground near Sylvania. The pine was floated down the Colorado from Bastrop, the weatherboarding was cottonwood, and the sleepers, rafters, and joists were live oak. The flooring and window frames were brought by boat from Bastrop.

Cut limestone was used for the foundation and set six feet deep. Brick was used for the floors and walls of the basement, which had steel bars set in brick over the windows. The house originally had white walls and green shutters. Simple, two-story columns support the roof of the mansion's front entrance porch, within which is a cantilevered second-story balcony. Four tall chimneys, two at each end of the house, originally served eight fireplaces.

The first and second floor had the same plan: two large rooms on each side with a long hall running from front to back. The attic is reached by stairs in the upper hall. The huge basement contains an old cistern for storing rain water and was also used to store plantation supplies. A widow's walk crowned the structure.

Dr. Tait moved his family into the town house in 1859 before it was finished. Sam Houston stayed there during his gubernatorial campaign. In 1863 Tait enlisted as a surgeon in the Fourth Texas Cavalry with the rank of lieutenant colonel. After he returned from the war in 1865, the house was completed when a two-story portico was added.[7]

During the early Reconstruction period, a Union colonel and his wife occupied a room in the Tait Town House during the winter while his men camped in the northern part of Columbus. The opportunistic Dr. Tait contracted with him to supply bacon for the soldiers and corn for the horses from Sylvania Plantation.

In 1842 Dr. John G. Logue came to Columbus after graduating from the Jefferson Medical College. Two years later he returned to Philadelphia and purchased a stock of drugs and chemicals for the first drugstore in Columbus and the Republic of Texas. (A state historical marker is at the site at Travis and Spring streets.) Dr. Logue's partner for a time was Dr. John H. Bowers. The census of 1860 showed merchant Logue as owning $60,000 in real property and $100,000 in personal property. Dr. Logue also served as first president of the Columbus Tap Railroad before his death in 1861.

John Henry Bowers was born in Alsace on November 6, 1817. He attended the University of Malhausen, where he first studied medicine. At age eighteen he traveled to China and India, where he learned to treat cholera and malaria. In 1836 he sailed from New York to Texas and joined Gen. Sam Houston at San Jacinto. After the battle Dr. Bowers served as physician to the prisoner Santa Anna and was later invited to visit the general at his Hacienda Corona in Mexico City.

Bowers walked from Matagorda to Houston to begin his medical practice. In 1851 he moved to Colorado County. He was married to Annie F. Griffitts and the couple had two daughters and one son. Dr. Bowers survived the yellow fever epidemic in 1873 and died at age eighty-nine in September 1907. At that time the mahogany clock given to him by Dr. Lawrence Washington was sent to his daughter in Galveston. Eventually it was returned to George Washington's home at Mount Vernon.

In 1845 Ira A. and Dilue Rose Harris moved to Columbus from a farm near Houston. Dilue was well acquainted with leaders of the Texas Revolution and the Republic of Texas.[8] The Harrises raised nine children in Columbus. Ira Harris served as sheriff of Colorado County from 1858 until 1862. Two of his sons were Confederate soldiers.

After Ira died in 1869, Dilue lived with her children. The Dilue Rose Harris home still stands at 600 Washington Street in Columbus.

When Mrs. Harris was seventy-four years old, she began to write her reminiscences in 1899. A major primary source of early Texas history, they were published in three parts in the *Quarterly of the Texas State Historical Association* and in the *Eagle Lake Headlight*. This important pioneer woman died at age eighty-nine on April 2, 1914, at Eagle Lake.

In July 1853, lawyer William J. Darden and his wife, Fannie, moved to Columbus.[9] From 1855 until 1859, Darden represented Colorado County in the state legislature. In the 1850s the Dardens traded a slave valued at $1,500 and the hire of other slaves for a year in return for Columbus property valued at $2,800 where they built a home at 726 Walnut Street.

In 1861 Darden enlisted as a private in Capt. John C. Upton's Company B, Fifth Texas Infantry Regiment, Hood's Brigade. William eventually became a quartermaster sergeant and suffered a paralyzed left foot during the war.

Darden served as a vestryman at St. John's Episcopal Church in Columbus. He died on May 29, 1881, and his funeral was the largest ever seen in town.

His wife, Fannie Darden, became known as the "poet laureate of Columbus." She wrote a good number of novelettes and stories, including "Romances of the Texas Revolution." In her book, *Living Female Writers of the South*, Ida Raymond ranked Fannie among the first of Texas authors.

Three of her poems — "Yokonah," "Grandmother's Baby," and "Nature's Festival" — were included by Sam H. Dixon in his book, *The Poets and Poetry of Texas*, in 1885. Her poems and articles also appeared in the *Houston Telegraph, Galveston News, New Orleans Times,* and in national magazines.

In March 1883, Mrs. Darden was named to the editorial staff of the *American Sketch Book* published at Austin.

In the 1880s, Fannie usually wrote "The Carrier Boys Address," a poem recited by "carrier boys" of the *Colorado Citizen* for their customers in hopes of receiving money gifts at the end of each year.

Mrs. Darden was also an artist, specializing in oil paintings, and taught art for many years at Colorado College.

After the first Episcopal church was built in 1874, Fannie played the organ there until her death. (Today there is a memorial window to her in the parish house at 325 Preston Street.)

Mrs. Darden survived an operation for breast cancer in November 1882. She kept a diary between 1885 and 1889 which is now in the possession of Mr. and Mrs. G.P. Wilburn of Glidden.

Fannie Darden died on January 4, 1890, and was buried beside her husband in the Odd Fellows Cemetery.

In 1855 William Harbert moved from western Tennessee to a large plantation between Columbus and Alleyton. He quickly established himself as a wealthy merchant, banker, and planter. In 1857 Harbert built a brick building in Columbus on the southwest corner of Milam and Walnut streets (the site of the present Columbus State Bank), where he conducted a general merchandise and banking business. The federal census of 1860 showed Harbert as owning $83,296 in real property and $200,808 in personal property.

He died intestate at age seventy on June 21, 1865, creating hardship and disaster for many of his debtors. Eight heirs sued in district court to obtain judgments for money owed the estate. After extended litigation, many property owners, including Dr. Lawrence A. Washington, lost everything.

In the summer of 1856, the prevailing paranoia of slaveholders over an alleged slave rebellion led to the hanging of three slaves and the severe punishment of some 200 others. At the time it was rumored that the slaves of Colorado County had a secret plot to murder their masters, steal their horses and guns, take their white wives, and fight their way to freedom in Mexico. Supposedly, the slaves were organized into units of two to ten men with each assigned to attack a particular home. They had secret signs and passwords along with the sinister motto, "Leave not a shadow behind," a vow of death. The slaves had accumulated guns, ammunition and knives to be used in a slave uprising planned for Saturday night, September 6,

1856. Rumor had it that many Mexican laborers recently arriving in Texas were also involved in the plot.

One slave, Richmond Norman, later said that his master tortured his slaves to induce them to confess to the conspiracy. He first placed them flat on their back in the cotton press, then ran it so tightly against them that they could not change positions for twenty-four hours. When this technique produced no results, the owner then laid his slaves on red ant beds for a short time, but they still refused to talk.

Once a Mr. Tooke (probably Isam) was warned of the plot in late August, some 200 slaves were arrested, including three ringleaders and a free black man named Frank who escaped. After a unanimous vote of county residents — but no trial — the three leaders were hanged on Friday, September 5, 1856. By that same vote it was decided to severely punish, but spare the lives of, the other offenders due to the potential loss of labor and property. One or two of them were whipped to death.

After the lynchings, the Columbus Corresponding Committee —John H. Robson, H.A. Tatum, and J.H. Hicks — wrote a letter to the editor of the *Galveston Tri Weekly News* which appeared on September 11, 1856. The letter read in part:

> .... Without exception, every Mexican in the county was implicated. They were arrested and ordered to leave the county within five days, and never again to return under the penalty of death....
>
> We are satisfied that the lower class of the Mexican population are incendiaries in any country where slaves are held, and should be dealt with accordingly. And, for the benefit of the Mexican population, we would here state that a resolution was passed by the unanimous voice of the county, forever forbidding any Mexican from coming within the limits of the county....

Sadly, later evidence casts considerable doubt that there *was* a planned slave rebellion in Colorado County. While Norma Shaw was writing her master's thesis in 1939, she interviewed a former slave, Charlie Phillips, who told her that "there was no uprising planned, that the entire trouble was caused by a lie that a Negro named Tom told his master, Mr. Tooke." (Five men with that last name owned slaves in Colorado County in 1860.)

This information ties in with a report on the rebellion in the *Galveston Tri Weekly News* on September 6, 1856, which identified the man who discovered the rebellion as "Mr. Toake." Ex-slave Phillips did not have access to 1856 editions of the Galveston paper in 1939. In hindsight, it also appears that the elaborate communication system and sinister motto credited to the slave conspirators was simply beyond the capacity of such ignorant and servile men.

In 1860 there were 3,559 slaves in Colorado County. The largest slaveowners were John H. Crisp — 146, John Matthews — 140, William Harbert — 123, and H.D. Rhodes — 103. During the year M.E. Newsom, a Columbus merchant, reported an attempt by slaves to set his store on fire. The plot was foiled when a store clerk shot the offender and he escaped.

By then the Knights of the Golden Circle had been formed, a secret organization aiming to create a slave empire encircling a diameter of 2,400 miles around Havana, Cuba. It was their objective to monopolize the world's supply of tobacco, cotton, and sugar. Local units were referred to as "castles." By December 1860, the Columbus castle was headed by Professor H.A. Tatum.

A future rail connection to Columbus was realized in 1859 when William Alley founded Alleyton three miles east of town. Alley had acquired this land from his brother, Rawson. On November 5, 1859, William Alley signed Deed No. 2057 giving the Buffalo Bayou, Brazos, and Colorado Railway Company right-of-way through his lands on the east side of the Colorado River and an undivided half-interest in 200 acres to be laid out as a townsite named Alleyton. Center Street was 150 feet wide with a rail line going down the middle, and the railroad company selected a site for a depot. On May 22, 1860, the first five purchasers of lots bought block 21 of the eighty-three surveyed blocks.

The BBB&C Railway Company was organized by Gen. Sidney Sherman on June 1, 1850, for the purpose of building a rail line from Harrisburg through the Brazos and Colorado river farm lands. Other incorporators included John Sealy, William Marsh Rice, B.A. Shepherd, John G. Todd, and W.J. Hutchins along with five eastern financiers from Boston, Massachusetts. The first spike was driven at Harrisburg in December 1852. The line reached Richmond on the Brazos in 1855 and Alleyton on the Colorado in 1860. The BBB&C originally intended to lay track up the east side of the Colorado to Austin, but construction stopped at Alleyton due to the Civil War.

On February 2, 1860, the Columbus Tap Railway Company was incorporated to tap into the BBB&C. John G. Logue was the first president, followed by E.P. Whitefield. C.W. Tait was treasurer of the line and C. Windrow served as clerk. The citizens of Columbus also voted a bond issue to construct a bridge across the Colorado. Thus the "Tap" could connect with the BBB&C at Smith Junction just north of Alleyton. However, the war delayed these plans also.

With the coming of the Civil War, Columbus voted for secession by a margin of 201 to 93 on February 23, 1861. Several local units served in the war. On July 22, 1861, the Columbus Greys were organized with John Mackey as captain, twelve other officers, and sixty privates. On August 21, 1861, the Colorado Rovers, a cavalry company, was organized with S.B. Lamb as captain, twelve other officers, and thirty-six privates. That same day Shropshire's Cavalry was organized with John H. Shropshire as captain, eleven other officers, and forty-four privates, among them the aging W.B. Dewees. The Colorado Home Guard, a reserve infantry company, was organized at Columbus on August 24, 1861, with J.W. Mathee as captain, eleven other officers, and twenty-seven privates.

Among the outstanding Confederate heroes from Columbus was John H. Shropshire, the leader of Company A, Fifth Regiment, Texas Mounted Volunteers. A Kentucky native and successful lawyer, John married Caroline L. Tait, a sister of Dr. C.W. Tait. The couple had one child, Charles T., born in Wilcox County, Alabama, in 1861 and educated at Columbus.

The 1860 census showed the twenty-seven-year-old Shropshire as owning $37,820 in real property, $50,550 in personal property, and sixty-one slaves.

The family was returning from a visit to Alabama in early July 1861 when their schooner, *Dart*, was captured by the blockading Union ship, *South Carolina.* Fortunately, her captain falsely assumed that Texas was full of Union men. When Shropshire wisely chose not to correct him, he was treated kindly and released the next day.

John's Company A was the first unit to join Col. Thomas J. Green on Salado Creek. Shropshire was promoted to major on February 21, 1862. Green's forces were a part of Gen. Henry H. Sibley's brigade, whose objective was to capture New Mexico and Arizona. Starting from San Antonio Sibley's brigade reached El Paso after a two-month march and short of rations, clothing and supplies. Their leader was also in poor health and drinking heavily.

General Sibley was victorious in the Battle of Valverde, in

which he suffered eight percent casualties. It was Shropshire who led his company in the last successful charge.

In the Battle of Glorietta Pass, Major Shropshire led companies A,B,C and D of the Fifth Texas Cavalry in a counteroffensive against federal troops from Fort Union. On March 28, 1862, he was killed early in the battle while cheering his men on.

Another prominent Confederate leader from Columbus was John Cunningham Upton, a Tennessee native who moved from California to Texas in 1859 and settled south of Columbus. During the war he led Colorado County's Company B, Fifth Texas Infantry Regiment, Hood's Texas Brigade. Upton's Company B included thirteen other officers and 112 privates, including R.E. "Bob" Stafford and the Baker brothers — Ben, J.D., and A. Hicks (who was killed at Sharpsburg). The brigade, which included thirty-two companies raised in twenty-six counties, reached Richmond, Virginia, about June 1861 and fought with Robert E. Lee's Army of Northern Virginia.

Hood's Texas Brigade played a prominent role in six major Civil War battles: Gaines' Mill, Second Manassas, Antietam, Gettysburg, Chickamauga, and the Wilderness. The Fifth Texas Infantry had 239 men shot down in the Second Manassas, including all seven color bearers, and Upton, who was buried on the battlefield where a marker was later erected in his memory. His performance also earned high praise from General Hood, who remarked that "the gallant Upton was, indeed, preeminent in his sphere as an outpost officer."

The famed Terry's Texas Rangers included twenty privates from Colorado County: two from Company B, three from Company C, twelve from Company F, two from Company I, and one from Company K.

Capt. Richard V. Cook and his infantry company from Colorado County were unsung heroes of the Battle of Sabine Pass. Cook, who had practiced law in Columbus since 1856, was commissioned on March 22, 1862, and raised Company A, 13th Regiment, Texas Infantry. All of Cook's twelve officers and thirty-four of his sixty-seven privates were from Columbus.

Sabine Pass was a narrow, six-mile strait and the Gulf outlet for both the Sabine and Neches rivers. Fort Griffin, a timber-and-mud stockade, was three miles from the Gulf of Mexico and guarded the pass a short distance above it. Capt. Frederick H. Odlum was commander of Confederate forces at Sabine Pass. While he was on furlough in Houston, command fell to Lt. R.W. "Dick" Dowling, a twenty-five-year-old Irish saloonkeeper from Houston. Dowling and his forty-seven-man artillery company, the Davis Guard, manned six small, smooth-bore cannon at Fort Griffin.

On September 1, 1863, a Union armada of four gunboats and seventeen transports carrying some 5,000 Federal soldiers and 2,500 sailors sailed from New Orleans with the objective of retaking Sabine Pass. Captain Cook and his infantry company were at Grigby's bluff fifteen miles up the Neches River when he was ordered to make a forced march to the relief of Fort Griffin.

At 3:00 P.M. on September 8, 1863, the lead Federal gunboats attempted to run by Fort Griffin at full speed. The first gunboat to make the break was the *Sachem* with seven rifled guns, followed by the *Clifton* with nine 32-pounders, and then the old *Arizona*.

Dowling's men put a ball through the steam drum of the *Sachem*, scalding most of the crew to death. They also tore off a propelling wheel on the *Clifton*, thus disabling both gunboats. Their cannon also disabled the machinery of the *Arizona*, which backed off out of range and managed to escape. In less than forty-five minutes, Dowling's forces fired their cannons 137 times, turned back the entire invasion force, and had not a man injured.

Although he received none of the historical credit or glory accorded Dick Dowling, an equally impressive feat was performed by Captain Cook and his Company A. While Dowling's artillerymen were firing away, Cook's infantrymen spotted a old steamboat, the *Uncle Ben*, lined with cotton bales and two guns on the upper deck lying alongside the wharf at Sabine City. While under enemy fire Cook ordered the steamer captain to hove up beside the *Sachem* and *Clifton*. He then ordered the troops on both gunboats to surrender and hand in their arms. Cook then took aboard some 375 well-armed and equipped Yankees and towed the disabled gunboats to the wharf.

After delivering the captured arms and ammunition at Sabine Pass, Captain Cook sent Lt. R.W. Putney and eight guards to carry the prisoners to Beaumont on the *Uncle Ben*, then on to Houston by rail. En route the tiny guard detail bluffed the Federals into believing that 6,000 Confederate cavalrymen were out in the timber. One of the guards, Benjamin F. Mitchell of Columbus, was later quoted in the Weimar *Mercury* as saying: ". . . That reconciled them. They could have taken our guns away from us, thrashed us and sent us home. Nothing like being brave, if you are a little scared. . . ."

Mitchell described Captain Cook as "a high-toned, educated gentleman and fine lawyer" who was tall and commanding in appearance.

On November 11, 1863, Captain Cook wrote a revealing letter to his wife, the former Elizabeth F. Moore, whom he had married in 1859 in Fayette County. He told her that Dr. C.W. Tait, the prominent Columbus planter, had met with less success leading a militia company he raised in Colorado County. It seems that Dr. Tait's company "got themselves into hot water" by refusing to go into Louisiana for twenty days. The men claimed they could not be ordered out of Texas since they were state troops. Major Tait immediately resigned, saying he would not command troops that didn't want to fight for their country. According to Cook, the men cursed and abused Tait and Adjutant Sam Harrington, who also resigned, at a most tremendous rate.

The outstanding local politician was Claiborne C. Herbert, a Virginian native and owner of a plantation at Reed's Bend on the Colorado twelve miles southeast of Columbus. After representing the Columbus district in the Texas Senate from 1857 to 1861, Herbert captained a home guard company at Eagle Lake and served as aide-de-camp of the Tenth District, including Milam, Burleson, Washington, Austin, and Colorado counties.

In November 1861, Herbert was elected to represent the Second Texas District in the Confederate House of Representatives and served in both the First and Second Congress from 1862 until 1865. After the war, Claiborne was elected to the 39th and 40th Congress in 1865 and 1867, respectively, but was denied his seat both times.

The Columbus Mutual Aid Association was formed in 1863 by such prominent local men as C.W. Tait, Stephen Harbert, E.P. Whitfield, Isam Tooke and A.M. Campbell. In conducting general mercantile business, they agreed to "sell to families of soldiers at cost." They also pledged to purchase and deal in provisions, family supplies and merchandise which would be sold to others at a profit not over twenty-five percent, thus protecting the people from speculators and extortioners.

During the war, Alleyton enjoyed boom times as a key point on the Confederate supply line, serving as an important cotton station and quartermaster depot. The town was the terminus of the cotton road leading to Bagdad near neutral Matamoros, Mexico. From there cotton was shipped to European markets. Cotton and freight was off-loaded from railcars at Alleyton, ferried across the Colorado, then carried by ox-drawn wagons or mule trains to Mexico.

In 1863 Alleyton was full of Mexican teamsters, cotton buyers and sellers, merchants, peddlers, speculators, foreigners, and soldiers. The predominant business was the "receiving, forwarding and commission agents" with "saloons" running a close second. The town had three hotels, a Ten Pin Alley, blacksmith shop, livery stable, barber shop, and a number of general stores, including the C.A. Dittman General Merchandise Store, established in 1859.

Some 2,000 Confederate troops were also stationed at Camp Webb on the outskirts of Alleyton in 1863. Due to friction between the soldiers and the citizens of Columbus, these men of the 22nd Brigade, Texas State Troops, camped in a field on a site named for Inspector General Henry L. Webb.

The reality of defeat hit home on June 24, 1865, when Maj. L.B. Hobson and the 23rd Iowa arrived quietly and took possession of Columbus. The *Times* optimistically noted that

> . . . The people are pleased with the officers. They were mild, generous, and forbearing, and by their course of proceedings have secured the respect and confidence of the people. The soldiers are quiet and as well disciplined a regiment as has ever been seen. They deserve credit and the people award it to them. . . .

The first incident of violence was reported in the *Columbus Times* on August 11, 1865. The paper noted that Mr. Trammell, the manager of Dr. J.S. Hick's farm, had used a shotgun to kill a black man who had advanced on him with a large knife.

Federal troops were stationed at Fort Columbus in "The Grove," an area in the northern part of town near the river with many huge live oaks and few houses. Before his death in 1966, Mr. J.H. Wooten enjoyed telling of a prank played on the black cavalry of the 23rd Iowa stationed at Fort Columbus.

According to Mr. Wooten, a group of local young men had a few too many drinks at an uptown saloon one dark, moonless night. They proceeded to tie several strong ropes together, then stretched it across Milam Street about knee-high to a horse. The daring youths then fired their pistols and rifles in the air, mounted their horses, and scattered.

Upon hearing the burst of gunfire, the officer of the day at the fort ordered the black cavalry troops to ride into town and quell the uprising. When the first of the troops reached the 800 block of Milam, their horses hit the taut rope, stumbled and fell; those behind continued the pileup of horses and men. Although the number of injured soldiers and animals is unknown, the prank resulted in a total sense of frustration, anger, and disgust among the black troops.

On July 21, 1865, President Andrew Johnson appointed A.J. Hamilton as provisional governor of Texas. Governor Hamilton appointed W.B. Dewees as county treasurer, John D. Gilmore as chief justice, and James B. Good as sheriff of Colorado County.

When country officials were again elected on June 15, 1866, J.B. Leyendecker became the new sheriff and Charles Schmidt was chosen as new treasurer. Dewees failed to turn over some $1,200 of missing county funds, claiming that thieves had stolen the money from a safe in the law office of Claiborne and Daniels in Columbus. Dewees lost the case in district court as well as an appeal in 1870. This incident ended his public life and blemished the good name of the "Father of Columbus."

According to the Colorado County census of 1870, Dewees was seventy and keeping a boardinghouse. He had real estate valued at $2,000 and a personal estate of $100. His wife, Angelica, was thirty-six and keeping house. Their seventeen-year-old son, Bufford, was still living at home.

On February 12, 1878, the commissioners court referred to Dewees as "an indigent and worthy person" and ordered the county treasurer to pay this county pauper $12.50 per month for his support.

W.B. Dewees died at seventy-eight on April 14, 1878. He was buried under an impressive monument in the first burying ground of Columbus, the City Cemetery. By 1885 all of his land was sold in pieces to twenty-five landowners.

After the war, a small Ku Klux Klan unit was organized in Colorado County. Most of the members were survivors of old Company F, Terry's Texas Rangers, including Dule Turner, Nicholas T. Ware, Buck Dunlavy, and William W. Wade. The local Klan hanged a white scalawag guilty of "preaching the equality doctrine in Columbus." After chasing him to Alleyton, the Klansmen strung him up on a big live oak beside the Old Spanish Trail near town.

On July 5, 1867, Col. C.C. Herbert was shot to death in Columbus. While drinking with a Mr. Spear in Brunson's saloon, the two had a slight altercation. A half hour later Herbert was sitting and talking under a large oak tree in front of the saloon. At that point Spear returned on horseback and called to "Charley" to bring him a drink. Herbert asked for identification, then took a candle and started toward Spear. The horseman drew his six-shooter and threatened to kill Herbert if he came any closer. A Mr. Howard then stepped between the two adversaries and tried to calm down Spear, telling him that Herbert was "perfectly harmless." As the two men continued to talk near the saloon door steps, Colonel Herbert suddenly appeared in the door. Without saying a word, Spear shot him in the abdomen and galloped off in the night. Herbert died minutes later from a burst aorta.

When Spear resisted arrest he was killed by a sheriff's posse. Colonel Herbert was buried beside the fresh grave of his wife, at Reed's Bend.

Brunson's saloon, the scene of the tragedy, was owned by Charles "Charlie" Brunson, who came to America from Germany at age fifteen in 1845. After chopping wood, quarrying rock, and driving stagecoaches and mule teams, Brunson settled in Columbus in 1866 and entered the liquor business. After building a large brick house in 1870, Charlie took his German bride, Margaret Huffman, to live there the next year.

In 1891 Brunson had a two-story brick building constructed. It enclosed an area of 33x90 feet and had stone and cypress wood ornamentation, a pitched tin roof, and a canopy supported by cast-iron pillar supports. From 1896 until 1908, the Lone Star Opera House occupied the second floor of the Brunson Building. [10]

Charlie Brunson closed his saloon and retired from active business at age eighty-three in 1913. He died three years later.

In November 1869, Radical Republican E.J. Davis was elected as Reconstruction governor of Texas, defeating the conservative former governor, A.J. Hamilton. Under the new regime, Texas and Louisiana were placed in the Fifth Military District. One of the seven Texas military posts was located in Columbus, and one infantry company was assigned to Fort Columbus.

In mid-October 1873, a yellow fever epidemic ravaged Columbus. There were five deaths by October 20, among them County Judge George W. Smith, who died in his home at the corner of Washington and Travis streets. Citizens fled town by train, carriage and horseback, leaving Columbus almost deserted and most businesses closed by October 22. There were 164 reported sick cases and thirty-three dead by November 1. A week later only 300 residents remained in Columbus. On November 18, Mayor John C. Miller died. Another prominent victim was Leopold Steiner, a prosperous Jewish merchant.

A grieving town found something to cheer about on January 17, 1874, when Democratic Governor Richard Coke was inaugurated to end nine years of Reconstruction in Texas.

In the postwar years, two Columbus cowmen were involved in an incident similar to a famous story, an episode illustrating the devotion of cattlemen Charles Goodnight to his older partner and father-figure, Oliver Loving. In the late summer of 1867, Loving died of a gangrene infection at Fort Sumner, New Mexico, after being chased down and wounded by Comanches. Before his death, Loving asked Goodnight to bury him in the home cemetery at Weatherford, Texas. Several months later his wooden coffin was placed in a charcoal-lined tin container and carried home in a wagon. In Larry McMurtry's novel *Lonesome Dove*, and the subsequent film, one of the two main characters performed such a deed for his friend.

Columbus can also claim such an incident. In the summer of 1870, a black cowboy named George Glenn accompanied his boss, Bob Johnson, on a trail drive to Abilene, Kansas. After Johnson died there in July, Glenn vowed to bury him in Columbus. Since it was too hot to travel with a corpse, Johnson's body was embalmed and buried near Abilene. With the coming of cold weather, Glenn had the body disinterred and loaded onto a wagon. The loyal cowhand then made the forty-two-day trip back to Columbus, sleeping beside the casket each night. At journey's end Johnson was buried beside his wife under a large monument in the City Cemetery.

Two years after this remarkable trip, George Glenn married Lucy Conner and settled down in the Columbus area. His dedication to his employer made Glenn somewhat of a celebrity when he later attended reunions of the old-time trail drivers. Ironically, in contrast to Bob Johnson, Glenn was buried in an unmarked grave near Glidden when he died in 1931.

Between 1865 and 1890, the most powerful, influential man in the Columbus area was cattleman Robert Earl "Bob" Stafford. Born in Glynn County, Georgia, on March 27, 1834, Stafford married Sarah Elizabeth Zoucks in December 1852 and brought his bride to Lavaca County in the fall of 1856. The couple would have five children: Julia Augusta, Warren D., Mary Sarah (who died in infancy), Myra E., and Robert Earl, Jr.

Bob Stafford has been described as a tough, hard-fisted, red-bearded, six-foot-two-inch cattleman who welcomed trouble and went looking for it.

After moving to Colorado County in 1857, the Staffords first lived three miles west of Columbus. During the Civil War, Bob enlisted as a first lieutenant in the Colorado Rovers, a cavalry militia company of fifty-one men led by Capt. S.B. Lamb.

After driving his first herd of cattle to Kansas in the spring of 1869, Stafford began to buy up all cow brands. Soon the prairie was full of his cattle all the way to Stafford Ranch headquarters thirty-five miles south of Columbus. In 1872 Bob signed a contract with Allen Poole & Company to supply beef for the Havana market. When the company failed in 1878, he bought their cattle and land.

Stafford's younger brother John, who was born on April 2, 1849, moved to Colorado County in 1867. He was joined by two other orphaned brothers, Benjamin Franklin and William. After becoming Bob's partner, John Stafford married Grace A. Walker in December 1874. They had three children: Carrie, Joe, and Stella.

In 1882 John Stafford built a 7,600 square-foot mansion four miles south of Columbus. The Stafford ranch house was three stories high with a widow's walk on the roof where John liked to stand and gaze over part of his ranching domain. Built on the highest point of the ranch, the house was known as the "sentinel of the prairie."

The cypress and pine mansion featured wide verandas wrapped halfway around the house on both floors, unique columns set in groups of five, towering chimneys, and two large, cast-iron dogs guarding the front entrance.

The ornate double doors of glass and carved wood opened into a broad foyer. All of the downstairs rooms — the living room, dining room, breakfast area, kitchen, and two bedrooms — were 20x20 feet with 16-foot ceilings. There were four bedrooms and a wide hall upstairs. All of the beds in the house had seven-foot-high blackboards. One of the front rooms on the second floor was the "ballroom," and the musicians were quartered in the hall.

There were six fireplaces in the mansion, all different hand-carved walnut mantels. The rooms were adorned with fine walnut furniture, full-length mirrors that tilted, and handsome dressers with marble tops. [11]

After the Civil War, the Staffords and the Townsends were the two great families in Colorado County. Asa Townsend was the oldest of seven brothers who came to Texas from South Carolina beginning in 1826. Stephen Townsend was elected the first sheriff of Colorado County in 1837. All of the brothers fought in the Confederate army. After the war, Asa Townsend and Bob Stafford shared the open range in the Columbus area.

The feud between the two families began over cattle in 1871, specifically the issue of accommodation branding. When a rancher gathered his stock, he would brand odds and ends of neighbors' herds, who expected him to pay fifty cents a head for doing so. However, carelessness and cases of doubtful ownership often led to hard feelings.

In the fall of 1871, Ben Stafford, who tended to be pretty quiet unless he was drinking, became riled over the issue. In early December he was coming out of a Columbus barbershop when he met neighboring rancher Sumner Townsend. Heated words were exchanged, both went for their guns, and six or seven shots were fired. Sumner was seriously wounded in the arm and shoulder. Ben was shot in the ankle, a severe injury requiring two years of recovery time and the wearing of a special shoe. Although there would be no further warfare for a long period, the two families henceforth avoided each other and refused to do business.

For years Bob Stafford also had his own private feud with Shanghai Pierce. Bob's free-grass range extended onto Pierce's proposed ranch across the Colorado River from Wharton. Shanghai's partner, Bill Kyle, grazed this land with the Staffords for two years with no friction. Once the Pierce-Kyle buffer partnership was dissolved, Bob Stafford considered cattle with the P-K brand as trespass-by-design and sought to convert the free-grass issue into a personal one.

Since Stafford cattle were also grazing on the Pierce-Ward pasture, Shanghai and Ben fenced their Crescent V Ranch from the Gulf to the Navidad River and drove out Bob's herds, prompting him to proclaim, "I resolve to shoot Mr. Pierce on sight." Soon after the warning, the two met face-to-face in the vestibule of a train stopped at a way station. When Pierce recognized his adversary, he turned his back and said plainly, "Bob Stafford is too much of a gentleman-of-the-code to shoot an unarmed man in the back." Once he walked off the train and disappeared into the village, Bob said, "I admire the colonel's quick thinking."

During this tense period, Pierce ambled into a Victoria hotel to register for the night. Peering at the hotel register, he saw in fresh ink the name, "R.L. Stafford — Columbus." Pointing at the name, Shanghai loudly stated, "Gentlemen, I know this is a comfortable hotel with ample accommodations for ordinary men, but, by God, Sirs!, it is entirely too small for Bob Stafford and Shanghai Pierce at the same time." He then quietly left the hotel.

According to Henry Calhoun Thomas, one of Stafford's cowhands, "Pierce got to spreading out and stuck up notices telling the Staffords to move their cattle west of the West Mustang (creek)." On August 9, 1877, the Committee of 25 Navidad printed a notice in the *Colorado Citizen* warning all stockmen not to work for or with either Sam Allen or Bob Stafford "under the penalty of entire destruction of the grass. . . ."

The same day Allen and Stafford published a blistering reply in the *Citizen* which read in part:

> This notice could not have emanated from any but a cowardly and dishonest band. It is doubtless the work of some parties who have been prevented from following their nefarious avocation of killing and skinning other people's cattle, . . . we do not propose to be driven from the pursuit of a legitimate business by threats of a set of cowardly cattle-skinners and thieves who have not the manliness to confront us with any charge of wrong dealing face to face. . . .

Stafford cowboys Thomas and Daniels were sent to the coast country to distribute 500 copies of the reply. The two were gone for ten days and were never molested.

Beginning in 1880 Pierce and banker Herman Kountze began to buy 200,000 acres of Stafford's prairie grasslands. This free-grass range between the Crescent V and Pierce's BU Ranch was either railroad-grant land or owned by non-resident Texas army veterans. The 200,000 acres purchased by Kountze and Pierce became the fenced K and KO ranches, cutting the heart out of Bob Stafford's free-grass domain. To further even the score, Shanghai had a devoted friend, Ed Taylor, take a Winchester and turn Stafford cattle out of the Kountze ranches 1 and 2.

Bloodshed began to dog the Stafford clan in the early 1880s. On the night of February 19, 1880, Bill Guynn was seen leaving Columbus with Ben Stafford, who had moved to the Pinchback Ranch, and Wes Ratcliff. Guynn was found shot to death the next morning, but neither of his companions was ever convicted of the murder.

On the night of December 27, 1882, a camper named J.W. Stidman shot and seriously wounded Warren Stafford in the shoulder en route to his Uncle John's house for a party. After Warren managed to reach the Stafford mansion, his enraged kinfolk set out to avenge the shooting. John and Will Stafford and a friend, Will Townsend, cornered the hapless Stidman, shot him as he tried to run, then hanged and shot him repeatedly for good measure. Both John Stafford and Will Townsend were arrested for Stidmen's murder, but the charges were dismissed in March 1886.

The old Stafford-Townsend feud that began over cattle in 1871 turned political after one of old Asa's sons, James Light Townsend, was elected sheriff of Colorado County in 1880. Asa's brother Mose had a son, Marcus "Marc" Townsend, reputed to be the smartest lawyer in South Texas. For years the two Townsends ran the county by telling blacks how to vote.

By 1890 Sheriff Townsend had hired two of his nephews, Larkin and Marion Hope, as peace officers. Both Hopes were young and undersized but handy with guns. Larkin served as city marshal, and sheriff's deputy Marion followed his brother's orders.

By July 7, 1890, the cornerstone for the new courthouse was to be laid followed by a grand ball in the evening. Sheriff Townsend had heard rumors of a plot against his life. It seems that Colorado County was tired of him and Marc Townsend retaining power simply by controlling the Negro vote. Thus both the sheriff and his deputies were on edge the day of the celebration.

Bob Stafford's son Warren got in trouble that day for being drunk. Bob had an understanding with the Hope boys: if Warren "outdid himself," he would not be bothered and his father would pay the fine and damages. This time, however, the Hope brothers arrested Warren and paraded him through the streets of Columbus handcuffed like a common thief. Although Warren was not actually jailed, his father was furious over the incident. According to the unwritten code, cautious peace officers should have asked Warren's friends to take care of him.

At 7:00 that evening, Bob Stafford and his brother John ran into the Hope boys just as they came out of the Nicoli Saloon on the southwest corner of the square. Bob was about to get into the wagon of ten-year-old Ralph Grimes when he saw the two lawmen. According to two eyewitnesses — Constable York and bartender Hugh Smith — Bob started a heated conversation and shook his finger in Larkin's face, who stepped back and drew his pistol. At this point Mrs. Larkin Hope happened to drive by in a buggy. When she tried to break up the confrontation, Larkin assured her that he was all right and told his wife to go home.

Soon thereafter Bob Stafford unleashed a barrage of "nigger loving" epithets; that was more than Larkin Hope could stand, and he began to fire away. His first shot hit John Stafford, who sat down in the door of the saloon. Larkin then turned his gun on Bob, who staggered into the saloon, where he was shot again from the side door. Hope then returned to the saloon front to be sure that John was dead. At this point the two Hopes calmly walked to the other side of the street, where their uncle, Sheriff Townsend, took charge of the two.

Bob's wife, Sarah Stafford, and their daughter, Mrs. Myra Early, became hysterical when they were taken to view the two bodies lying on the floor of Nicoli's Saloon. Later a mile-long procession followed the bodies of the brothers to the family burial plot in the Odd Fellows Cemetery.[12]

The Hope brothers were indicted for double murder and stood trial in several counties but were never punished because of hung juries and postponements.

Shanghai Pierce was en route to New York when brother Jonathan relayed the news: "Staffords got their Just Deserts in the Long race." To Shanghai's great embarrassment, the Hope brothers sent him a letter asking for $1,000 "to help us out of our trouble in the Stafford killing." After receiving a subpoena to appear as a witness on the Hopes' behalf, Pierce escaped the jurisdiction of the Texas courts by going on a grand tour of Europe.

On September 25, 1890, Sheriff Light Townsend was asked to resign his office after a citizens' meeting. He stepped down for a time and was replaced by Sam H. Reese of Oakland. Reese was the handsome husband of Light's cousin, Keetie. In the fall of 1890, Sheriff Reese brought his wife and five children to the new jail. The Reeses were a kindly, home-loving family. Mrs. Reese cooked for the prisoners and made sure they were warm on cold nights.

Light Townsend was reelected sheriff in 1892. When he died in office on November 14, 1894, Sam Reese was appointed sheriff. Although Sam was considered a good officer, he did not get along with the Townsend clan.

Friction between Reese and precinct constable Larkin Hope over court costs led Hope to run against Sam for sheriff in 1898 with the blessing of Marc Townsend. During the hotly contested campaign, Larkin was shot and killed on Milam Street on the night of August 3. A mysterious gunman put two shotgun charges of buckshot into his victim before riding out of town. Jim Coleman of Alleyton was indicted for the murder of Hope amid rumors that Sheriff Reese was behind the killing. Marc Townsend's brother-in-law, Will Burford of Osage, was put on the ballot and beat Sheriff Reese at the polls. After Coleman's murder trial was first tranferred to Fort Bend County, he was eventually acquitted at San Antonio.

The murder of Larkin Hope was to lead to a new round of blood-letting, the Reese-Townsend feud. At 5:30 P.M. on March 16, 1899, Sam Reese was tying his pony at the horse rack in front of Brunson's Saloon as deputy W.D. "Willie" Clements talked with Ed Scott. Marc Townsend was sitting eating cheese next door in Bob Farmer's grocery store. Suddenly, a street fight broke out between Reese and Clements. In the melee that followed, as many as twenty shots were fired and Reese was shot dead through the neck. Farmer Charles Boehm was also hit by a stray bullet and died instantly while getting in his wagon. A small boy, John Williams, was hit in the hip and crippled for life while watching the fight from his father's gate. When the firing stopped, Walter Reese ran out of a nearby store and found his father's gun empty. As he cradled the dead man's head in his lap, Walter vowed to get the man who killed his father.

Willie Clements, Marion Hope, and Marc Townsend were all arrested and jailed. After being released on bond, they were charged with manslaughter before the case was dismissed. At that time Marc Townsend moved to San Antonio, where he died in 1915.

After declaring a "pressing" emergency, Judge Kennon wired Governor Sayers requesting help from the Texas Rangers. Famed Capt. Bill McDonald came to Columbus from the Panhandle and was met by four Ranger privates and a town divided into two armed camps. Sheriff Burford had deputized many of his friends and supporters, and they were faced by a small army from the Reese faction on the other side of the square.

In this explosive situation, Captain McDonald presented himself, alone, to Judge Kennon and said, "Come on. I believe I can stop it. We can see a mighty good fight, anyhow." Because of this determined Ranger, there was no fight. McDonald persuaded both sides to lay down their weapons and sent his privates to patrol the streets, disarming those with any kind of weapon. The only disturbance came on the evening of March 28, when someone tried to shoot Willie Clements through his own window. Four days later, the worst was over and McDonald left Columbus.

At 9:00 P.M. on May 18, 1899, deputy sheriffs A.L. "Step" Yates and J.G. Townsend shot Dick Reese of Orange, the brother of the ex-sheriff, and his black driver, Dick Gant of Alleyton. The two were killed instantly in their buggy near the east end of the Colorado River bridge. The two officers had been sent there by order of Sheriff Burford to intercept pistol carriers. They claimed that Dick Reese, who had one paralyzed arm, tried to draw his pistol when they ordered him to halt at the bridge. When the runaway horses were found down the Alleyton road at 3:00 the next morning, the two corpses were still in the buggy. The Reese family contended that the twin killing was actually a cold-blooded ambush.

Again, Judge Mansfield sent for the Rangers. A unit headed by Captain Sieker remained in the Columbus area for an extended period, and there was no serious trouble for five months.

Deputies Yates and Townsend were both indicted for murder. By the time Townsend stood trial at Bastrop on January 15, 1900, Yates had died of tuberculosis. About 300 people from Columbus took the train by way of LaGrange to attend the trial. There was a detachment of Rangers there to confiscate firearms. However, the legal proceedings took only a few minutes after a motion for continuance was granted. Willie Clements left the courthouse walking with Sheriff Burford's son, Arthur, who had just finished a law course at the University of Texas. This bright, promising young man was considered a friend by both factions. Just as they passed the Golden Rule Saloon, a burst of gunfire struck them. Clements, the intended target, dodged behind the innocent Burford, who died instantly from a shot to the head. Willie Clements survived a bullet hole through the lungs and eventually recovered.

Walter Reese, Jim Coleman, and Tom Daniels were arrested and held in Bastrop, where they were indicted by the grand jury. Their case went to San Antonio on a change of venue and was dismissed.

Walter Reese moved to Rosenberg, where he had trusted friends, but trouble followed him there. On July 31, 1900, he and Jim Coleman were involved in a shootout on the train station platform with Willie Clements, Marc Townsend, Frank Burford and A.B. Woolridge, who were riding through town in a passenger coach. Reeese and Coleman were badly wounded in the fracas. Although Townsend and Burford were arrested, there was no further legal proceeding against them.

There would be one final fight in the Reese-Townsend feud after the Reese family returned to Columbus. On the night of June 30, 1906, Marion Hope intentionally burned Herbert Reese's face with his lighted cigar as Herbert passed the new roller skating rink set up near the square. Reese was whipped in the fight that followed, went home, and returned armed along with his brother Walter. Hope was awaiting them hidden in the Zumwalt Drugstore. When the Reeses neared the Franz Saloon, Marion jumped out of hiding and fired his shotgun at them. Both brothers were wounded in the arms and legs but not seriously. The wild shooting left Hiram Clements of the Townsend faction shot from behind and mortally wounded while standing near the post office. A mule was shot in the head, and numerous bullets shattered shop windows and lodged in awnings and door facings.

Once the shooting stopped, the armed citizens of Columbus rallied and escorted the Reese boys to their home, where their wounds were attended to. After Clements died Dr. Joe Lessing, brother-in-law of the Reeses, was charged with murder. Although he was arrested and jailed along with the Reese boys, the grand jury for the fall of 1906 term of district court no-billed the three men.

Sheriff Dick Bridge again requested that Governor Lanham send in a Texas Ranger to keep peace and settle the Reese-Townsend feud. On July 16, 1906, Capt. John R. Hughes and three privates arrived in Columbus.

Due to the epidemic of killings, Mr. Joseph Odom called for a mass citizens' meeting at the courthouse on July 19 to discuss "ways and means for the betterment and relief of the depression which has settled upon all our people." As many as 300 residents attended the meeting and elected James W. Towell as chairman. A committee of five, including Baptist minister G.M. Parker, was appointed to draft resolutions "expressing the sentiment of our people in regard to recent occurrences in our town." Resolutions adopted that afternoon opposed the storing of easily accessible firearms or offensive weapons and condemned the carrying of pistols and loaded firearms. Resolution 9 requested that the mayor and city council of Columbus reestablish the office of city marshal, which had been abolished in 1903. A petition to that effect was also signed by over 125 citizens, but the council rejected the proposal by a vote of 3-2.

Chairman Towell, the co-owner of Towell and Shaw Gin, then asked the greatly incensed people of Columbus to reassemble the next morning, July 20. At that meeting W.L. Adkins proposed the abolition of the corporation of the town of Columbus. In an election held on August 7, 1906, disincorporation was approved by a vote of 99 to 35. The voters considered this decision a step in the right direction toward securing peace. It was thought that the affairs of Columbus would be better served by the county commissioners court with the preservation of law and order left in the hands of the county sheriff, his deputies, and one Texas Ranger stationed in town, J.C. White. Columbus would remain unincorporated until 1927.

In January 1907, Ranger Capt. Bill McDonald twice disarmed members of the opposing factions in the Reese-Townsend feud, and the killing finally stopped.[13]

On September 21, 1866, an act of the state legislature authorized the Buffalo Bayou, Brazos, and Colorado Railway Company to purchase the Columbus Tap Railway. In February 1867, Irish workers began to drive piles in the river to support the first railroad bridge across the Colorado at Columbus. Under the direction of superintendent Wheeler, the new bridge was completed by November. The locomotive, *General Sherman,* first crossed the bridge on November 10, 1867, and reached Columbus about 3:30 p.m. This momentous occasion prompted the *Columbus Times* to report that "new buildings are going up and the spirits of the merchants are high." Later that month the *Times* observed that "Alleyton is pulling up stakes and moving to Columbus."

With the new bridge Columbus became the terminus of the BBB&C and was soon shipping 48,000 bales of cotton yearly. Columbus was now a hub for trade to Galveston and Houston with an estimated $5 million in annual business. By 1878 the town had a population of 4,500. Until 1883 the bustling trade center was the division point of the railroad between Houston and San Antonio, having a roundhouse, extra switch tracks, and storage facilities.

In March 1869, a right-of-way survey began to extend the railroad west to San Antonio. On July 27, 1870, the legislature passed a bill enabling the BBB&C to build toward San Antonio under the new name of the Galveston, Harrisburg and San Antonio Railway Company. Maj. James Converse began construction westward in 1870, and the main line reached San Antonio on February 5, 1877.

In 1870 T.W. Peirce purchased the railroad and brought the locomotives *Jupiter* and *No. 42* to Columbus to be used as switch engines.

The reorganized GH&SA had its main headquarters in Columbus until 1880. The railroad hospital there was managed by Dr. R.H. Harrison, Sr., chief surgeon of the railroad. Dr. Harrison, a close friend of T.W. Peirce, was called to Boston to attend his illnesses. Dr. Harrison was unhappy with the noisy and smoky roundhouse and shops being so near his home and the hospital. Backed by similar complaints from Columbus residents, Harrison persuaded Peirce to have the yards and shops moved to three miles west of Columbus.

There was also a practical reason for the relocation of the facilities: Since every westbound train had to be pushed over Glidden Hill, the switch engine should be located closer to the incline.

On December 21, 1882, the railroad puchased 159.64 acres of land from T.J. Oakes. The tract was located on Abstract 18 of the W.B. Dewees League. By January 1883, a large roundhouse was built and a substantial amount of switch track was laid. Initially, the new location was referred to as the "new Columbus yards" or Converse.

On May 27, 1885, cheif engineer James Converse filed the first official plat of Glidden, Texas. By this time the GH&SA had been absorbed by the Southern Pacific Railroad, whose president, E.H. Harriman, named the new railroad terminal for his nephew, a railroad engineer named F.J. Glidden.

By 1886 there were fifty families living in the new town. Glidden had a station office, passenger depot, freight depot, section house, roundhouse, turn-table, deep well, two railroad-owned hotels, a church house, a restaurant, and two Oakes & Company stores. Two years later a post office was established at Glidden.

On February 5, 1880, the Columbus office of Dr. Robert H. Harrison was destroyed by fire. As a result he purchased a two-story hotel building on the southwest corner of Spring and Live Oak streets. Dr. Harrison then converted the structure into a hospital with ten private rooms and four wards for six to eight patients each.

Although it was intended to be a private hospital, Thomas W. Peirce, president of the Galveston, Harrisburg and San Antonio Railroad, arranged with Dr. Harrison to use the facility as his company's hospital two months after the opening. It was then named the

GH&SA Railroad Hospital, and railroad employees were charged a small fee to help maintain the first railroad hospital in Texas.

Dr. Harrison served as medical director and was in full control of the hospital, which also admitted other patients. He reported that in the first twenty-two months, 1,404 cases were handled by the hospital; only twenty-six of those resulted in the death of the patient with six of them considered hopeless at the time of admission. Dr. Harrison claimed this was the best record for recovery from disease or injury of any hospital in America at the time.

By 1882 Mr. Peirce was making plans for a newer, larger hospital to be located on land he purchased in San Antonio. He was determined, however, to keep the services of Dr. Harrison, who wanted to stay in Columbus. Even though the Columbus city council agreed to right-of-way and land donations in order to have the $50,000 hospital built there, the future site of the new railroad hospital was still undecided when Peirce died in New York in October 1885.

Dr. Harrison retired from private practice in July 1883. The next month he completed the expansion of his hospital by opening a two-story bath house next door. The first floor was open to the public with the second level reserved for hospital patients.

In June 1887, officials of the Southern Pacific Railroad, which had absorbed the GH&SA, decided to end their affiliation with the Harrison hospital in Columbus and to build a new hospital in San Antonio. Dr. Harrison then announced plans to modernize his facility, add a third story to the building, and open it as a private hospital and sanitarium.

Shortly after midnight on September 12, 1887, a fire broke out in the hospital kitchen, and the entire structure was soon engulfed in flames. Volunteers working until dawn managed to save only part of the hospital library and to keep the fire from spreading. Dr. Harrison also lost the major part of his medical library. Since the hospital was insured for only $15,000, he chose not to rebuild, leaving Columbus without a hospital until October 1928.

Banking in Columbus dates from 1873, when James Hendly Simpson of Hallettsville opened the private Simpson Bank in the old Harbert-Boedecker Building built by William Harbert's slaves in 1857. (It was located where the Columbus State Bank now stands.) Simpson and his partner, Carey Shaw, operated the bank until

Simpson's death in 1889. At that time ownership passed to his son Friench and Shaw.

The Simpson Bank was forced to close for good in October 1914. Selling off bank real estate brought in $54,000 to help pay creditors, but little was left for depositors. At the time of its closing, the bank had $89,936.68 of time deposits and $89,533.57 of demand deposits.

In 1882 rancher R.E. "Bob" Stafford established the R. E. Stafford Bank with himself as sole owner on the corner of Milam and Spring streets.

On January 25, 1913, the First State Bank was organized at Columbus by Ike T. Pryor, former vice-president of the Stafford Bank, and E.A. Hutchins, Owen G. Hoegemeyer, R. Lee Hastedt, and H. Lee Johnson. All five became directors and their bank received a charter from the state in February. The First State Bank opened for business on March 1, 1913, in the Stafford Bank Building. The accounts of the two banks were gradually merged until the Stafford Bank was liquidated in 1914. First State Bank remained there until 1916, then purchased the property of the Simpson Bank at the corner of Walnut and Milam streets. That facility was occupied until 1923, when a new brick building was erected at a cost of $36,512.63.

Columbus State Bank opened on August 19, 1919, with capital of $50,000. It was organized by investors from Columbus, Eagle Lake, Weimar, and Alleyton with E.B. Mayes as president.

Two Columbus attorneys, Wells Thompson and George McCormick, were elected to high state offices in the late 1870s. Wells Thompson was born in Marengo County, Alabama, on December 12, 1837. In the early 1840s, his family came to Texas and settled in Matagorda County. In 1859 Thompson graduated from the University of North Carolina. Two years later he was first in his class in the law department of the University of Georgia. During the Civil War, he advanced from private to captain in the Confederate army and was twice wounded.

Thompson was elected district attorney in June 1866, only to be removed by the military. He was also the Democratic nominee for lieutenant governor and state senator in 1869 and 1870, respectively, but lost both races to Radical Republicans.

On February 28, 1871, Wells married Caroline Tait, daughter of Dr. C.W. Tait, and the newlyweds lived in the Tait town house for a short time.

Thompson was elected to the state senate in 1876 and served as president pro tempore during his one term. In 1878 he was elected to a two-year term as lieutenant governor of Texas.

In the 1880s, Thompson was one of the leading stockraisers in Colorado County. He was also an Odd Fellow, an Episcopalian, and a member of the board of regents of the Agricultural and Mechanical College of Texas. He died at Bay City on January 17, 1914.

George McCormick came to Columbus from Virginia in 1858. After being elected Colorado County clerk in June 1866, he was disqualified and replaced in April 1869. The commissioners court appointed him as the first county attorney in September 1870.

McCormick was elected attorney general of Texas in November 1878, and served for two years. On July 15, 1882, he was one of sixty-nine lawyers who met in Galveston to organize a state bar association.

Judge McCormick died in October 1905 and was buried in Weimar beside his wife, Myrah Thatcher McCormick, who preceded him in death in 1902.

Two present-day Columbus landmarks were built in 1883 and 1891, respectively. In 1883 the town's first water tower was built by Capt. R.J. Jones on the southwest corner of the courthouse square at Spring and Milam streets. The circular structure cost $25,000 and included 400,000 handmade bricks in walls thirty-two inches thick. There was a fire house with engines in the lower part of the tower; contemporary photographs reveal that the fire wagon could barely squeeze through the doorway. The large wooden water tank on top of the tower was later replaced with a galvanized tank. This water tower was used until 1912, when a steel tower was erected.[14]

On October 1, 1889, a $54,000 contract was let for a new Colorado County courthouse and jail built to replace the 1857 structures. The cornerstone was laid on July 7, 1890, and the new courthouse was accepted by the county commissioners on April 4, 1891. It was built in Second Empire Style with brick made from Colorado River clay and Belton stone detailing.

On February 24, 1891, a grand ball was held in the District Court Room of the new courthouse. All white citizens were invited, and music was provided by the "Weimar Band."

The magnolia trees that now surround the courthouse were planted in 1905.

On July 21, 1909, a hurricane nearly destroyed the courthouse. The clock tower and roof were torn off, and the interior rooms suffered extensive water damage.

Repairs were completed in September 1910. The original clock tower was replaced with a Neo-Classic copper dome and a magnificent stained glass dome in the District Court Room. Other outstanding features included hand-carved newel posts and wainscoting of red heart pine.

In 1939 a basement was added to the courthouse. During World War II, the iron fence surrounding the courthouse square since 1881 was used for scrap iron.

(A major restoration of the courthouse began in 1980 and was completed in September 1981. During this time the exterior was thoroughly cleaned and repainted. A false ceiling was removed, the glass dome was restored, and a chandelier was installed.)

The courthouse was named a recorded Texas Historic Landmark in 1969 and listed in the National Register of Historic Places in 1976. The grand old structure was designated a State Archaeological Landmark in 1981.

Two modern conveniences also date from this period. On March 31, 1887, telephone service connected Columbus and Weimar. By 1900 there were forty-seven telephones in Columbus.

In 1893 an electric power system was installed in Columbus. It consisted of a 100-horsepower steam engine and a 75-kilowatt direct current generator. The machinery was operated by Carey Shaw and Jim Towell. This was the first electric plant installed between Houston and San Antonio. In the early years the electric system operated only at night.

In 1887 Henry Ilse built one of the grandest homes in Columbus at 1100 Bowie Street. Patterned from the symmetrical Victorian style, the two-story structure is made of cypress with pine floors and jigsaw patterns. The interior pine woodwork still has the original grained painting. There are three fireplaces with the original marble mantels. The roof is made of stamped metal rectangles. The fine taste of Mr. Ilse is reflected in the brass dust catcher, carpet rods on the stairway, and the Victorian bronze hardware. This mansion was occupied by the builder until 1954.[15]

Another fine home dating from this period is the Senftenberg-Brandon House at 616 Walnut Street. The home was built in the late 1860s by the Tate family. This four-room Greek Revival structure had four fireplaces and a full basement constructed of hand-made bricks. In the 1880s, the Senftenberg family added a Victorian second floor with verandas and an ornate stairway.[16]

R.E. "Bob" Stafford was already well on his way to becoming a millionaire when he built a refrigerated meat-packing plant in Columbus in 1883. The Columbus Meat and Ice Company, the first of its kind in Texas, was built near the North Bridge at the site of Robson's castle. The plant was valued at $250,000 and could process 250 head of cattle and forty tons of ice per day, enabling Stafford to ship refrigerated meat to England and Holland.

On May 14, 1883, Charles Crary's livery stable and the old Bond Hotel on the southeast corner of Milam and Spring streets were destroyed by fire. The area lay vacant until December 1885, when Stafford purchased the lots for the purpose of constructing two brick business buildings along Spring Street and a new personal residence facing Milam Street behind the buildings. Once his plans became known in the *Colorado Citizen,* a citizens' petition asked Stafford to unite the top floors of the two business buildings into one large hall as an opera house. He agreed to the request and decided on just one longer two-story brick structure with his home next door on Spring Street.

The imposing building cost $50,000, and the Second Empire architecture was designed by the famous Nicholas J. Clayton, who built so many of Galveston's grand buildings. The first floor, which housed the R.E. Stafford & Company Bank and the Senftenberg Brothers Mercantile Company, was completed by August 1886. The mercantile store carried dry goods stock valued at $75,000.

Work on the second floor Stafford Opera House went on into 1887. This first-class facility seated 800 on the 90x66-foot main floor and another 400 in the U-shaped balcony. The stage was 30x30 feet with wings eighteen feet wide.

Bob Stafford wanted kerosene or oil lamp lighting, but Clayton preferred the new safer gas lighting, which gave a whiter, more brilliant light. The architect won the argument. His original gas light wrought-iron chandelier had a brass ring eight feet in diameter, holding sixteen glass globes with sixty jets produced by compressed gasoline vapor.

Stafford spent an additional $10,000 on a stage curtain hand-painted in oils, wings, and stage equipment. The stage curtain was one of only two by a nationally known artist; the other hung in the Hancock Opera House in Austin.

The first-floor facade was composed of iron columns cast at the Galveston Foundry and fourteen-foot cypress and glass doors and transoms. The four colors of handmade brick were fired at the Quinn Walker place on Skull Creek, then placed in highly detailed Roman and Byzantine relief. The mansard roof had ventilating gables with ornate metal detail. The second-floor grand hall was spanned with heavy timber trusses.

The unique cornerstone has a steer's head sculpted with a lasso looped over its horns and hay at its mouth. In the upper right-corner is a hand holding a rope; N.J. Clayton, arch., and J.F. Taman, supt., is inscribed below. "R.E. Stafford's building" is written diagonally through the center with the date 1886.

Bob Stafford also built his new house next door in 1886. Local legend has it that the upper story windows were placed so that Bob could stay in his bedroom and have a full view of the stage next door. With his windows open there were no sound or vision problems.

Stafford chose Ed Sandmeyer, a local attorney and cashier of the Stafford Bank, to manage the opera house. On October 28, 1887, the Stafford Opera House had its grand opening with Louise Balfe starring in *The Planter's Wife*. She had opened the season at Pillot's Opera House in Houston in *Dagmar,* the drama in which she starred in Columbus on the second night, October 29. Nearly 700 in formal dress attended the premier, and the *Colorado Citizen* described Miss Balfe as having a "fine figure, expressive face, and graceful carriage." The opening night crowd was smaller then expected, possibly because *The Planter's Wife* had already been presented in Columbus at Ilse's Hall, a large room occupying the second floor of Ilse's Saloon, which began to host theatrical performances of traveling companies in the 1870s. Ironically, Bob Stafford was not present to bask in the spotlight at the opening of his opera house; he had gone on vacation some weeks earlier.

From the beginning there was regular attendance from Eagle Lake and Weimar. Special trains sometimes ran from as far away as Schulenburg and returned after the performance.

The first season also included appearances by Lizzie Evans, Katie Putnam, McIntyre and Heath's Modern Minstrels, and the Mendelssohn Quartet. The great blackface team of James McIntyre and Tom Heath were the forerunners of the style of parody culminating in the *Amos and Andy* radio and television series. Their sketches included "The New Telephone" and "The Ham Bone."

The Mendelssohn Quartet closed the theater that first season. Although this accomplished group did not typically play rural halls, they agreed to fill an opera date at Columbus en route from Houston to San Antonio after being guaranteed a minimum by local residents.

The artistic "low" of that first season was a show by the Chinese Students on February 23, 1888. The troupe was sponsored by women of the Methodist church and advertised displays of Chinese artifacts and the serving of a genuine Chinese meal. The *Colorado Citizen* described the show as being "a miserable farce." When the audience jeered and hissed throughout the performance, the company manager came out on stage to announce that the city and its citizens were "the worst place and worst people" he had ever seen. As the company boarded the train the next day, some of the still-angry audience pelted them with fresh — not rotten — eggs, a final "review" that knocked off hats and stained clothes of the Chinese Students.

The 1888-89 season was highlighted by three performances. The first was an appearance by Thomas M. Keene in the popular play *Richelieu* on the evening of October 18. The *Citizen* called his appearance "the greatest dramatic event in the history of Columbus" and referred to Keene as "one of the finest actors in the world."

Near the end of the season, the MacCollin Opera Company of New York, with a cast of thirty-five, presented the only genuine operas ever heaard in the Stafford Opera House. On March 8, 1889, the three-act opera *La Mascotte* was presented, followed the next day by William Gilbert and Arthur Sullivan's delightful operetta *The Mikado.*

There were only six performances in the 1889-90 season. All six of these productions also played Galveston, Houston, or in both cities. The only major theatrical event featured Lewis Morrison in *Faust* on March 4, 1890.

The 1890-91 season was opened on September 20 by James H. Wallick with the historical drama *Sam Houston*, a play full of historical inaccuracies. The Texas audiences were unimpressed by a production that put Houston in command of forces at the Alamo and had him utter the famous vow of William Barret Travis, "I shall never surrender or retreat."

The most popular plays tended to be very melodramatic. Typical was *The Two Orphans,* performed in the Stafford Opera House on November 20, 1890. This story was about two beautiful young orphan girls, Henriette and the blind Louise, who journey to Paris and have a series of misadventures.

The season closed on April 24, 1891, with Henry Watterston

lecturing on "The Money Devil." This newspaper editor was destined to win the Pulitzer Prize in 1917 for his pro-war editorials.

The highlight of the 1891-92 season was the appearance of the renowned actor Frederick Warde in *The Lion's Mouth* on January 13, 1892. He had toured as Lillie Langtry's leading man in California in 1888 and was possibly the foremost actor in America after the retirement of Edwin Booth.

The sixth and final season (1892-93) of the Stafford Opera House was highlighted by the performance of James O'Neill in his new play, *Fontenelle*, on February 7, 1893. This period drama was set in France during the reign of Louis XV. O'Neill was already famous for perfoming the role of Edmond Dantes thousands of times in the theater classic, *The Count of Monte Cristo.*

The Stafford Opera House all but went dark after 1893. The last known professional dramatic performance in the history of the opera house was Katie Putnam's production of *The Little Maverick* on January 10, 1894. This was the only attraction that season.

During its glory days sixty-five of the eighty-two productions that played the Stafford Opera House in the years between 1887 and 1894 also played in either Houston or Galveston the same season.

The demise of the opera house can be traced to two deaths. Bob Stafford was killed in July 1890. The theater never made money but was kept open by the financial backing of the Stafford family. When his bitter widow withdrew this support, the theater simply could not operate. The practical end of the opera house came with the death of manager Ed Sandmeyer in 1895.

The opera house came to life again briefly on February 5, 1898, when Lillian Lewis performed *For Liberty and Love.* She did the same play in Houston and Galveston only days later. A particular favorite of Columbus audiences, this was the fourth appearance of Miss Lewis at the Stafford Opera House. It is likely that she arranged this return to the city herself since the storied theater was not under any active management at the time.[17]

On December 31, 1896, the Lone Star Opera House opened on the second floor of the Brunson Building in Columbus. Unable to lure prime circuit attractions, this effort to replace the Stafford Opera House failed shortly thereafter. After being used for local talent productions and area social events, the Lone Star Opera House closed permanently in August 1908.

In 1916, E.C. Guilmartin purchased the opera house building

from Mrs. Ike T. (Myra) Pryor, the daughter of Bob Stafford. Two years later, Guilmartin opened a Ford dealership on the lower floor. A Ford agency remained there under different ownership for fifty-four years.

Over the years the second floor was used for lodge meetings and as a roller skating rink and dance hall. It also served as a court for high school basketball games and as a prize fight arena. Then the stage area was remodeled into apartments by the father of Arthur J. Willrodt, who owned it in the 1940s and 1950s. The theater finally became a pigeon roost and storage space for an auto agency until 1972.

From October 28 to November 1, 1909, Columbus hosted the first Colorado County Fair. The event featured a welcome home reception for U.S. Secretary of Commerce and Labor Charles Nagel, who was born on a Colorado County farm on August 9, 1848. After moving the family to Austin County in 1855, his father Hermann worked actively against the Confederate cause during the Civil War. In November 1863, Charles left home with his father to avoid service in the Confederate army.

After settling in St. Louis, Missouri, Charles Nagel became an attorney. One of his first clients was the powerful Adolphus Busch, president of the Anheuser-Busch Brewing Company. His opposition to the growing prohibition movement led Busch into presidential politics. Attorney Nagel labored diligently for the election of William Howard Taft and became the first native-born Texan to be appointed to a president's cabinet, serving from 1909 until 1913.

On November 1, 1909, Nagel arrived by special train at Columbus for the closing day of the Colorado County Fair. After making a speech, the secretary led a parade to the fairgrounds before touring the proposed power plant on the Colorado and viewing a water power exhibit. Nagel then had supper at the Kulow Hotel in Columbus and attended a local play, *The Beauty Machine*, at the Stafford Opera House. The festivities concluded with a three-course banquet in the Stafford Hall.

Nagel maintained a close association with the Busch family the rest of his life. When it became apparent that prohibition was going to be repealed, Anheuser-Busch began to plan an advertising campaign. Nagel then suggested a soon-to-be-famous corporate symbol — a team of Clydesdale horses pulling an old style beer wagon. The board of directors accepted his idea on December 28, 1933. Charles Nagel died on January 5, 1940.

Columbus celebrated her 100th birthday on August 24, 1923, with daylong festivities attended by as many as 6,000 people. Honored guests for the Columbus Centennial celebration included Texas Governor Pat M. Neff, Brig. Gen. Jacob F. Wolters, and the army band of the Second Division from Fort Sam Houston.

The celebration was highlighted by a huge barbecue supper and a pageant at dusk on the east banks of the Colorado. A cast of 500 presented seven historical scenes on a 210x175-foot stage illuminated by 200 footlights. The seven acts ranged from the landing of LaSalle in 1685 to the return of the troops after World War I. Each of the scenes had appropriate dances and costumes. The pageant was conceived by Mayor O.A. Zumwalt, local pharmacist and historian, and written by Mr. and Mrs. A.P. Hinton. Visitors from Houston and San Antonio marveled that nothing like this had ever been attempted in their cities.

In the fall of 1935, the normal tranquility of Columbus was shattered by a murder-rape and subsequent lynchings involving three local teenagers. On Thursday morning , October 15, nineteen-year-old Geraldine Kollmann, the valedictorian of Columbus High School, rode her horse to the Cummins Creek bottoms to find out who had been stealing pecans from the family grove. When she failed to return to the family farm house, her anguished mother sent Geraldine's younger brother, Milton, to look for her at about 4:00 P.M. When he reached the pecan grove, he noticed his sister's horse tied to a fence post near the creek. The horrified boy then spotted her body floating face down in the nearby creek swimming hole. Her breeches were unbuckled and a shoe and stocking were missing.

It was first assumed that the pretty, vivacious young woman had either drowned or committed suicide. A medical examination quickly revealed, however, that she had been strangled and was dead when her body was thrown into the water about noon that day. On Friday morning, a local doctor informed Sheriff Frank Hoegemeyer that Miss Kollmann had also been criminally assaulted by two different men after her death.

The sheriff began his investigation by picking up three pecan raiders who had earlier been ordered off the Kollmann farm. After these suspects were released, a break in the case came on Saturday morning. Sheriff Hoegemeyer found a black witness, Alex Alley, who had seen two black youths, Ben Mitchell and Ernest Collins, walk over the Colorado River Bridge on Highway 71 on Thursday morning and then head up the dirt road toward Cummins Creek. The sheriff then traced their route through four farms, where they had sought work as pecan harvesters.

When sixteen-year-old Mitchell and fifteen-year-old Collins were arrested on Saturday afternoon, the day of Miss Kollmann's funeral, both denied any knowledge of the crime. When the sheriff told Mitchell that he could prove that the two were on Cummins Creek about noon on Thursday, the suspect admitted the fact. After being coaxed with a huge bag of candy and questioned for hours, Mitchell finally confessed that he and Collins had killed Geraldine Kollmann.

On Sunday afternoon, Sheriff Hoegemeyer took his prisoners to the Houston city jail for safekeeping. That night Mitchell signed a written confession. He said that Miss Kollmann had found the two black youths sitting in the family pecan grove and accused them of threshing a nearby tree. As they followed her to the tree in question, Ernest Collins picked up an elm stick and whispered that they might assault her. When they reached the tree, Collins struck her with the stick, pulled her from her saddle, and strangled her to death as Mitchell held her down. (Then followed a crudely vulgar and detailed account of the rapes.) About an hour later the two threw her body into the creek and fled the scene.

Once both boys made written confessions in Houston, it was assumed that the maximum penalty of the law — death by electrocution — would be assessed Mitchell and Collins when they were brought to trial. Popular anger and racial tension began to mount in Columbus when it became general knowledge that the confessed slayers were juveniles, and that under state law their most severe sentence would be confinement in a state reformatory until the age of twenty-one.

In the month that followed, secret plans were made by the outraged white citizens of Columbus. Spotters began to watch the movements of Sheriff Hoegemeyer and Deputy Berry Townsend.

Shortly after noon on Tuesday, November 12, 1935, the two lawmen were seen slipping out of town headed east for Houston. They intended to bring Mitchell and Collins back to Columbus for an examining trial in juvenile court the next day. The sheriff was hoping to secretly slip the prisoners into town on Tuesday night by leaving the main highway at Eagle Lake and taking a dirt road detour through Altair.

About 7:00 that night, a sentinel at Eagle Lake reported that the sheriff had passed there headed for Altair. When Hoegemeyer's car reached the Colorado River bridge four miles from Columbus, he was halted by cars blocking both ends of the bridge. Ten heavily armed and masked men stepped out of the cars with license plates covered. They quickly disarmed the sheriff and deputy, took their car keys, and forced the chained prisoners into one of their vehicles. A procession of cars then sped off toward Columbus.

Awaiting their arrival was a lynch mob estimated at from 300 to 500 surrounding a giant oak tree one mile north of town on Highway 71. After ropes were looped around the necks of Mitchell and Collins, Rev. Charles Gresham Marmion, Jr., rector of Saint John's Episcopal Church in Columbus, leaped onto the fender of an old Ford Model-T and shouted for silence. The young minister then pleaded with the men not to take this "barbaric and sinful" step — to let the law take its course. As he finished his speech, there was a chorus of boos and Marmion was jerked from the fender by a burly man. He then left in disgust and horror and drove back to the parish hall.[18]

In the meantime the black youths were marched beneath the tree and ropes thrown over a ten-foot-high limb. Ten men seized the end of each rope and pulled the boys' feet from the ground. Collins, who was large for his age, grabbed the rope and pulled himself up, shouting, "Oh, Lord, help me!" Three of the lynchers decided that he was "dying too easy" and jerked him violently downward, breaking his neck instantly.

By then Mitchell had started to babble out a new confession, claiming that there was a third black youth who had planned the whole thing and was the first to rape the girl. Mitchell's body was vigorously yanked from the ground, and he died when his head struck the tree limb. (Some members of the mob went looking for the other alleged accomplice to the crime, only to find that he had been warned and left the country.)[19]

By 10:30 P.M. the crowd had silently dispersed, leaving the bodies swinging from the limb. When Sheriff Hoegemeyer arrived at the grisly scene, he cut down the bodies. With him was Justice of the Peace O.E. Thrower, whose inquest verdict in the lynchings was "death by hanging at the hands of a mob." (It should be noted that not a single shot was fired during the entire proceeding.)

The families of the two black boys did not claim the bodies, presumably because they feared for their own safety. The remains were turned over to the local Negro undertaker, then buried by the county in a country cemetery.

The two ropes, each with a hangman's noose, were placed on display in a Columbus drugstore. Ever since that deadly night, the oak where the lynchings took place has been called the "Hanging Tree" in Columbus.

The next day, November 13, 1935, the lynchings in Columbus provided the front-page headlines and lead columns in the *Houston Post, Houston Chronicle,* and *Houston Press.*

The local official response to the lynchings was defiant and defensive in nature. County Attorney O.P. Moore issued the following statement: "I do not call the citizens who executed the Negroes a mob. I consider their action an expression of the will of the people." County Judge H.P. Hahn said, "I am strongly opposed to mob violence and favor orderly process of the law. The fact that the Negroes who so brutally murdered Miss Kollmann could not be adequately punished by the law because of their ages, prevents me from condemning those citizens who meted justice to the ravishing murderers last night." The Columbus Chamber of Commerce wrote a letter to at least two Houston newspapers defending the action of the mob and saying that they were tired of listening to criticism. It was the chamber's view that the mob action took place only because of the state legislature's failure to adequately deal with juvenile criminal law.

Justice Thrower immediately announced plans for holding a court of inquiry into the lynchings, and Texas Ranger E.M. Davenport was sent to assist in the investigation. In spite of this flurry of activity, no indictments were ever returned by subsequent grand juries against anyone who took part in the lynchings.

The year 1961 marked a turning point in the history of what had become a rather sleepy, complacent little town. In that year a handful of farsighted residents had a vision: turning a neglected asset — a large number of historic homes and buildings — into a much needed boost to the local economy. Since that time tourism has become a major focus through two remarkably successful ventures: the annual Magnolia Homes Tour and the more recent "First and Third Thursdays" walking tours of downtown Columbus.

In 1961 ten local citizens formed the Magnolia Homes Tour with local architectural designer Arthur J. Willrodt as first president. The group opened four century-old homes to the public in conjunction with the Live Oak Art Club's annual spring show. Since that time Magnolia Homes Tour has conducted tours through selected historic homes and buildings on the third weekend in May each year. In addition, groups consisting of a minimum of thirty persons may make reservations for guided tours on scheduled days during the year.

In 1968 the organization incorporated as a nonprofit corporation for further preservation, restoration, and education. In that year Magnolia Homes Tour, Inc., purchased the Tate-Senftenberg-Brandon House. In 1972 the group acquired the Stafford Bank and Opera House from H.P. Meyer for $30,000. The Alley Log Cabin was donated to the corporation in 1976.

Restoration of the Stafford Opera House proceeded in phases as funds became available. A.J. Willrodt directed the first phases of restoring the exterior, the roof, and the first floor of the imposing brick structure. The downstairs area was turned into commercial office space, and an elevator was installed to the second floor and balcony. This project was followed by electrical and plumbing work upstairs.

In 1983 coordination of the theater interior restoration was placed in the hands of Houston architect Barry Moore, FAIA, who had experience in both historic preservation and theater projects. Moore researched the Nicholas Clayton papers in the Rosenberg Library in Galveston. He also read all of Clayton's correspondence of 1885 and 1886 when he was designing the Stafford building, including his letters to Bob Stafford.

In 1985 work began on restoring the stage to its original state. Two years later, the stage was complete with dressing rooms, lights, sound system, and a new hand-painted curtain.

Then came the remaining phases of restoration, including audience seating, coverings for floors and windows, and refreshment facilities.

All restoration work was done in painstaking detail. Stage and scenery are copies of the original facility as is the beautiful hand-painted curtain. Moore and Eddie A. Morrow of Alcon Lightcraft Company in Houston made a faithful copy of the original light fixture. Moore and Houston stage designer John Bos recreated the original scenery, working from 1900 and 1909 black-and-white photographs. Their project included a grand garden backdrop and stately column flats on each side. All restoration woodwork was done by Columbus carpentry and wood-turning artisan Mark Potter, a thirty-two-year-old, fourth-generation native of Colorado County. His work included a circular eight-foot-wide ceiling medallion above the chandelier.

The restored Stafford Opera House now has 500 handsome stacking chairs on the main level, which may be cleared for parties, balls, and the like. The reconstructed U-shaped balcony will seat 100. The reproduction antique theater chairs installed in the balcony are decorated by painted motifs at the end of each row. These permanent seats were purchased by opera house underwriters for $1,000 each.

Laura Ann Rau served as chairwoman of the Stafford Opera House Restoration Committee. Among the early contributors were the Moody Foundation of Galveston and the Myra Stafford Pryor Foundation of San Antonio. The Texas Historical Commission awarded the opera house its first restoration grant, an early boost of $115,000 from the U.S. Department of the Interior.

After eighteen years of dogged restoration and the raising of $1,400,000 by the Magnolia Homes Tour, the Stafford Opera House had its Grand Gala Re-opening on October 13, 1990. The opening show included a performance by the sixty-piece Brazosport Symphony Pops Orchestra.

In 1991 Magnolia Homes Tour decided to open the opera house to a variety of entertaining programs and dinner theaters by producing a "Season at the Stafford." These performances are presented every third Saturday each month from September through May. Those who come to "play" the Stafford Opera House are immediately impressed with the true acoustics and the intimacy of the inclined stage in relation to the audience.

New museum space adjacent to the first floor meeting room displays furniture, documents, and objects from the Stafford family. There is also office rental space downstairs.

"First and Third Thursdays" began in September 1987 as an outgrowth of the popular annual festival presented by Magnolia Home Tours, Inc. The Thursday "Historic Walking Tours" were organized by R.F. "Buddy" Rau, a founder of Magnolia Homes Tour and a sixth-generation Texan with deep roots in the Columbus area.

The mini-tour starts at the Chamber of Commerce office at 425 Spring Street in the corner of the opera house. There the visitor receives instructions and a walking map listing fifteen stops, all concentrated in a five-block area. The visitor will find residents in period dress waiting to welcome him at each stop.

The mini-tour includes the Stafford Opera House, a historic document collection, the Confederate Memorial Museum, the Colorado County courthouse stained-glass dome, an early Texas maps and currency collection in the Columbus State Bank, the Live Oak Art Center, the Preston Kyle Shatto Wildlife Museum, the Senftenberg-Brandon House Museum, the Alley Log Cabin Museum, antique shops, country gifts and collectibles, three bed and breakfast inns, Thursdays Treasures (a plain front building with twenty-seven arts and crafts shops featuring local talent), and the Magnolia Room (a gracious tea room serving homemade soup, salads, and sandwiches).

In 1992 Columbus was designated by the governor and legislature of Texas as the Official Christopher Columbus Quincentennial Town of Texas. (Corpus Christi received a similar designation as the Quincentennial City of Texas.) Queen Isabella and Christopher Columbus, portrayed by local residents Pamela and Henry Potter in authentic costumes, acted as hosts for quincentennial functions in Columbus.

The celebration began on May 8, 1992, with a trail ride. Groups from all parts of the state brought national flags from foreign sister cities and the official 1992 Quincentennial Flag. The contingents arrived at 5:00 P.M. at the old Beeson's Crossing historical marker on U.S. Highway 90 one mile east of town. Flags in the ceremony represented Spain, France, Mexico, the Republic of Texas, the United States, Italy, Portugal, Scotland, England, Wales, Northern Ireland, and Germany.

The celebration culminated in the 32nd Annual Magnolia Homes Tour, which began on May 9-10 and continued through May 17, 1992.

Tourism has joined the cattle business, heavy construction, medical services, rental merchandising, trucking, and gravel mining as the major industries in Columbus. A recent brochure distributed by the Columbus Area Chamber of Commerce is titled "America. . . Discover Columbus." The pamphlet lists nineteen restaurants, three hotels or inns, and bed-and-breakfast lodging facilities.

The brochure touts such tourist attractions as the annual Magnolia Homes Tour and Live Oak Arts and Crafts Festival, the "First and Third Thursdays" monthly historic walking tours, the "Season at the Stafford" featuring an entertainment activity every third Saturday from September through May, the annual ColumbusFest celebrating the town's German and Czech heritage, and the weekly Saturday Night Jamboree featuring country music talent in the Nashville manner.

Because of the careful preservation and faithful restoration efforts of a band of energetic Columbus residents, the brochure can truly promise the visitor that "the past is our present to you."

C. W. Tait, ca. 1880 — doctor, engineer and planter.

— Photo courtesy Archives of the Nesbitt Memorial Library, Columbus, Texas

Tait Town House (1856), 526 Wallace St.
— Photo courtesy J. C. Hoke, Wharton, Texas

Tait Plantation House, six miles south of Columbus on S.H. 71, then left on County Road 101 for three miles.
— Photo courtesy J. C. Hoke, Wharton, Texas

Tait slave cabin.
— Photo courtesy J.C. Hoke, Wharton, Texas

Tait Family Cemetery, one mile from present site of house.
— Photo courtesy J. C. Hoke, Wharton, Texas

Dilue Rose Harris, ca. 1890, pioneer of the Texas Revolution.
— Photo courtesy Archives of the Nesbitt Memorial Library, Columbus, Texas

Dilue Rose Harris House Museum, 600 Washington St.
— Photo courtesy J. C. Hoke, Wharton, Texas

Fannie Darden and Home, 1886, the "Poet Laureate of Columbus."
— Photo courtesy Archives of the Nesbitt Memorial Library, Columbus, Texas

Alley Log Cabin (1836) — the oldest structure in Columbus.
— Photo courtesy J. C. Hoke, Wharton, Texas

R. E. Stafford, ca. 1885 — Cattle baron and the most influential man in the Columbus area between 1865 and 1890.

— Photo courtesy Archives of the Nesbitt Memorial Library, Columbus, Texas

John Stafford, ca. 1885 — Younger brother and partner of R. E. "Bob" Stafford.

— Photo courtesy Archives of the Nesbitt Memorial Library, Columbus, Texas

Stafford-Miller House, built in 1886, Spring St. facing courthouse square.
— Photo courtesy J. C. Hoke, Wharton, Texas

Stafford Opera House, 1886.
— Photo courtesy J. C. Hoke, Wharton, Texas

Water Town, Opera House, R. E. Stafford House, ca. 1905.

— Photo courtesy Archives of the Nesbitt Memorial Library, Columbus, Texas

John Stafford House, built in 1882, four miles south of Columbus. Destroyed by fire in 1994.
— Photo courtesy Archives of the Nesbitt Memorial Library, Columbus, Texas

Brunson Saloon, ca. 1898. Charlie Brunson, third from left.

— Photo courtesy Archives of the Nesbitt Memorial Library, Columbus, Texas

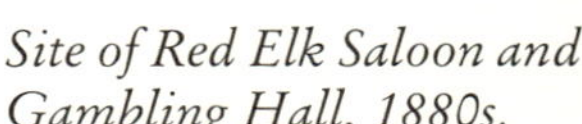

Site of Red Elk Saloon and Gambling Hall, 1880s.

— Photo courtesy J. C. Hoke, Wharton, Texas

Dr. R. H. Harrison, ca. 1885 — Medical director of the GH & SA Railroad Hospital.

— Photo courtesy Archives of the Nesbitt Memorial Library, Columbus, Texas

GH & SA Railroad Hospital, 1886.

— Photo courtesy Archives of the Nesbitt Memorial Library, Columbus, Texas

Wells Thompson, ca. 1895 — State senator and lieutenant governor of Texas.

— Photo courtesy Archives of the Nesbitt Memorial Library, Columbus, Texas

George McCormick, ca. 1890 — Attorney General of Texas.

—Photo courtesy Archives of the Nesbitt Memorial Library, Columbus, Texas

John H. Bowers, ca. 1885 — Pioneer Columbus physician.

— Photo courtesy Archives of the Nesbitt Memorial Library, Columbus, Texas

Colorado College, 1886.

— Photo courtesy Archives of the Nesbitt Memorial Library, Columbus, Texas

Columbus Water Tower, built in 1883 — Now United Daughters of the Confederacy Museum.

— Photo courtesy J. C. Hoke, Wharton, Texas

Colorado County Courthouse, ca. 1910.
— Photo courtesy John Hastedt, Jr.

Colorado County Courthouse.

— Photo courtesy J. C. Hoke, Wharton, Texas

Colorado County Citizen *Building.*
Photo courtesy J. C. Hoke, Wharton, Texas

Columbus railroad bridge, 1870s.
— Photo courtesy John Hastedt, Jr.

Senftenberg-Brandon House Museum, built in 1860s, 616 Walnut St.
— Photo courtesy J. C. Hoke, Wharton Texas

Raumonda (the former Henry Ilse Home), 1887, 1100 Bowie St.

— Photo courtesy J. C. Hoke, Wharton, Texas

Light Townsend, ca. 1890 — Sheriff of Colorado County.

— Photo courtesy Archives of the Nesbitt Memorial Library, Columbus, Texas

George Glenn, a Columbus cowboy who went on trail drives to Abilene, Kansas.

— Photo courtesy *The Colorado County Citizen*

The Hanging Tree (Columbus), one mile north of Columbus on S. H. 71.
— Photo courtesy J. C.Hoke, Wharton, Texas

Geraldine Kollmann, murder-rape victim, October 1935.
— Photo courtesy *Famous Detective Cases,* July 1936

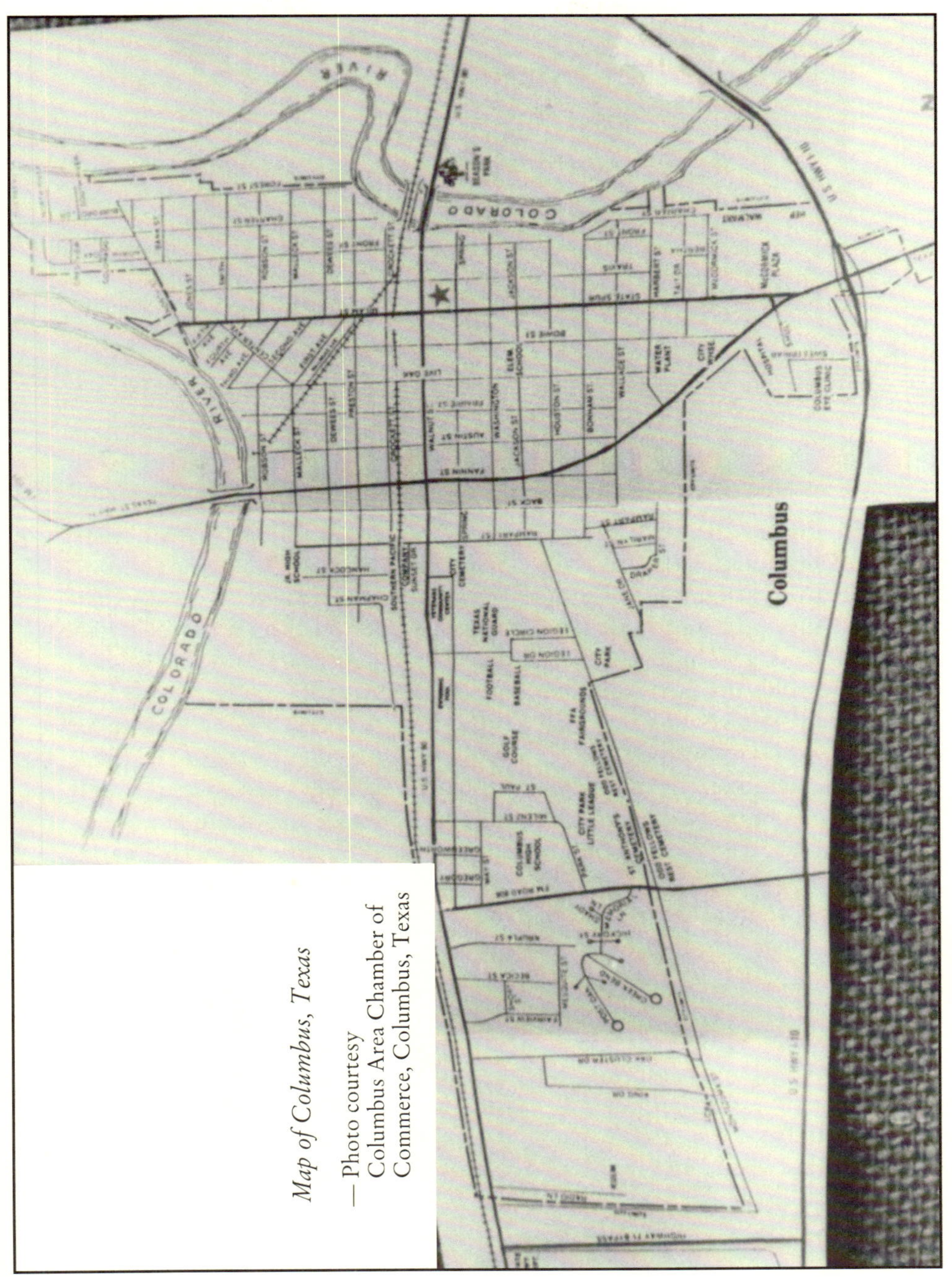

Map of Columbus, Texas

— Photo courtesy
Columbus Area Chamber of
Commerce, Columbus, Texas

III

Jefferson: The Old South Revisited

In 1872 the wharves of Jefferson were lined with steamboats and crammed with brick warehouses. The northeast Texas river port was the sixth largest city in the state and second only to Galveston in commerce and industry. This cultivated, cosmopolitan city had the first gas lighting system in Texas. A year later, however, Jefferson's economy drained out to sea when the Red River raft was blown. The town went into a rapid decline and a sleepy existence, only to be revived in the 1950s by the dedicated efforts of the local garden club. Capitalizing on such historical assets as a storied hotel, a famed railroad car, a sensational murder case, and some grand old homes, thirty-five women brought life and vitality to a dying town through tourism. Today Jefferson enjoys a national reputation as a tourist center because of the annual historical pilgrimage.

Allen Urquhart, the founder of Jefferson, arrived in Texas on April 11, 1837. A North Carolina native and surveyer by trade, Urquhart was entitled to 1,280 acres of land as a head of family by the Republic of Texas. On August 3, 1838, he appeared before the Board of Land Commissioners of Red River County as a married man and took half of his headright in Daingerfield. Allen also claimed as a potential townsite a slender, irregular-shaped, 640-acre tract between Big Cypress Bayou and Black Cypress eight miles to the north.

The site of Jefferson was conveyed to Urquhart on August 23, 1841, and surveyed on November 19. Located at the head of navigation and on the bend of Big Cypress, the townsite was wide enough for a turning basin and was also near the point where Trammel's Trace crossed Big Cypress headed south to Nacogdoches. Although Urquhart continued to live on his plantation in Daingerfield, he made weekly trips to Jefferson to collect his share of the tolls from the ferry he owned across Big Cypress.

The town of Jefferson was probably named for Thomas Jefferson and first appeared on a map published by Sidney E. Morse and Samuel Breese in New York in 1844. The first permanent resident of Jefferson was Berry H. Durham, the operator of Urquhart's ferry who later sold town lots and served as postmaster. On October 2, 1842, Durham bought sixty acres of land from Urquhart for $2 an acre. The first influx of settlers arrived that year from Smithland after a faulty land title led them to accept Urquhart's offer of property on the banks of Big Cypress.

On January 28, 1843, Urquhart became the owner and agent of the Jefferson Town Company. He also signed a permit allowing D. and Tinsly Weaver to operate the ferry boat until June 1, 1844. The plan for Jefferson was drawn up by Hugh Hensey on January 4, 1846. He laid out lots and streets parallel to the bend of Big Cypress in the southern portion of the Urquhart headright. One-half of the 125 blocks were residential with each block containing four large square lots in the northeast and southwest part of town. The central business district was laid out along the water front with six smaller rectangular lots in each of the wharf and commercial blocks. The courthouse square covered two blocks. Urquhart's choices of street names are still on the city map today.

Allen Urquhart never lived in Jefferson, choosing instead to commute from Daingerfield, where he died in 1866. After his father's death, lawyer John McNiel Urquhart moved to Jefferson with his family.

Daniel N. Alley, the co-founder of Jefferson, moved to Texas with his family from Jefferson County, Indiana, before 1840 and helped build cabins in the northwest corner of present Marion County along a tributary of Big Cypress named Alley Creek. On March 31, 1852, Daniel was named as first postmaster of the new settlement of Alley's Mill.

On August 29, 1845, Alley purchased a 586-acre tract for

$2,000 from Stephen and Lucinda Smith of Lamar County. This land adjoined Urquhart's tract on the northwest and became known as the "Alley Addition" of Jefferson. Since Alley's land was above the turning basin, his streets followed the points of the compass with Line Street dividing the two tracts. The streets intersected on the east at forty-five-degree angles, resulting in triangular and irregular fractions of blocks. From the beginning the Alley Addition was intended to provide a genteel residential environment for stately homes.

Daniel Alley established a real estate office in Jefferson and deeded a city block for a courthouse and jail after Marion County was organized in 1860. He was also a breeder of fine horses and the builder of the Alley Race Track. Alley died in Jefferson in 1868 and was buried in Oakwood Cemetery there.

The actual town of Jefferson owes its existence to a privately funded navigation project. It was apparent in the early 1840s that the point farthest upstream on Cypress Bayou would control the commerce to the north and west. Jefferson was the last port founded on the stream because the six miles of Cypress Bayou between Smithland and the Jefferson townsite were choked with fallen trees and other obstructions which prohibited steamboat navigation.

A project to clear this channel began on April 9, 1844, at a meeting of cotton planters and merchants at Daingerfield. Those present pooled their resources and hired a contractor "to open the navigation" with work to begin on July 4 and end on December 25. The contractor for the job was William Perry, a steamboat captain, who completed the clearing project on schedule in December 1844. He left the debris in-channel, where it was flushed out by the spring rise on Cypress Bayou.

Captain Perry's successful project was reported in the *Northern Standard* of Clarksville, a Red River steamboat port to the north. On October 16, 1844, the newspaper noted that several houses were going up at the townsite of Jefferson and that several stocks of goods would be opened there within two or three months. On January 16, 1845, the *Northern Standard* observed that the navigation of the Big Cypress had been cleared, quite a number of buildings were going up, and a town would be there immediately.

In the early spring of 1845, Captain Perry brought the first steamboat to Jefferson. The sixty-six-ton *Llama* followed the Red River to Shreveport, then steamed north to Twelve-Mile Bayou and on through Caddo Lake into Big Cypress Bayou. According to tradition, Captain Perry's wife, Sardinia, gave birth to the first child born in Jefferson.

Steamboat passage to Jefferson was made possible by the Red River raft. Since the days of the early Spanish and French explorers, a huge raft of logs, brush, and mud had clogged the Red River north of Natchitoches, Louisiana. Some sections of the raft were solid log masses twenty-five feet deep and bonded together by roots, moss, weeds, vines, and cemented silt. Willows and cottonwood trees grew out of this solid formation. This river raft backed water into Caddo Lake and Big Cypress, thus raising the water level to allow steamboats to reach Jefferson.

In 1828 scientist Jospeh Paxton of Mount Prairie, Arkansas, wrote a report pleading for the removal of the Red River raft. He argued that removing the raft would reclaim flooded lowlands for fertile farming areas in southwest Arkansas, North Texas, and southern Indian Territory. The United States Congress responded on May 23, 1828, by approving $25,000 for planning purposes.

In 1832 a former steamboater, Capt. Henry Miller Shreve of the Army Corps of Engineers, was appointed to direct the removal of the raft. Shreve, the superintendent of the Western Waters Department, reported on September 29 that the best and least expensive method of removal was to loosen the timbers and allow them to float downstream.

After designing the snag boat *Archimedes*, Captain Shreve arrived at the Great Raft on April 11, 1833. At that time the raft was 130 miles long. Using four snag boats to extract the logs one by one, Shreve removed seventy miles of the raft in the first three months, but the raft replenished itself in the off-season. In 1838 his yearly appropriation for the task reached $75,000.

Captain Shreve developed improved snag boats referred to as "Uncle Sam's Toothpullers." These double-hulled vessels had snag beams and powerful lifting machinery capable of breaking a seventy-five-ton log snag.

In March 1838 a steamboat channel was finally cleared through the head of the raft. When heavy rains resulted in a new raft blocking the channel in April 1839, work stopped on the project. Shreve gave up direction of the effort in the spring of 1841 and retired to St. Louis. Although the engineer failed to remove the river raft, his efforts resulted in the founding of Shreveport on the west bank of the Red River in 1837.

On May 13, 1844, a citizens' meeting of the Southern Division of Red River County met in Daingerfield with Isaac Hughes presiding. Those present voted to raise $2,000 in cash or cotton to clear a channel from Jefferson to Port Caddo in order to reopen the route to steamboats.

Jefferson offered one great advantage to steamboats: a wide turning basin formed where the two branches of the Big Cypress come together after being divided by Saint Catherine's Island. The turning basin at the eastern tip of the island was at the foot of Polk and Walnut streets.

Jefferson's beginning as the second greatest port city in Texas can be traced to April 12, 1845, when the second steamboat, the *Gazelle,* arrived with 130 passengers on board. From that time on, it was the major East Texas reception center for immigrants, lumber, and supplies. The thriving town was also an outlet for Texas exports of hides, tallow, and cotton brought there by wagon train.

One of the arrivals that spring day in 1845 was Buck Barry, who was to win fame as a Texas Ranger, Indian fighter, and state legislator from Bosque County. Before his death in 1906, Barry wrote an autobiography in which he described his first impressions of Jefferson. He recalled seeing only one finished house in town, a log cabin without a nail in it. His first meal there was breakfast cooked over an open fire with a large pine log serving as his table. To have a roof over his head, Barry went home with a farmer named Steward, who lived twenty miles away.

When English visitor Edward Smith arrived by steamer from Shreveport on May 24, 1849, he found sixty good houses and several large, well-supplied stores in Jefferson. There was also one warehouse and a small saw and grist mill.

It was cotton exports that made Jefferson the largest inland port in Texas. The new town was the closest port to many East Texas cotton fields, the crop of choice and major money-making cargo. By providing a water connection to the major cotton port of New Orleans, Jefferson became the favorite port for many Texas cotton growers, who brought their crop by wagon caravan. By the end of the 1840s, steamboats were making regular scheduled runs from New Orleans, which was 450 land miles away. The winding voyage to Jefferson might take a week or two, depending on stopovers and river conditions.

At this time the architecture of Jefferson homes began to resemble the Greek Revival and raised cottage style of New Orleans' Garden District, including the columned porch and four rooms with central hallway, fancy millwork, hardware, and ornamental iron.

The best example of such architecture is the Presbyterian Manse, one of the oldest homes in Jefferson. This one-story structure was built in 1853 at the corner of Alley and Delta streets. Soon ox teams began to cut this corner too close and pass down Delta Street to the boat landing. To protect the Manse, an old iron post with a large wheel design near the center was positioned at the corner to hang far out over the street.[1]

The first steamboat fleet to service Jefferson was owned by George L., John, and Ben B. Kouns with headquarters on Front Street in New Orleans. They were later joined by William Tiley Scovell. All of their boats were named the *Era* and numbered from 1 to 13. Single trips to Jefferson netted a profit of $20,000, bringing construction materials and store stocks, then returning to New Orleans with cotton.

Due to the narrow water passages between Caddo Lake and the turning basin at Jefferson, the steamboats were all sternwheelers. When tree limbs loomed ahead, the hinged smokestacks were lowered by pulley to lay atop the pilot's cabin. The boats drew only twelve inches of water and could carry 1,000 bales of cotton on three feet of water. The largest steamboat, *Era No. 11,* was 245 feet long, carried 4,500 bales of cotton, 700 head of cattle, and had four classes and prices of passenger rates. On the *Grand Era,* the main cabin salon was 202 feet long, and a daily paper was issued for passengers.

Jefferson, the northwestern end of Red River navigation from New Orleans, was a rival port of Shreveport, located only sixty miles away. The "River Intelligence" columns of Shreveport newspapers included a steady stream of jokes, barbs, and satirical remarks about competitor Jefferson, which received a boost in 1856 when the state legislature approved $21,298 to clear Big Cypress from Jefferson to the state line.

On March 20, 1848, Jefferson was incorporated by an act of the state legislature. A city charter was obtained two years later, and S. H. Ellis was elected as first mayor of Jefferson in late 1850. Among the early city ordinances was one of 1854 requiring any steamboat captain or owner discharging freight on Sunday to pay a fine of $50; the consignee was not required to receive such goods.

One of Jefferson's finest homes, the Freeman House, was built in 1850 by planter Williamson M. Freeman, the owner of a 1,000-acre cotton and sugar plantation. Built in the Greek Revival style by slave labor, the "big house" was constructed with pine, cypress, and hand-made bricks. The framing timbers were cut, notched, and pegged by hand. The brick walls on the lower floor are fourteen inches thick, and the outside walls on the upper, main floor are cypress. Across the wide gallery, centered by a staircase, are four tapered columns made of pie-shaped bricks. When Jenny Lind visited Jefferson, she sang in the beautiful drawing room of the Freeman House.[2]

The first Jewish businessman in Jefferson, Israel Leavitt, purchased land from Berry H. Durham on September 5, 1845. His "kitchen house" or tavern was located between Dallas and Lake streets. Other Jewish merchants started dry-good stores, confectionaries, and liquor stores. The 1850 census showed six other Jewish families clustered along Houston Street in the southwestern part of town, an area known as Jew Town.

Led by Jacob Sterne, the Hebrew Benevolent Association paid $150 for land in the southwest corner of the old graveyard and founded Mount Sinai Cemetery, the fourth oldest Jewish cemetery in Texas. The Jefferson Hebrew Society was the second such organization in Texas.

The town's first newspaper, the Jefferson *Democrat,* was established by Gen. W. N. Bishop in 1847. Four months later he sold the paper to Berry Durham, who in turn sold out to Rev. Job M. Baker in early 1848. Reverend Baker brought a printing press from Rome, Georgia, and renamed the paper the *Spirit of the Age,* with R. W. Loughery as editor.

On December 8, 1848, the *Age* printed the prospectus for the *Jimplecute,* which was to be published by E. C. Beasley at a subscription rate of $4 per year. This unique Jefferson institution was published by Ward Taylor, Jr., and his family from 1865 intil 1926. During the big fire of 1866, the Taylor family was living in the Irvine Hotel (later the Excelsior House). Thinking they might have to escape quickly, they tied all their favorite clothes and articles in bundles.

After Ward's death in 1894, his son, M. I. Taylor, and daughter, "Miss Birdie," ran the paper together until 1915. She then took over entirely until selling the paper in 1926.

There are several local explanations for the newspaper's name. Some say that "Jimplecute" is a possible acrostic for the town motto: "Join, Industry, Manufacturing, Planting, Labor, Energy, Capital, in Unity Together Everlastingly." The name may have been inspired by a common mid-nineteenth-century Texas coloquial expression which means "sweetheart." Ward Taylor, Jr., envisioned the Jimplecute as a mythical, terrifying monster and hired a commercial artist to draw a scary picture for the newspaper masthead in 1867. Whatever the origin of the newspaper name, it has served to bring fame to Jefferson.

From 1925 until 1937, the name *Jimplecute* was discarded, and the paper became the Jefferson *Journal.* After first restoring the old name, publisher Tom Foster renamed his paper the Jefferson *Daily Jimplecute* in April 1937.

Churches in Jefferson date from 1844, when a Methodist congregation was organized, and James W. Baldridge was appointed as minister by the East Texas Conference. By the end of 1845, the church had fifty white and three slave members. In 1848 Allen Urquhart "sold" (gave) the Methodist trustees a lot for $100. Two other lots were later acquired in the same block for the parsonage, and the present church still stands there on the foundation of the brick building erected in 1860.

To assure a silvery tone, church members collected 1,500 Mexican silver dollars to be melted down and cast into a bell. The principal donor was trustee F. A. Schulter. A church committee then accompanied the valuable cargo to Troy, New York, where the Menneley Bell Foundry produced their church bell in 1858. After being returned to Jefferson by steamboat, it was placed in the church belfry in 1860. The bell was later positioned in the Gothic spire of the new wooden building finished in 1883.

In the late 1840s the Jefferson Cumberland Presbyterian Church was organized by minister Solomon Awalt, who held services in a small frame building on the corner of Line and Jefferson streets. In 1872 John Ligon started construction of the largest sanctuary in town, a structure of intricate brick designs with a towering spire topped by a globe. When completed it was considered the finest building of a Cumberland Presbyterian congregation in Texas. In May 1875 the first Cumberland Presbyterian general assembly to convene in Texas met in the church.

Instead of mechanical clocks, false clock faces were painted on four sides of the steeple base with the fixed hands showing the starting times of services. This unusual feature of the church disappeared in 1981, when the steeple was remodeled.

The Jefferson Baptist Church was organized on March 24, 1855, with the family of planter William Freeman comprising seven of the eleven charter members. The deed to the church lots was recorded on October 11, 1860. The first pastor, George B. Tucker, was succeeded by David Browning Culberson, Sr., in 1861. Reverend Culberson was the father of a longtime U. S. congressman and the grandfather of a Texas governor and U. S. senator. The congregation first met in Freeman Hall, Judge Patillo's school, and the Methodist church. Under the leadership of Pastor C. S. McCloud, a brick church building was completed on Polk Street in 1864. Six years later an imitation pipe organ was installed at a cost of $1,000.

On May 7, 1874, the Jefferson Baptist Church played host to the first meeting of the Southern Baptist Convention held west of the Mississippi River. Over a thousand mesengers attended the five-day convention. The Baptist visitors were then given a free tour of the state by the Texas and Pacific Railroad.

On June 8, 1860, sixteen charter members organized Christ Episcopal Church with Bishop Alex Gregg presiding. The church first met in a building on Main Street.

In 1863 Father Jean Marie Giraud, a native of France, led the first Mass in Jefferson, marking the beginning of the Immaculate Conception Church, the oldest Roman Catholic parish in the Dallas Diocese. His congregation of twenty-two first met in a private home. In April 1866, James M. Murphy and Allen Urquhart donated lots 10, 11, and 12 at the corner of Polk and Lafayette streets for building a church. Giraud's flock finished a wooden church building there in September 1867 with money sent from Lyon, France. Because of noise and traffic congestion, the building was dragged over logs by ox teams to its present site at the corner of Vale and Lafayette streets.

Father Giraud returned to France in 1868 and obtained $6,000 from the French Society of the Propagation of the Faith to found a school in Jefferson. The next year he purchased a private home built in 1860 by Robert W. Nesmith, a contractor of stagelines. This two-story structure at the corner of Henderson and Market streets was to serve as a Catholic convent and school.

In 1869 six nuns from the Catholic Sisters of Charity in Emmitsburg, Maryland, were sent to staff the school. On October 18, 1869, the sisters opened St. Mary's School with five pupils. They also operated a hospital behind the building. Due to lack of students, the nuns left Jefferson in 1875. At that time the property was sold to the Sinai Hebrew congregation.

There was no Catholic school in Jefferson for nine years. In 1884 four sisters of St. Agnes Convent, Pond due Lac, Wisconsin, opened St. Joseph's Academy with twenty-two pupils. The academy closed in 1888 due to declining population and river trade.

On June 2, 1873, Jefferson's Sinai Hebrew congregation was formed. On November 20, 1875, they paid $2,000 to the Sisters of Charity for the St. Mary's School. At that time the Jewish congregation built an adjoining structure as their synagogue. (This building is now the Jefferson Playhouse.) The original house — the old Catholic convent — became the home of their rabbi, who came to Jefferson from Dallas. (This building is now the Ruth Lester Memorial.)[3]

The first iron furnace in the Jefferson area was built by Jefferson S. Nash on the Walter H. Gilbert headright in 1847. Located seventeen miles northwest of Jefferson on the Coffeeville road, the Nash Iron Works used oak and pine charcoal to stoke the furnace. The melted ore gathered in pools at the bottom of the smokestacks. Although the process was slow and expensive, the Nash Iron Works was producing over 10,000 pounds of pig iron by 1858. The iron was converted into kitchen utensils, wash pots, and kettles. In 1861 the Nash company made some cannon balls as Confederate ammunition. Two years later, the company suffered a blow when the state legislature refused to grant aid to "a business already established" for making military equipment. The holdings were then sold to the George Kelly Iron Company, and the equipment was moved to Kellyville (formerly Four-Mile-Branch), four miles west of Jefferson.

George Addison Kelly, a Scotch-Irishman, was born on October 17, 1832, in Green County, Tennessee. In 1849 he moved with his family to Natchitoches Parish, Louisiana. Three years later, Kelly moved to Jefferson as a steamboat mate at age twenty. After working there as a mechanic, George in 1854 became slave foreman in a small iron foundry John A. Stewart operated at Four-Mile-Branch west of Jefferson.

Initially, small crude plows were produced, but Kelly persuaded Stewart to make cast-iron stoves, cooking utensils, and thousands of cow bells. In 1858 the business became known as Kelly and Stewart, but George became sole owner when John died two years later. In 1860 he designed and made the famous Kelly Blue Plow, adapting it to the sandy land of East Texas.

During the Civil War, Kelly built a furnace using costly charcoal for fuel and began to smelt high-grade pig iron. In 1861 he raised a company of Confederate soldiers and was commissioned a captain. His company was accepted for battle, but George was detailed to stay at home and make plows and cast iron for cannon balls.

By 1874 Kelly was worth more than $250,000 and was making every type of cooking stove in domestic use. In the late 1870s, however, the uninsured Kelly Iron Works was totally destroyed by fire. In 1882 salvage from the foundry and factory wreck at Kellyville was moved to the new rail center of Longview. There the G. A. Kelly Plow Company was organized, and a rebuilt factory using cheaper coke fuels produced a wide variety of plows and farm implements.

George Kelly married Lucy Anne Stewart, the sister of his former partner, and the couple had three sons and four daughters. George served as mayor of Longview for four years and died there on October 2, 1909. He was buried in Greenwood Cemetery, and his son, Robert Marvin, became president of the family-owned Kelly Plow Company.[4]

From the beginning Jefferson residents *wanted* railroads to complement their inland port. On February 2, 1854, locals incorporated the Jefferson Railroad Company seeking connections with a transcontinental line. The charter required that twenty miles of track must be completed within five years. Although the charter was renewed in 1860, it expired with no road being built.

When the Memphis and El Paso and Pacific Railroad was incorporated in 1853, Jefferson was not included on the route but was designated as the initial point of construction for the line. The contractor was to ship building supplies to Jefferson and to construct the Metropolitan line forty-five miles from there to Moore's Landing on the Sulphur Fork of the Red River. The Metropolitan line got under way in August 1860, but only five miles of track were laid before the Civil War stopped construction and dashed Jefferson's hopes for a rail link with Texarkana.

In the spring of 1858, plans were announced to lay off lots for Oakwood Cemetery. By then Jefferson had stagecoach lines running northwest to Clarksville and south to Marshall (daily) and Nacogdoches (tri-weekly).

In 1859 and 1860, the cotton export trade of Jefferson was 88,000 bales and 100,000 bales. The comparative figures for Galveston were 118,000 bales and 148,000 bales.

On February 8, 1860, Marion County was organized with Jefferson as the county seat. Carved out of Cass County, it was named for either Francis Marion, the "Swamp Fox" of the American Revolution, or for Dr. Marion DeKalb Taylor, a Georgia native who was instrumental in creating the county while a member of the Texas House of Representatives. In December 1863, Dr. Taylor was elected as House Speaker during the Civil War.

The 1860 federal census showed Marion County with a population of 3,977; of that total 2,017 were slaves. Slaveowners in the county made up 43 percent of all taxpayers. The census showed Jefferson's population as 988, with 266 of those residents being black.

These figures help explain a city ordinance of November 25, 1857, which placed numerous restrictions on slaves with punishment including up to thirty-nine lashes on the bare back. For example, slaves could not assemble at any time for a ball or other amusement; they could not ride any type of conveyance or animal within the city limits for their own amusement.

In 1861 Dan N. Alley, Sr., the co-founder of Jefferson, built a Greek Revival cottage as a wedding gift to Dan, Jr. This structure is located at the corner of Main and Walker streets. Just inside the entrance is a large box used by family members for storage. It bears the name of Dan N. Alley, Jr., and was first used to ship his bride's personal effects and wedding gifts brought by the newlyweds from New Orleans and Port Gibson, Mississippi. (Three generations of the Alley family owned this house until 1991.)[5]

On February 22, 1861, Marion County voted for secession with 467 for and none against. When the Civil War erupted, several county officials left their posts for military service, including J. P. Durr, Henry Mimms, N. A. Birge, Royal Francis Lockett, and John K. Cocke.

Several Jefferson units served in the war, including Captain Black's infantry company which saw action in Virginia. Capt. H. P. Mabry's company was reorganized into a regiment, the Third Texas Cavalry, at Dallas. In June 1861, the Jefferson Guards were organized by Capt. William M. Duke and other members of Christ Episcopal Church. Before the men departed for Missouri, Miss Fannie Benners made a stirring speech in presenting a banner and flag "bedewed by women's tears" to the unit; the banner motto was "The brave may fail, but never yield." Fannie was the daughter of the Rev. Mr. Benners, the first resident minister of the church.

In late July 1861, H. P. Mabry recruited another company, the "Dead-Shot Rangers," as an element of the South Kansas Texas Regiment. On March 31, 1862, Capt. W. L. Crawford recruited a company of sixty-six men. On April 12 of that year, Col. W. B. Ochiltree enlisted a company of ninety-eight men for three years at Jefferson. The 107 men who joined the Marion Rifles in March and April of 1862 became Company A of John Bell Hood's First Texas Brigade.

Most Jews opposed slavery, and only 105 of them joined the Confederate army. Four of these soldiers were from Jefferson: Mark Pinski, J. Nussbaum, James M. Jacobs, and Gus Leavitt. Thirty-seven-year-old Jacob Sterne hired farmer John L. Bird as his substitute in 1863, then served as a Confederate quartermaster at home. J. Nussbaum stayed at Jefferson and was awarded a Confederate contract in 1864 to manufacture soap and candles for the army in Texas.

During the war, Jefferson was a major supply depot for the Confederate army in the Trans-Mississippi Department. There was a brick, three-story Confederate clothing factory, meat-packing plant, and shoe factory in town. J. B. Dunn supplied the Confederate army with 150 beeves a day. Under terms of an 1863 contract, the Confederate government provided beef cattle and salt with Dunn doing the slaughtering and packing. The dressed meat was then carried to New Orleans.

The Confederate army quartermasters who were supplied from Jefferson brought a much-needed economic boost and enlivened the social life of the town. The river port had the advantage of offering the lowest cost for military transportation: freight was only five cents a mile by boat, as opposed to six cents by wagon, twenty-five cents by railroad, and forty cents per mile by stagecoach.

Jefferson escaped invasion during the war, with the closest engagement being ninety miles away, the Battle of Mansfield, fought on April 8, 1864. Gen. Nathaniel P. Banks with a Union army of 25,000 and a flotilla of gunboats moved up the Red River from Alexandria, Louisiana, intending to capture the port of Jefferson and the

Confederate shops at Marshall and Henderson. Awaiting Banks' advance fifty miles below Shreveport was Gen. Richard Taylor and 11,000 troops from Texas, Louisiana, and Arkansas. Taylor's men attacked on April 8, routing and driving back the Federal invaders by late evening. The Confederates captured 2,000 prisoners, twenty pieces of artillery, and twenty wagons. The loss at Mansfield ended Banks' Red River campaign, and he fell back to the Mississippi River.

Three Jefferson units fought in the Battle of Mansfield: Capt. John K. Cocke's Company D, 18th Texas Infantry; Capt. W. L. Crawford's Company A, 19th Texas Infantry; Capt. T. D. Sedberry's Company F, 19th Texas Infantry. Among the Jefferson soldiers wounded in the battle was Gus Durrum, whose leg bone was shattered just above the knee. The day after the battle, Gus wrote his parents a letter from the College Hospital at Mansfield, asking them to come for him in a hack (carriage) since he could not survive a buggy ride. Tragically, young Durrum died of his wounds before his parents arrived with the hack.

A large force of Union soldiers occupied Jefferson at the end of the war. Federal officers stayed in the Haywood House, a four-story brick hotel on Dallas at Market Street built in 1865 by local lawyer Hinch P. Mabry. Proprietor W. T. Rives advertised the Haywood House as the "largest and finest hotel building west of the Mississippi." Transient customers were charged $3 per day, $15 per week, and $1 for a single meal. When the hotel manager learned of a plan to kill Mabry and his brother-in-law, Joe Haywood, the two fled to Canada and Tennessee, respectively, until it was safe to return.[6]

Union enlisted men stayed in camps erected on leased grounds at the edge of Jefferson. The infantry camp was a sandy slope at the southwest corner of town along Big Cypress. A 137x55-foot cypress log stockade was erected in this "Sandtown" area at the intersection of Common and Texas streets. This infamous structure consisted of two buildings and a guardhouse for those regularly held under military arrest.

A local resistance movement was led by Cullen Baker, who moved to the Jefferson area in 1842 and committed his first murder at the age of nineteen. During the war, Baker led daring raids on Federal supply trains. In August and September of 1867, he attacked and killed United States soldiers, then carried off their mules, wagon, and supplies. On January 6, 1869, Baker was killed by a group including his father-in-law and was buried in Jefferson's Oakwood Cemetery.

Among the most sensational acts of violence during this period was the Bonfoey case. David Brainerd Bonfoey, the former mayor of Marshall and Harrison County judge, was appointed U. S. collector of internal revenue for the Fourth District of Texas in 1865. One of Bonfoey's duties at the Marshall office was the collection of the lucrative cotton tax.

In the late summer of 1867, Bonfoey learned that W. H. Fowler, his deputy collector in Jefferson, was conspiring with cotton dealers in the subdistrict to defraud the government of the tax. Armed with a pistol, Bonfoey traveled to Jefferson on August 7 to investigate and demand settlement of Fowler's unexplained deficit of $18, 140.23. When confronted with the matter, Fowler refused to cover the shortage and threatened to kill Bonfoey unless he wrote a receipt clearing Fowler of the indebtedness. When Fowler put his pistol on the table while preparing the bogus receipt, Bonfoey reached for his own gun and killed his deputy collector. He then surrendered and was placed in the Jefferson jail.

Upon hearing the news, Mrs. Bonfoey requested a federal guard detail for her home; the safe contained $13,000 of personal funds and $34,000 in federal collections. On the night of August 28 or August 29, she was savagely beaten and her skull was split open during a robbery attempt. No money was taken but Mrs. Bonfoey went into a coma and died days later. The two soldiers on duty at her home were arrested and charged with the crime. After being detained in the Harrison County Jail, they were released by military order, put on a train, and never seen again.

Six weeks later, bail was arranged for Mr. Bonfoey. Upon arriving in Marhsall he went straight to the cemetery, where he fell unconscious on his wife's grave. He died a day later at his home, a victim of strain.

During this period thousands of privately owned cotton bales in Jefferson warehouses were confiscated by U. S. treasury agents. After local citizens accused R. L. Robertson and A. O. Carolan of cotton theft and swindling, the grand jury of Marion County set a trial date for February 1866. The trial was stopped by Capt. J. B. Jones, who declared their arrest was unlawful over the protests of Judge B. W. Gray.

On the first Saturday in March 1868, a fire swept through four blocks of downtown Jefferson at 11:00 P.M. Since there was no fire company to fight the blaze, more than fifty buildings were destroyed with over $1 million in losses. Local residents blamed the fire on a newcomer, George Washington Smith, who had come to Jefferson from New York and controlled the black population as head of the Loyal League. Nicknamed "Dog" by the white population, Smith had told the ex-slaves they could not govern the town until it was burned.

On the night of October 4, 1868, a group of outraged citizens broke into the Jefferson jail, killed Smith in his cell, and murdered two of his black companions, Steward and Grant, in the street. No one was arrested for two months while R. W. Loughery, the publisher of the *Jefferson Times,* justified the death of agitator Smith as being "demanded by public safety."

In May 1869 stockade trials began for the twenty-four prisoners charged with the death of Smith. Among the influential citizens on trial were William B. Ochiltree, Col. W. L. Crawford, Lt. Col. Phillip Crump, Maj. W. P. Saufley, and Capt. Charles L. Pitcher. Representing the stockade prisoners was the finest legal talent, including B. H. Epperson and David Browning Culberson. The military commission of eight officers was headed by Gen. Edward Hatch, who began the trial at Freedman's Hall on May 24. Testimony began two days later and ended on August 9.

On August 23, 1869, the military commission rendered a decision, finding six of the accused guilty on various counts. Two of the men, George Gray and Oscar Gray, were sentenced to life imprisonment at the Huntsville penitentiary, but there is no record of their confinement there. Hatch, the president of the commission, was openly critical of the outcome, charging that only "minnows" had been convicted while such "whales" as leading suspect Phillip Crump went free.

On January 2, 1869, Capt. William Perry was murdered on the sidewalk near his home on Clarksville Street. The Jefferson pioneer brought the first steamboat to town and built the hotel later named the Excelsior House. The military government claimed the shooting was a result of mistaken identity; the intended victim of assassin Charles Bostwick was Bud Connor. Bostwick and Sgt. C. H. Grimley were charged with murder, but Judge Winston Banks allowed bail and determined that the two were not guilty since they were acting under lawful military orders in executing an arrest warrant.

During this epidemic of gunplay, Daniel Nelson Alley, Sr., built the Magnolias at 209 E. Broadway Street as a wedding gift to his daughter, Virginia Alley Crawford, in 1867. This stately Greek Revival home began as a modest townhome. In the 1870s, the dining room and kitchen area — the two largest rooms in the house with fifteen-foot ceilings — were added along with the steep stairs in the back hall.

The central hall is divided into two sections by an ornate wooden elliptical arch. Double drawing rooms on the east side of the hall are separated by a pair of sliding pocket doors with etched glazed panels.

As a sign of the times, there are two cabinets on both sides of the front entrance hall. One is a gun closet; the other is a fake said to be a secret crawl space to the attic for lookout purposes and clandestine meetings during the Federal occupation of Jefferson. The front door was unlatched only with proper indentification.[7]

During the Reconstruction period, Alley, the most active home builder in Jefferson, dismantled forty-eight of his houses and burned the lumber. This destruction was either an emotional reaction against the undesirable newcomers or a business decision to reduce the large home inventory on which he paid high taxes.

During this violent period after the Civil War, Jefferson enjoyed a burst of prosperity. Ignoring the boycott advice of newspaperman Loughery, town leaders chose instead to conduct business as usual with the Radicals. The war's end brought high cotton prices and a surge of immigration. The population of Jefferson increased from 1,988 in 1860 to 4,190 in 1870, making the inland port the sixth largest city in Texas and second only to Galveston in commerce and industry.

During this "Golden Era" of Jefferson, one-fourth of the trade of Texas passed through town. The port city was a distribution point for lumber and manufactured goods destined for Sherman, Dallas, Paris, Fort Worth, and Greenville. Distances were measured from Jefferson. All roads led there, and they were crowded with wagon trains and stagecoaches. Trading was done on a cash basis with the money stashed in tow sacks in the bottom of wagons. Cotton buyers gave a free jug of whiskey to their customers.

In this lusty, brawling metropolis of East Texas, one could find cock fights and horse races on the outskirts of the city. The Haywood House was a famous hotel, while the Lady Gay and

Charlie's Palace were home to professional gamblers, dancing girls, and blaring orchestras.

The cultural life of Jefferson was enhanced when Mr. Gustave Frank came from Dormstadt, Germany, and settled there about 1863. Professor Frank taught music and led a twenty-five-piece band for years. His wife was an accomplished organist in Jefferson for twenty-five years. The couple raised five children — only one of them their own — and gave them musical educations. Professor Frank's home had doors which could be thrown open, allowing the seating of up to 100 for concerts. Both his wife and their daughter-in-law, Mrs. F.H. Frank, played violin in his orchestra.

By 1870 Jefferson was shipping more than 75,000 bales of cotton by steamboat annually. In that year 87,623 pounds of wool were brought to town in ox-drawn wagons and exported by steamer. To facilitate trade the Marion County commissioners court had a dredge boat built at a cost of $20,000. In 1872, 226 steamboats with a carrying capacity from 225 to 700 tons docked in Jefferson.

Among the palatial New Orleans steamboats that visited Jefferson were *The Danube, Bessie Warren, Red Cloud, Iron Cities, Koontz, John T. Moore,* and the *Lizzie Hopkins*. Many items from these early steamers are displayed in the Jefferson Historical Museum today. Each carried an Italian band that played at landings, at meals, and for evening balls. The elaborate dress for such occasions was carried on board in huge trunks with two or three compartments for hats only.

The steamers used large oil lamps with reflectors for headlights. They also carried red and green signal lights on the smokestacks on the left and right, respectively. The largest boats could carry 6,000 bales of cotton.

Since the black deckhands could not read, freight was distributed by placing playing cards over the names of towns: Jefferson was the "King of Spades." Few errors were made using this system.

Deckhands labored eighteen to twenty hours without rest, singing as they worked. Their songs were weird, haunting melodies known as "Coonjines." Some of these tunes can still be heard today along the shores of Caddo Lake.

The Jefferson Gas Light Company, the first artificial gas plant in Texas, was created in 1870-71. Gas was made from rich pine knots cut and placed in iron drums called "retorts" about seven feet long and tapered off at one end like the mouth of a jug. The bottom opened with a door. When the retorts were subjected to intense heat, the steamlike substance exuded from the heated pine escaped through an opening in the top and into iron mains or pipes. The gas was then conveyed over the business section of town to ornamental hollow posts with large globes on top. These streetlights were lighted at night and turned off in the morning. The water that accumulated in the pipes was removed by hand pump during the day. The gas was forced through the mains by a large drum affair raised during the day. As the drum gradually sank at night, its weight forced the gas through the pipes. The ruins of the large, brick foundation on which the drum rested still stands along Big Cypress.

One of Jefferson's more colorful pioneers was Green Berry McDonald, an engineer of Scottish ancestry who came to town from Louisville, Kentucky, in 1870 after receiving the contract to build the artificial gas plant. As superintendent of the Mississippi Valley Land and Navigation Company, it was McDonald who checked out the boat, the *Robert E. Lee,* before the famous race.

He later owned a flour mill, gin, and machine shop in Jefferson. Reticent to the point of rudeness, G.B. and his beautiful wife spent much of their time at home, where he had an extensive library on engineering, drafting, mechanical drawing, advanced mathematics, history, poetry, English literature, and philosophy. McDonald also enjoyed playing the rosewood Chickering concert grand piano in his living room. It was one of only eight such instruments in the United States. Above the rare piano was an oil painting of McDonald as a young man.

Jefferson could also boast of the first artificial ice plant in the United States. In 1874 Mr. Boyle and partner Henry Scott built a patented, steam-powered machine that produced cakes of ice four or five feet long, two or three feet wide, and one inch thick. The ice plant site was just beyond Willard Hill on Highway 49 in the city limits. After only one year of operation, Mr. Boyle, the originator of the idea, went north in search of financing and never returned. Henry Scott soon went into bankruptcy, and the plant was moved to Harrisburg.

Mr. B.J. Benefield worked for Boyle and Scott as the first dispenser of the artificial ice. Using his own wagon and team, Benefield sold the ice for ten cents per pound. One of his first customers — a prominent local citizen — naively purchased 1,000 pounds of the ice and placed it in his cistern so his family would have an unlimited ice supply during the hot summer months. When it all melted, he became a *daily* customer of Benefield.

Beginning in the 1870s, the "Queen Mab" celebration was held in Jefferson in imitation of the Mardi Gras in New Orleans. At the time Jefferson fancied herself a little Crescent City; many of her citizens came from there. Riverboats from New Orleans brought fancy furnishings, manufactured goods, and fashions to the East Texas river port. There were even similarities in architecture; Jefferson's raised cottages and Greek Revival homes were like those on Canal Street or St. Charles Avenue.

The name for Jefferson's daylong "Queen Mab" celebration was taken from the queen of the fairies in an Irish myth. A street parade several miles long featured elaborate floats carrying flowers and grotesque fairy folk, with "Queen Mab" as the central figure. Jesse Allen Wise was crowned Queen Mab of the 1875 festivities, which ended with a grand ball in the drawing and dining rooms of the Excelsior House. The 1875 Queen Mab Ball featured 150 costumes borrowed from New Orleans mixed with hundreds of local creations. Party delegations from Shreveport and Texarkana packed thirty railroad cars to Jefferson, and the steamboat *Col. A. P. Kouns* brought a boatload of revelers.

On April 2, 1875, the editor of the *Shreveport Times* gave the following glowing account of the festivities:

> The ball opened at ten with the entrance of her Majesty and the ladies of her court. Their fair faces which, during the day, had been hidden behind masks, were now unconcealed and beautiful with all the witchery of loveliness. . . . So numerous were the costumes, so varied, so brilliant that it was almost impossible to individualize them. . . . It resembled a beautiful garden in which a world of gorgeous flowers had been gathered, of every hue, of every clime. . . .[8]

Ironically, the greatest shipping disaster in the Jefferson area occurred during this boom period: the burning and sinking of the *Mittie Stephens* steamboat in Caddo Lake. This 312-ton, 160-foot-long sidewheeler was built in Madison, Indiana, in 1862. J. L. Stephens, the owner and member of a prominent Missouri family, named the vessel for his two-day-old daughter, Mittie. The steamer was valued at $45,000 in 1864 and was utilized that year as a Union troop transport during the Red River campaign.

The *Mittie Stephens* left Shreveport bound for Jefferson on Thursday, February 11, 1869, at 4:00 P.M. There were 109 people on board, including eight children. She was also carrying a shipment of hay, eight or ten kegs of gunpowder, and as much as $100,000 in gold as payroll for the Reconstruction troops in Jefferson.

By midnight the boat was near Swanson's Landing and only ten miles from Jefferson. Suddenly, steersman Lodwick, standing at the wheel with pilot Swain, saw smoke rising from the hay. A pine knot torch used as a guide light had sent a spark flying to the load of hay stacked at the front of the vessel. The alarm was sounded, and the boat made a five-minute race to the shore.

By then the forward part of the steamer was engulfed in flames, causing the passengers to run its length away from shore to the stern where the water was ten feet deep. After the overloaded yawl sank, men, women and children were faced with the choice of burning to death or drowning. Some suffocated or were trampled to death. Even the best swimmers were sucked under the churning paddlewheels or drawn under by others holding to them or by waves caused by the boat's wheels. Many who jumped overboard were blinded by the glare of the fire and could not see land.

Of those women who refused to leap overboard, only four were saved, all of them on the lower deck. Amelia Jordan, a beautiful, dark-haired mother with long hair, jumped into Caddo Lake clutching her little boy to her breast, only to disappear seconds later. All of the children died, some later picked up tied to floating furniture.

In only thirty minutes, the boat was a wreck with sixty-three passengers dead. Boat carpenter Phillip Hill saved many lives by quickly removing the powder kegs from the hull, then throwing them overboard. Some who escaped were rescued by the skiff of the *Dixie*, and Capt. Thornton Jacobs carried the forty-three survivors to Jefferson by dawn.

The search for bodies lasted more than a week, but that of James Christian was never found. Although he was commended for his heroic efforts to save passengers, Captain Kellogg quit the river after seeing the *Mittie Stephens* sink in flames. Tradition has it that the payroll gold was lost with the boat, although eyewitness Lodwick claimed that the vessel's safe was removed to the *Dixie*.[9]

During the postwar period, Jefferson was home to three famed political figures — David Browning Culberson, Benjamin Holland Epperson, and Charles Allen Culberson.

David B. Culberson was born in Troupe County, Georgia, on September 29, 1830. After reading law at Tuskegee, Alabama, he was admitted to the bar in 1850 and moved to Gilmer in Upshur County, Texas, in 1856. Culberson was judge of the Sixth District Court and a member of the Texas legislature in 1859-60. An opponent of secession, he resigned that post and moved to Jefferson in 1861.

During the Civil War, Culberson rose from private to first colonel in the 18th Texas Infantry before health problems led to his reassignment to Austin as adjutant general of Texas. In 1864 he was elected to the state legislature from Marion County.

After being elected to the state senate in 1873, Culberson went on to serve ten consecutive terms in the United States Congress, from 1875 to 1897, and in that position was known as "The Silent Member" and "Honest Dave." A brilliant lawyer, he defended Abe Rothschild in the famed Diamond Bessie murder trial.

In 1880 David and his wife, Eugenia, built the Culberson House at 403 N. Walnut in Jefferson. Built in the Greek Revival style, the house has pine board floors six inches wide, fourteen-foot ceilings, five fireplaces, a secret passageway, wood-pegged interior doors, and old New Orleans plantation shutters.[10]

David B. Culberson died in Jefferson on May 7, 1900, and was buried in Giraud Cemetery.

His son, Charles Allen Culberson, was born in Dadeville, Alabama, on June 10, 1855, and moved to Jefferson with his parents in 1861. He graduated from Virginia Military Institute in 1874 and from the University of Virginia law school in 1877. After beginning a law practice in Jefferson and serving as Marion County attorney, Charles married Sallie Harrison on December 7, 1882, and moved to Dallas in 1887.

Charles Culberson was elected attorney general of Texas in 1890 and reelected to that position two years later. He was successful in defending the reforms of Governor James S. Hogg, including the law creating the Railroad Commission.

In 1894 Charles was elected governor of Texas. Known as the veto governor, he was a champion of rigid economy and administrative reform. After being reelected governor in 1896, Culberson was elected to the United States Senate in 1898 and served for twenty-four years. A very handsome man known for his immaculate attire, Charles was very reserved and did not speak often in the Senate. When the Confederate Monument was unveiled in Jefferson near the intersection of Broadway and Polk on July 10, 1907, Senator Culberson delivered the dedication address.

After being defeated in the Texas primaries in 1922, Charles stayed on in Washington, died there on March 19, 1925, and was buried in Fort Worth.

Benjamin Holland Epperson was born in Amite County, Mississippi, in 1826. He attended Princeton University but did not graduate there. Epperson moved to Clarksville, Texas, before 1847 and represented Red River County in the House of the Second Texas Legislature. A Unionist, he also served in the Eighth Legislature in 1859-60 and supported his personal friend and confidante, Sam Houston, for governor. While practicing law with M. L. Sims at Clarksville, Benjamin was elected a member of the First Confederate Congress in 1861-62.

In 1866 Governor J. W. Throckmorton appointed Epperson as financial agent. He was elected to the U.S. House of Representatives in 1867 but was not seated. After the Civil War the Memphis, El Paso and Pacific Railroad Company was reorganized with Epperson as president and promoter. The line was later absorbed by the Texas & Pacific.

After representing the stockade prisoners — those accused of killing G. W. Smith — in July 1869, Benjamin moved to Jefferson in 1871. The next year he built the House of the Seasons in the style of a two-story Italian villa with widow's walk and cupola on the third floor. The house is Greek Revival in plan and overall form, but the style is Victorian in detail. It takes its name from the different colored stained glass in each side of the cupola symbolizing the four seasons: blue glass from Germany on the north for winter, red glass from France on the east for summer, amber glass from Belgium on the west for autumn, and green glass, with tiny air bubbles imitating raindrops, from England on the south for spring. The sun rays striking these windows also heated the bathing water for the house. The most interesting interior feature of the house is the magnificent inner dome containing beautiful frescoes, which can be viewed from the first floor through a well-like opening. Many of the parlor furnishings are original to the house.[11]

In 1874-75, Epperson represented Marion County in the House of the 14th Legislature. Epperson and his law partner T. J. Campbell were two of the state prosecutors in Abe Rothschild's trial.

Benjamin died at Jefferson on September 16, 1878, leaving a

widow and five children. In 1931 his papers and letters were donated to the University of Texas by his son. These documents cover the period from 1859 to 1872 and are now in the Archives Collection of the University of Texas.

Jefferson's days as a river port were numbered after the U.S. Congress, responding to the national need for cotton, appropriated $150,000 for removal of the Red River raft on June 10, 1872. Raft work resumed that winter with Capt. C.W. Howell, engineer in charge, using a new explosive, nitroglycerin, rather than black powder. Two- to five-pound charges of nitroglycerin were sunk in cans near the bottom of the river. The powerful explosions loosened the mass and broke the long logs into small pieces that would float away in a rising river. On Thanksgiving Day, 1873, a steamboat channel was opened in the Red River when the last portion of the raft was permanently removed.

The chief engineer who actually removed the raft, Lt. E .A. Woodruff, knew that clearing the raft would have devastating effects on steamboat navigation into Jefferson. In his view, however, Jefferson's welfare was secondary to that of settlers along the upper Red River, who had seen their farm land destroyed by the log raft. Sensitive to the town's plight, Lieutenant Woodruff recommended that a dam and lock be built at Albany Point on Caddo Lake to compensate for the lowering in the lake's water level. However, the relief plan was condemned by his superior, C. W. Howell, captain of engineers in the New Orleans office. In a report dated May 15, 1873, Captain Howell expressed "grave doubts" as to whether the lock and dam at Albany Point would have permanent results.

With a meager appropriation of $10,000, Lieutenant Woodruff began the work of improving Big Cypress Bayou on December 18, 1872. With such limited resources, Woodruff eagerly accepted the offer of the city of Jefferson to use the city-owned dredge boat, the *Lone Star*. The plan involved dredging a three-mile channel from Boon's Bend to the city wharf. The channel was forty-five feet wide and six to seven feet deep. By June 1873, the dredge boat excavated 44,000 cubic yards and deposited it on the slope of the bank.

As the water level receded in Caddo Lake and Big Cypress, Jefferson slipped beyond the range of steamboat navigation. Her population dropped from a federal estimate of 7,297 in 1872 to 3,260 in 1880. In contrast, thriving Shreveport more than doubled in size to a population of 12,000 in 1885 and became the major Red River port.

The Army Corps of Engineers allowed the port of Jefferson one "last hurrah" by spending $45,000 between 1866 and 1896 to improve Cypress Bayou, thus allowing two boats, the *New Haven* and the *Friendly*, to make thirty-three round trips between Jefferson and Shreveport in 1889-90. By 1894, however, only the *Rosa Bland* from New Orleans linked the two towns with freight service. In 1903 she became the last steamboat to dock in Jefferson on a regular cargo schedule.

During the early years of Jefferson's decline, local attention was diverted by the sensational murder of "Diamond Bessie" Moore. Born Annie Stone in Syracuse, New York, in 1854, the black-haired beauty was given the surname of Bessie Moore at age fifteen by a hometown young man who took her as his mistress. After becoming a prostitute, Bessie traveled from Cincinnati to New Orleans to Hot Springs. A substantial inheritance from her father and a dazzling collection of diamond gifts from her admirers led to the nickname of "Diamond Bessie."

While plying her trade in Hot Springs, Bessie met a handsome young traveling jewelry salesman, Abraham Rothschild. Abe's father, Meyer, was a prominent jeweler in Cincinnati and was distantly related to the famed European banking family. Once Bessie became his common-law wife, the drinking and party-loving free-spender began to procure men for her; by then Abe had been disowned by his wealthy family.

After spending two days at the old Capitol Hotel in Marshall, Abe and Bessie arrived in Jefferson by train on Friday afternoon, January 19, 1877. Registering as "A. Monroe and wife," the strikingly dressed couple checked into Room Four of Brooks House Hotel on Vale Street. Rain kept them in their room all day Saturday, and chambermaid Jennie Simpson heard quarreling and sounds like blows and weeping coming from Room Four.

On Sunday morning, January 21, Abe purchased two picnic lunches at Henrique's restaurant, and the couple strolled across the Big Cypress foot bridge west of the turning basin and disappeared in a thick fog. After hiring a black boatman to put him over the river by a different route, Abe was seen alone around town later that afternoon. On Monday, he told inquirers that his wife was visiting friends in the country and would join him to leave the next day. Room Four was empty at daybreak on Tuesday, January 23.

Rothschild left Jefferson that day on an eastbound passenger train with his and Bessie's baggage.

On Monday, February 5, Sarah King was out looking for firewood southwest of town when she found the body of a young woman on a snow-covered embankment just east of Big Cypress ferry. There was a single bullet in the temple of the corpse, which was untouched by birds or animals. Between 4:00 and 5:00 P.M., the body was observed by P. M. Graham, the foreman for the coroner's court. According to Graham,

> . . . the body did not have much appearance of decomposition to me. The appearance of the body to me was that it had been dead four or five days. The body looked very near natural. . . . I think the body lay square on its back.

At this time the identity of the corpse was unknown. Local residents collected $150 to pay for a coffin and burial plot in Oakwood Cemetery. Late in the afternoon on Wednesday, February 7, the sexton interred the body of Diamond Bessie and (legend has it) her half-formed unborn child.

After an inquest a warrant was issued for the arrest of A. Monroe for the murder of an "unknown woman." Soon a new warrant identified the murder suspect as Abe Rothschild and the victim as Bessie Moore. Before being located in Cincinnati by Marion County Sheriff John M. Vines, Abe attempted suicide in late February. He fired a pistol at his head outside a saloon but managed only to blind his right eye and disfigure his face. While recovering in the hospital, he was arrested, then placed in jail to await transfer back to Texas.

Since Abe would not voluntarily return to Jefferson, Texas Governor R. B. Hubbard appealed to his Ohio counterpart for a warrant of extradition. Because Rothschild was physically unable to travel at the time, an Ohio court granted a twenty-day stay of delivery. On April 11, 1877, Sheriff Vines and Deputy G. W. Stroll arrived in Jefferson by train with the prisoner. A curious crowd of several hundred watched as Abe was taken to jail by carriage.

Rothschild's father had a change of heart toward his wayward son and hired the best available defense attorneys for Abe, including Congressman David B. Culberson. To prosecute the case, Governor Hubbard appointed the Jefferson law firm of B. H. Epperson and T. J. Campbell.

Since there was extreme local prejudice against Abe, motions were filed for a change of venue, and Judge B. T. Estes of the Fifth Judicial District of Texas ordered Rothschild transferred to the Harrison County jail for trial in Marshall. The trial was delayed until December 1878 due to the absence of two witnesses and the political duties of some of the attorneys. After three days of concluding arguments, a unanimous jury on December 24, 1878, concluded that Abe was guilty of murder in the first degree. Six days later the judge pronounced the sentence: death by hanging.

When the decision was appealed to the Seventh Texas Court of Appeals, Judge J. Clark found the trial court in error and reversed the case. It seemed that juror William Sanders had stated he had an opinion on the case, thus denying Rothschild a fair and impartial trial. After this unpopular decision, Abe was returned to the Jefferson jail.

A third indictment from the Marion County grand jury came on December 2, 1880, and a new murder trial began in Jefferson on December 14. More than 150 men were examined before a panel of twelve qualified jurors were found, including two black citizens. During the two-week trial, the jurors were lodged at the Excelsior House. On December 30, after only four hours of deliberation, the jury found Abe not guilty. A carriage waiting at the rear door of the courthouse whisked him away before angry citizens could render "more exact justice." That night Abe left town with his family by train, bound for Cincinnati.[12]

Local legend has it that twelve $1,000 bills were passed down through the jury room ceiling in the Marion County courthouse, courtesy of "Mama Rothschild." According to folklore, each of the jurors later received a fine piano, and they all met a violent death within a few years.

Bessie Moore's death is still listed as an unsolved murder in the official records of Marion County, although almost all the evidence points to Abe as her killer. There is still one troubling aspect in the case: How could the body be so well preserved after lying in the woods from January 21 until it was discovered on February 5?

This murder trial was the last one conducted in the Marion County courthouse. Designed by Dan Alley, it was built with $70,000 in bonds in the "Frogtown Hill" area of town in 1874. The structure was abandoned soon after the trial. It was later used as a black public school and burned in 1937. (Today a middle school is on the site at Highway 49 and Crawford Street.)

The only Jefferson portraits of Abe and Bessie are based on

photographs made by Sloan's Picture Gallery during the Jefferson trial and sold for twenty-five cents each. In January 1938 a staff artist of the *Dallas Morning News* drew portraits from the original faded photos. Pastel versions of the original photos can be found in the Diamond Bessie suite of the Excelsior House.

Since 1955 the highlight of the annual Jefferson historic pilgrimage has been a courtroom drama called the "Diamond Bessie Murder Trial." Staged by citizens of Jefferson in the old Jewish synagogue (now the Jefferson Playhouse), the play was written by Mrs. Lawton Riley, wife of the local Episcopal rector. In a setting of flickering gas lights and antique furnishings, the drama is presented to an audience of about 250 in a theater-in-the-round. The actual handcuffs worn by Abe Rothschild are used in the play.

Local legend has it that Jefferson leaders tried to obstruct the coming of the railroads. However, there is no factual basis for this myth. To the contrary, the town sought a rail connection to supplement existing water navigation as early as 1854.

On August 5, 1870, the State of Texas granted a charter to the International Railroad Company for the construction of a line from Fulton, Arkansas, to Laredo by way of Austin and San Antonio. The charter required that either a trunk line pass through Jefferson or that a branch line up to thirty miles connect the city to the main track.

In February 1871, an eager Jefferson donated $200,000 in city bonds to the International Company. In addition thirty-two acres were granted for a machine shop site, four city blocks along Big Cypress for a depot site, and a right-of-way through town for a trunk line and spur line.

Hoping to develop the western half of the townsite, the W. W. Alley family in March 1872 gave the International Railroad twelve blocks of right-of-way from the northern limits of the Alley survey to the southern boundary where the line would cross Big Cypress south of Speak Street. In turn, the city was to give $20,000 to W. W. Alley and his brother-in-law, M. L. Crawford, to reimburse them for the right-of-way.

When the International line stopped forty miles short of Jefferson at Longview in 1873, the Alley grant became the right-of-way for the Texas & Pacific, which built through the center of the Alley addition only ten blocks west of the business district. In addition,

Dan Alley in December 1872 transferred twelve lots in three blocks to the city to be used for a depot.

On June 21, 1872, Col. Thomas A. Scott, president of the Texas & Pacific Railroad, arrived in Jefferson on the steamer *Lotus* seeking financial aid for his company. Upon Scott's nighttime arrival, a band played "Hail to the Chief," cannons fired a salute, and a ball was given in his honor. After touring Jefferson the next day, Scott's party of ten returned to Marshall.

Shortly thereafter, $125,000 and $175,000 in county and city bonds, respectively, were overwhelmingly approved and donated to the Texas & Pacific. The city also offered a five-year tax exemption if machine shops were built in Jefferson instead of Marshall. A local committee also selected and offered land for a depot site that was closer to the business district.

In March 1873, the first Texas & Pacific track was laid from Marshall to Marion County; eight miles of track was completed by June 19. The completion of the line to Jefferson was celebrated with a public barbecue and grand ball on July 8, 1873.

On July 25, Jefferson was linked to Dallas when the Texas & Pacific completed its rails west to the Trinity River. This vital rail connection also meant that Dallas would soon supplant Jefferson as a trade center.

The false local legend linking Jay Gould's curse to the decline of Jefferson is rooted in the register of the Excelsior House dated January 2, 1882.[13] At the top of that page is the drawing of a bluejay followed by the surname Gould and the address, New York City. This entry is followed by a large X, indicating that the person left without paying the bill. Below other names in the register for that date is the bold phrase "End of Jefferson, Texas," in what appears to be the same handwriting. However, a "flag r" is used in "New York City," and a "stump r" is used in the "End of Jefferson."

Out of this hotel register entry grew the strong and longtime tradition that Jay Gould cursed Jefferson because his Texas & Pacific line did not get a free right-of-way from the city in 1872. Gould, however, was in no way connected with the coming of the first railroad to Jefferson in 1872-73. It was not until April 15, 1881, that a depressed and financially broken Thomas A. Scott sold his interest in the Texas & Pacific to Gould for $4 million.

Moreover, none of the newspapers in Marshall, Longview, Texarkana, Galveston, Dallas, or Fort Worth make mention of Jay

Gould being in Texas in either December 1881 or January 1882. Also, none of the dozen Gould biographies report him as being in Jefferson during this period. After viewing the famous jaybird signature in the hotel register in March 1982, Gould biographer Maury Klein, professor of history at the University of Rhode Island, wrote the following letter to Mrs. G. W. Carpenter, in charge of the Excelsior House:

> The signature in your register is certainly not that of Jay Gould. It does not resemble his handwriting at any point in his life. More than that, he never in his life, to my knowledge, ever used the drawing of a bird as part of his signature. It was not his logo in any sense. . . .
>
> The story of Gould threatening the end of Jefferson, Texas, and all the rest is simply preposterous on the face of it. That behavior is wholly out of character for Gould, and at this point, I know him better than any living soul. He was a quiet, soft-spoken man of immense self-control. His anger rarely showed, and certainly not in the form of vague, wild threats.

Although there is no factual basis for the "curse on Jefferson" legend, Jay Gould did visit the town on April 21, 1890, when his private rail car stopped there during a Texas tour. According to the *Fort Worth Gazette*, Gould received a cordial reception and remarked that Jefferson was "destined to be the iron city of the South."

The 1880 census showed Jefferson to have a population of only 1,331, including twenty-six Jewish households. Even in her period of decline, the town remained a leading cultural center. The Taylor Opera House seated 500 and rented for $35 a night. It hosted minstrel shows, magic shows, and such plays as Shakespeare's "As You Like It" in 1879 and "A Winter's Tale" in 1884. During these performances the actors stayed at the Excelsior House. Mr. H.C. Barrow, a scenic artist from Chicago, completed fifteen new stage scenes for the productions by May 1883.

On Wednesday morning, December 11, 1880, all Jefferson business houses closed for a community-wide memorial service to honor Jefferson Davis. At 11:30 A.M., the same hour of his funeral in New Orleans, eulogies were delivered at the Cumberland Presbyterian Church.

The 1881 Club, the oldest woman's club in Texas, was organized in Jefferson in October 1881, at the home of Mrs. W. B. Ward.

Initially a chautauqua circle for both men and women, the group elected Capt. J. P. Russell as first president and Ben Epperson as secretary. It was soon merged into a woman's club and renamed the Review Club. (Today the 1881 Club meets weekly but disbands from the second Saturday in May until the first Saturday in October.)

The rapid loss of population did not diminish civic pride. On July 27, 1891, the Board of Aldermen passed an ordinance requiring all able-bodied male citizens between the ages of eighteen and ninety to work three days a year repairing and clearing out city streets and alleys. Those reporting for such work details were to bring an ax, hoe, pick, or spade. One could, however, send an able-bodied substitute or pay a dollar a day in lieu of service. A person could be fined $10 for not cooperating.

During this period, Jefferson claimed a prominent Texas historian. In 1888 Mrs. Anna Hardwick Pennybacker wrote *A New History of Texas for Schools,* a standard Texas history textbook widely used in the public schools. Anna wrote most of the manuscript while living in Jefferson, where her father, Dr. J.B. Hardwick, was pastor of the First Baptist Church. Surprisingly, her textbook makes no reference to Jefferson.

The federal census of 1890 showed Marion County to have a black population of 7,001 and a white total of 3,861. Late in the decade, the white minority became convinced that the old Reconstruction system of black political bosses and the buying of votes were still present in the county. Reacting to this perceived threat, the whites began to organize a white citizens' primary in Marion County.

In 1897 secret meetings were held in Jefferson and other places in the county to form "vigilante committees" to end the buying of elections. Fearing possible federal charges, they kept no minutes or membership rolls. These white citizens' committees would surround the church or schoolhouse where black voters were to assemble, then issue a stern warning to the leaders to cancel the meeting. Some were threatened or escorted to their homes. Two who refused to cooperate were said to have been killed.

In the spring of 1898, some 400 of the "best white men" in the county met at the courthouse to form the Citizens White Primary. Their objective was the organization of a nonpolitical white primary to elect a citizens' ticket for the county. After being elected chairman, Mr. William Clark defined their purpose:

> . . .we are here simply as a band of law-abiding citizens . . . to devise ways and means by which she (Marion County) can be taken and lifted from the low plain to which she has fallen morally, by reason of the unholy, immoral, disgusting and degrading influences and conditions that face and surround every campaign that has been conducted within her borders for the last ten or fifteen years, at which her people have become supremely disgusted, and to which they will no longer submit, . . .

The goal of the Citizens White Primary was to have all white voters participate in a primary election for nominating all county and precinct officers and to support that nominee at the next general election. It was also agreed that participants would support only those candidates who submitted their names to the primary.

The first such white primary was held on July 21, 1898. Thereafter they were held in April and followed by necessary run-off elections a few weeks later. These early election dates were popular with farmers since they came before the busiest farming season. Both Democrats and Republicans abided by the primary outcome and supported single candidates for each office in the general election.

It is noteworthy that the Marion County white primary was the first of its kind in Texas and continued through the elections of 1948.

At the turn of the century, two attempts were made to bring a college to Jefferson. In 1901 the Twenty-seventh Legislature passed an act to create "an industrial institute and college for the education of white girls in arts and sciences." After Governor Joseph D. Sayers appointed a committee to decide the location of the college, Mr. Rudolph Ballauf presented a strong case for Jefferson in a printed pamphlet. His proposal offered the abandoned county courthouse as the college site with new wings added to provide student housing for 100. The Ballauf plan called for converting the jail into a residence and dormitory. Campus grounds would extend to "Lover's Leap" on Big Cypress. Since fish was considered to be brain food, the college would be supplied with fresh fish twice a week from the plentiful area supply.

Ballauf also reminded the site committee that East Texas deserved at least *one* public institution of higher learning. However, his efforts were to no avail. The college located in Denton and opened in September 1903 as the Girls' Industrial College. (The name was later changed to the College of Industrial Arts, then to Texas Woman's University.)

The county commissioners also talked of making a bid to remove Emerson College to Jefferson. This struggling school of 200 was located near Greenville in Hunt County. Emerson officials wanted $8,000 to relocate the college in Jefferson along with free use of the vacant old county courthouse. Local interest in the project waned after the spring of 1905, and the college closed in 1907.

During this time the ladies of the Jefferson Library Association provided a rallying point to revive city pride. In 1902 the Women's Auxiliary of the Jefferson YMCA began to collect books, library furniture, and funds. One of the book donors, Mrs. W. J. Sedberry, was elected president of the newly organized library association. Mr. Allen Urquhart then wrote to steel tycoon and philanthropist Andrew Carnegie and explained the need for a permanent library home.

In 1907 the Jefferson Library Association received a grant from Mr. Carnegie for $7,500 to build a library on the condition that the city be responsible for its upkeep. On April 15, 1907, a bid of $8,750 was awarded to J. F. Berry of Morris County for construction of the Carnegie Public Library. Located at the corner of Market and Lafayette streets, this imposing two-story brick structure has a columned entrance. It is only one of four such buildings still existing as libraries in Texas, along with those at Ballinger, Stamford, and Palestine.

In the beginning the first floor was library space. The large open space on the second floor was utilized for various meetings and functions. It was initially referred to as the "Auditorium" and later as the "Old Opera House." When fires destroyed Jefferson schools in the late 1940s and again in 1959, classes were held in the library.

In 1949 the new Jefferson Historical Society and Museum moved into the first floor, and the library relocated on the second level. Since 1965, the historical museum has occupied its own building, the old Federal Courthouse located one block to the south.[14]

At the left front corner of the library block is the Sterne Fountain. In 1913 the children of Jacob and Ernestine Sterne had a bronze fountain cast in behalf of their parents by J. L. Mott Foundry in New York. The fountain dispensed water at levels convenient for horses, people, and pets. The Italian sculptor Giuseppe Moretti recreated Hebe, the mythological Greek goddess of youth, on the pedestal above.

One of the great myths of Jefferson concerns the missing line on the old Confederate Monument. Interest in such a local monument increased after Jefferson veterans were invited to participate in the dedication of a Confederate monument in Marshall on January 19, 1906. After three years of discussion, a granite shaft from Llano, Texas, was finally ordered for Jefferson. Upon it stood a mature Confederate soldier of gray bronze designed by Frank Teich.

The monument first rested in a small park on the north side of Broadway at the corner of Line and Polk streets. It was unveiled at 4:00 P.M. on July 10, 1907. The inscription read as follows:

Erected by Gen. Dick Taylor Camp, UCV
Lest We Forget
In Memory of Our Dead
1861-1865

The local Confederate veterans group, the Dick Taylor Camp, was named in honor of Gen. Richard Taylor, son of President Zachary Taylor and hero of the Battle of Mansfield, Louisiana, April 1864.

The ceremony included thirteen little girls dressed in white with red sashes, one for each of the Confederate states. After placing wreaths of flowers at the base of the monument, each girl pulled ribbons to release buntings of red, white, and blue over the monument. A stirring dedication address was then delivered by U.S. Senator Charles Allen Culberson, who started his career as an attorney in Jefferson.

The *Jimplecute* devoted a full page to the event, including a quote of the inscription on the monument. However, there was no mention of an erased line, nor the fact that it had been removed before the dedication.

Ever since that time, Jefferson tradition has the missing line as being "For a Lost Cause." As the story goes, the line disappeared in 1911, when Hood's Brigade held their reunion in Jefferson. It seems that one irate veteran took notice of the inscription and shouted, "Hell, it was no Lost Cause." Legend has it that he and some comrades then removed the offensive words.

For years the bronze soldier on the monument had his back to the north. This positioning troubled Joe McCasland, who became county judge in the late 1930s. Upon taking office, Judge Mc-

Casland had the county surveyor determine true north. The judge then moved the Confederate Monument six blocks to the courthouse lawn and relocated the soldier to face his northern enemy.

The missing line on the monument inscription remained a mystery for seventy-five years. Then, on a Sunday afternoon in July 1982, a persistent seeker of the truth attacked the riddle with a lady's powder puff. Accompanied by Katherine Ramsay Wise, a member of the Marion County Historical Commission, he unleashed several flurries of Faberge powder on the monument's blank line. The white dust soon revealed the definite letters. As the two investigators continued to guess about the faint ones, they suddenly realized that the message was "In Oakwood Cemetery."

After this discovery a search of old newspaper files *before* the unveiling revealed that the Dick Taylor Camp had initially chosen the cemetery as the monument site. By the time they changed to the small park location, the monument was already ordered. When it arrived camp members quickly removed any reference to Oakwood Cemetery — thus the missing line.

On October 12, 1907, an election was held to vote Jefferson dry for the first time in history. This local movement was started by Mrs. Lizzie Moseley Haywood, who received staunch support from Mrs. J. H. Rowell, Sr., Miss May Belle Hale, and Mrs. H. A. Benefield. A week before the election, two hundred local women signed their names at the end of a *Jimplecute* advertisement which blamed "three-fourths of all the crime, nine-tenths of all the poverty, and nearly all the sorrows that have come to women on the saloon. . . ." The signers then appealed to chivalrous male voters for protection from this "burden."

On election day the dry forces carried Jefferson and Precinct 3 by a margin of forty-seven votes. Church bells heralded the good tidings, and a victory rally was held on Sunday morning at the Presbyterian church.

Jefferson women also supported a statewide prohibition campaign. Particularly effective was a weekly Women's Christian Temperance Union column in the *Jimplecute* by Mrs. H. A. Benefield. On November 10, 1909, she informed her readers that "three beers a day for one year ($54.75) would bring a long list of food to the home."

When the Texas prohibition election was held on July 22, 1911, the proposition was narrowly defeated by 6,000 votes out of 468,489 ballots cast. In the spring of 1918, the state legislature approved the Eighteenth (Prohibition) Amendment to the U.S. Constitution. By then 168 Texas counties had already outlawed alcohol.

In 1909 a short-term "Pearl Rush" came to the Jefferson area when fishermen Tom Allen and Will Teel began to use the soft white flesh of mussels as trot line bait. Mussels were abundant in the shallow water of Caddo Lake. Surprisingly, high-quality pearls were also found during the mussel hunts.

In July 1912, a woman wading in a bathing suit found a pearl worth $1,075 in the lake. The most successful pearl hunter was a Japanese man, Sachihiko Ona Murata, who found over $3,000 worth of pearls in one year in Marion County. Since hunters had to get down on all fours to gather mussels, they were referred to as "pearl hogs." The pearl boom ended after only three years when the Mooringsport dam increased the depth of Caddo Lake by several feet, thus covering the mussel beds in deep water.

In the 1920s, a revived Ku Klux Klan appeared in Jefferson. This second organization was known as the Invisible Empire, Knights of the Ku Klux Klan, and appeared soon after showings of the movie *Birth of a Nation* throughout the South in late 1915.

On June 10, 1922, the Klan in Marion County made an announcement in the *Jimplecute* explaining its purpose and requirements for membership. It was signed by the "Exalted Cyclops, Jefferson Klan, Realm of Texas." Among the principles announced by this secret organization were white supremacy, the protection of pure womanhood, preventing the causes of mob violence and lynchings, and the limitation of foreign immigration.

Claiming to be composed of "some of the most prominent, patriotic and best men of our country," the local Klan welcomed any male Gentile who was at least eighteen, a native citizen, and a believer in the Christian religion.

The proclamation assured all moral, law-abiding people — white or black — that they had nothing to fear. However, the Klan warned the immoral, the undesirable, and law violators that their presence would not be tolerated in the community.

On December 21, 1922, the first Klan parade was held in downtown Jefferson. A crowd of 1,000 watched as some fifty white-robed and hooded people followed a leader bearing a fiery cross. In spite of rumors that the parade would be stopped by Sheriff W. S. Terry, "everything passed off quiet and peaceful," according to the *Jimplecute*.

Cloaked in anonymity, the local Klan incited racist crimes, lynchings, and floggings during this period. They held regular meetings on the second floor of the old Kahn Saloon at the northeast corner of Austin and Vale streets.

The best known incident of Klan-associated violence occurred on Saturday, October 16, 1923. It seems that Sheriff B. B. Rogers and Will Proctor, a constable for the previous sheriff, had opposing views of law enforcement with regard to Klan activities. Their disagreement led to a fatal shootout with both men lying dead in an alley between Austin and Lafayette streets.

As was true throughout the South, the Jefferson Klan had its heyday in the mid-1920s. By the time of the Great Depression, its power and mystique were gone.

It was during this period that Jefferson produced major figures in both music and literature. Vernon Dalhart, known by some as the "Father of Country Music," was born Marion Try Slaughter on a farm southwest of Jefferson on April 6, 1881. His stage name was derived from two Texas towns, Vernon and Dalhart. The lad had a turbulent childhood in Jefferson, where his father, Robert Marion ("Bob") Slaughter, was known as the town bully. Bob was under indictment for murder when he was killed by his brother-in-law, Bob Castleberry, who thought Slaughter was mistreating his sister. When the two met on the morning of March 2, 1883, at Kahn's Saloon at the corner of Austin and Vale streets, Castleberry shot his adversary dead with a pistol after a loud argument. Murder charges were dismissed after it was determined that Castleberry was acting in self-defense.

Mrs. Slaughter moved into town and lived with the family of her husband's killer at 406 Line Street. Before Try Slaughter left Jefferson as a teenager, he received music lessons from Miss Eva Eberstadt and Miss May Belle Hale. Blessed with a natural, clear tenor voice, he sang for some of his first audiences at Kahn's Saloon. His most requested number, "Can't Yo' Heah Me Callin' Caroline," was a black dialect song that Try sang to perfection. It was released by the Edison Company in June 1917 as his first important recording.

Try moved from Jefferson to Dallas, where he married Sadie Lee Moore of Livingston and served as paid soloist at the First Baptist Church.

After moving his family to New York, Slaughter broke into professional grand opera in 1912. Following his first record release in 1917, the Edison Company sent "Vernon Dalhart" on national "tone-testing" tours. One of his concerts was at the Marshall City Hall Auditorium on April 8, 1919, but Dalhart did not visit Jefferson, possibly because of some bad childhood memories. By then his mother had sold her Jefferson cemetery lots after marrying a Mr. Onstadt in Dallas.

At the peak of his career in 1924, Vernon earned a million dollars from his hit, "The Prisoner's Song." During a two-week engagement on Broadway, he sang just that number. From 1924 until 1928, Dalhart was the busiest of all singers on record. His song "If I had wings like an angel. . ." was the first million seller for the recording industry.

Dalhart's records sold 75 million copies. By releasing songs under 112 names, he was able to record the same song for several different companies. There was no single distinctive personality in his recordings. Among the most versatile singers who ever lived, he was equally adept performing spirituals, sentimental ballads, and period songs.

By 1930 Vernon had burned himself out and lost his personal fortune. He attempted an unsuccessful comeback in 1939 with a group called Vernon Dalhart and his Big Cypress Boys. After dropping from sight, he was working as night clerk at the Barnum Hotel in Bridgeport, Connecticut, when he died in September 1948. Dalhart was buried there at the Mountain Grove Cemetery under a modest tombstone which reads, "Marion T. Slaughter, 1883-1948."[15]

Writer Barry Benefield of Jefferson achieved fame through his short stories, novels, and movies based on his writing. Barry's father, B. J. Benefield, served with an Arkansas regiment and was taken prisoner in the Civil War. He then moved to Jefferson and married Harriet Adelaide Barry in 1869. B. J. was the first ice man in Texas, making wagon deliveries from the first ice-manufacturing plant in the state.

Barry Benefield, one of five children, was born in Jefferson in 1871. As a boy he worked in his father's feed store and wagon yard. Barry was barely five feet tall when he graduated with honors from Jefferson High School. He enrolled at the University of Texas in the fall of 1898, became editor of the university magazine, and won short story prizes as a student. Upon graduation Benefield worked one year with the *Dallas Morning News*, then spent eight years on the staff of *The New York Times.*

In 1911 his short stories began to appear in *The Century, Scribner's, Collier's, Ladies Home Journal,* and *Smart Set.* Barry's best known novel, *Valiant is the Word for Carrie,* is about a prostitute from Crebillon, Louisiana (the fictional name for Jefferson). She adopts two children and moves to New York, where she achieves success as a dress maker. The novel became a Paramount film in 1936. Two other Benefield novels — *The Chicken-Wagon Family* and *Eddie and the Archangel* — also became Hollywood films. Barry also wrote the screenplay for the movie *Love Affair,* in 1939. His romantic, happy-ending novels offered the reader a welcome escape from the grinding realities of the depression years.

In November 1949, Benefield wrote a feature story for the *Ford Times* titled, "My Favorite American Town — Jefferson." After retiring in New York, Barry and his wife Lucille returned to the Jefferson family home. Lucille, a teacher by training, died in 1960. Her famed husband died at age ninety-four in 1971 and was buried beside Lucille in Jefferson's Oakwood Cemetery.

Jefferson's Excelsior House ranks with San Antonio's Menger Hotel as the two oldest hotels in continuous operation in Texas. The original portion was built by Capt. William Perry and his wife, Sardinia. On September 17, 1858, Perry purchased town lots 10 and 11 and block 20 of Austin Street and began construction of what became Excelsior House. The northeast wing, built in the Classical Revival style, was completed before 1860.

On January 2, 1868, Captain Perry sold his hotel to William Tumlin, who named it the Exchange Hotel and then Fulton House. During the Reconstruction period, Tumlin added a commercial wing to the southwest side of the hotel with a total of nineteen chimneys in the building. New owner Dr. A. A. Terhune renamed it the Commercial Hotel. In 1871 proprietor A. Britton advertised the building as the Irvine Hotel and announced that stagecoaches arrived and departed daily.

In 1877 Mrs. Kate Wood purchased the property and restored the original name of Excelsior House. Mrs. Wood was a widow who also ran a restaurant on Austin Street. During the thirty years she operated the hotel, Kate's guest register was signed by Presidents

Rutherford B. Hayes and Ulysses S. Grant, John Jacob Astor, P. S. Chrysler, the John Drew and Ward Barrymore troupe, and Oscar Wilde using the alias of John Gibbs.

In 1888 Mrs. Wood donated land on adjoining property to the east of the Excelsior House for construction of the Federal Building. The red-brick, three-story structure was of Romanesque design. The $36,000 project was started in May 1888 and occupied on April 1, 1890.

As was the custom in her native Germany, Mrs. Wood took a pitcher to be filled with beer at the corner saloon each evening. This daring daily ritual seemed to contradict her many ladylike qualities and caused talk in town.

Kate's fondness for beer was equaled only by her love for dogs. When she died in 1907, she was buried beside her two pet dogs, Jessie and Lily, in Oakwood Cemetery.

Amelia Wood McNeely inherited the Excelsior House when her mother died. Amelia's dog, Frank, had a gold tooth and wore a diamond studded collar. Local legend has it that when Frank died, he was picked up by a hearse and buried in Oakwood Cemetery, although no marker has been found.

Each afternoon Mrs. McNeely sat in a wrought-iron chair in front of the hotel dressed in colorful silks, satins, and French embroidered hose. Behind her were dozens of canaries in a large outdoor cage. Since her establishment was full of nineteenth-century furniture, travelers called it the "Canary Hotel" or the "Antique Hotel."

Longtime friend and hotel employee George Neidermeier inherited the Excelsior House when Mrs. McNeely died in 1920. Like his two predecessors, George had a pampered dog, Teddy, who was the hotel mascot during the 1920s. (Today a picture of the dog hangs in the hotel lobby.)

When George died in 1928, his sister and heir, Miss "Mamie" Neidermeier, sold the Excelsior House to Mrs. James I. Peters of Shreveport. A very wealthy woman in her earlier years, Mrs. Peters brought with her a priceless collection of antique furniture. In 1955 she installed a New Orleans-style fountain and courtyard behind the hotel. During her years of ownership, Mrs. Peters continued to live in a grand style beyond her current means. When she died in 1961, the Excelsior House was passed on to her sister, Mrs. Clarence Messer, who put it up for sale.

Fearing that the historic hotel might be torn down and its contents scattered, the Jesse Allen Wise Garden Club agreed to purchase it for $35,000 in August 1961. Although club officers had no property to offer as collateral, they were loaned $25,000 by the Marshall Building and Loan Association on the strength of their signatures. When the club took out another $7,000 loan at the Jefferson bank, husbands were required to sign the note for their wives.

After addressing some major structural and electrical problems in the hotel, a volunteer "army" of club members and their husbands began the time-consuming task of scraping paint, varnishing woodwork, polishing brass, weeding the grounds, and so on. One early decision was to give the famous canary birds away and remove the cages, thus eliminating a mite problem and a large feed bill.

An early task was the selection of "documentary" wallpapers, reproductions of authenticated papers from the era. For example, "Transportation" paper was chosen for the Jay Gould Room. Most of the hotel furnishings in 1961 were original, and the ladies refinished each piece.

Mrs. Lucille Terry was elected the first chairman of the nonprofit corporation set up by the garden club to operate the hotel. She served as chairman of the hotel committee for the first fourteen years until the loans were paid in full. Utilizing a totally volunteer staff, the Excelsior House stayed open to paying guests. Two club members even temporarily assumed night duty after three paid managers quit in rapid succession.

On March 2, 1962, all of Jefferson was invited to a linen shower at the hotel. The resulting gifts of white sheets, pillow cases, and towels amply stocked the hotel's linen closets.

At the formal opening of the Excelsior House in March 1962, Governor Price Daniel came to Jefferson to present an award to the garden club for the year's outstanding project in historical preservation.

In 1964 widow Cissie Benefield McCampbell became the hotel resident manager and served in that capacity until her death in 1981. Her day was declared in Jefferson on July 29, 1979. It was Cissie and Ruth Lester who created the famous plantation breakfast which always consisted of freshly squeezed orange juice, fluffy scrambled eggs, cured ham, grits, plum jelly, orange blossom muffins, and bite-sized biscuits.

Among the ghost stories associated with the Excelsior House

is one told by famed film director Steven Spielberg, who claimed to have visited Jefferson in the early 1970s while looking for locations for the movie *The Sugarland Express.* After checking into the hotel at 10:00 P.M. with two companions, each was given a stateroom with a canopy bed. Spielberg sensed something standing over his shoulder, then stepped into an ice-cold area of the warm room. When a companion observed that his room was also "real spooky," the three left town at 2:00 A.M. and checked into the nearest Holiday Inn. There is another twist to the mystery: Hotel manager Cissie McCampbell did not remember or have any written record of Spielberg's alleged visit.

When Lady Bird Johnson brings friends to Jefferson, the Excelsior House is her favorite place to entertain. A native of nearby Karnack, she lived in Jefferson in the mid-1920s while finishing her high school education. The garden club furnished the Rosewood Room in her honor, and Mrs. Johnson was a frequent guest in the 1960s. During the 1965 historical pilgrimage, Lady Bird paid a surprise visit. Impressed by their success in restoring the Excelsior House, Mrs. Johnson sought the advice of the garden club as she prepared her husband's Johnson City home for public tours. In the fall of 1972, Lyndon Johnson signed the Excelsior House register with his wife just months before his death.

The renovated hotel has fourteen guest rooms available, each decorated to reflect a time in Jefferson's past. The rooms are filled with antique maple, cherry, and mahogany furniture. There are marble-topped dressers, button and spool beds, and hardwood floors covered with oriental rugs.

Four of the guest rooms are on the ground floor: the much-in-demand Diamond Bessie Suite with wicker furniture on the sun porch, the Victorian Parlor, Blalock Room, and the Sleigh Bed Room.

The second floor contains four rooms in the original building. The Hayes Room and Grant Room in the Presidential Suite are named for two nineteenth-century presidents who stayed in the hotel. The red-decorated Hayes Room has a large antique canopy bed, and the Grant Room features tiger mahogany furniture and hand-carved walnut cornices. The jury room which once had six double beds is now the Jay Gould Room. The Rosewood Room or Lady Bird Room has rosewood furniture, pink lusters on the mantel, and a clock Mrs. Johnson donated.

There are smaller guest rooms on the second floor of the commercial wing of the hotel.

In the hotel lobby is a large glass case displaying yellowed register pages. There is a small museum between the lobby and the ballroom. The chandeliered ballroom has a pressed metal ceiling, a white Italian marble mantel, and columns from a Grecian hillside.

The adjoining dining room features a Sevres porcelain chandelier over a large Chippendale table with six matching chairs. The plantation breakfast is served there each morning from a modern kitchen added to the rear.

The old cast-iron hitching posts are still in front of the Excelsior House. A grand view is offered looking down from the upper grill-work of the hotel. The historic, white-brick structure is now one of the state's best traveling addresses, a favorite weekend getaway for city dwellers from Dallas and Houston.[16]

Directly across the street is Jay Gould's restored palatial railroad car, the *Atalanta*, which has proven to be a boon to Jefferson. Named for the beautiful, swift heroine of Greek legend, this private coach was ordered by Gould on November 18, 1886. He always spent the night on this coach car during his frequent trips, often traveling with his daughter Helen. His personal chef and physician also accompanied the financial wizard.

The *Atalanta* included four staterooms (each with a separate toilet), an observation lounge seating six with velvet cushioned wicker furniture, a butler's pantry, kitchen, observation platform, and a dining room with a large built-in china cabinet and silver from Tiffany's in New York.

After Gould died in 1892, the car was used by his heirs, then served as an office car for railroad company executives before being operated by the federal government during World War I. In 1933 James T. Davis, yardmaster at Overton, wrote to railroad officials in St. Louis asking for assistance in finding housing during the East Texas oil boom. As a result the *Atalanta* was sent to Texas and parked near the Overton depot after being lifted off its wheels. Davis, his wife, and two children moved into the coach car and air-conditioned it in 1935. They named their new family home the *Prairie Bell.*

When Davis was transferred to Houston in 1946, the *Atalanta* was moved to Pitner's Junction in Rusk County. There J. T. Davis, Jr., his wife, and son moved into it and stayed there until 1953, when he was moved to Shreveport. For more than a year, the unattended car deteriorated in a weed patch.

Fortunately, an East Texas oil field worker told his brother-in-law, Dan Lester, about the abandoned car. Dan and his wife, Ruth, had come to Jefferson with Shell Oil in 1937. Rather than be transferred in 1939, Lester formed his own drilling company in Jefferson and purchased Guarding Oak, one of the oldest homes in the Alley addition. In 1951 Dan was elected to the first of several terms as mayor of Jefferson. Ruth Lester was appointed to the new Texas State Historical Survey Committee and was elected president of the garden club in 1954.

In April 1954, Mrs. James T. Davis agreed to sell the *Atalanta* to the Lesters for $1,200; they in turn presented it to the garden club. Henry Eldridge then donated a site for the car directly across the street from the Excelsior House as a memorial to the Eldridge family.

On May 10-11, 1954, Stroud Brothers Trucking of Joinerville moved the eighty-eight-foot car over a 100-mile circuitous route to Jefferson. The 40,000-pound *Atalanta* was carried on an 8,000-pound trailer towed by an 18,000-pound Mack truck. The trip took two days at a speed of 10 to 15 miles per hour.

When the members of the garden club first saw the *Atalanta*, it had a wooden house roof, was rusty, and badly in need of a paint job. The thirty-five members of the club undertook the restoration of the car without seeking any federal assistance. Help did come from W. G. Vollmer, president of the Texas & Pacific, who on June 8, 1954, authorized repairing the roof, putting one coat of primer and two coats of paint on the exterior, and varnishing the interior. After removing the house top, the garden club ladies had a metal canopy built over the car.

Jay Gould's railroad car was first opened to tours during the 1955 historical pilgrimage. Wearing costumes of the 1880s, trained garden club members and high school students acted as hostesses. The *Atalanta* is now opened to tours throughout the year.

This "palace on wheels" was last used by George Jay Gould and his actress wife, Edith Kingdom Gould. The stateroom which she occupied is lavishly decorated in velvets and satin, and her monogram is on the headboard. George Gould's stateroom has a gold brocade coverlet on the bed and a picture of his wife hanging over it. George expected his guests aboard the private train to wear full evening dress for dinner.

In November 1937, Curtis Morris, editor of the East Texas Chamber of Commerce magazine, made a fateful speech to the

Young Men's Business Association of Jefferson. Citing the town's historical significance and the scenic beauty of nearby Caddo Lake, Morris challenged local leaders to follow the example of Natchez, Mississippi, and begin an annual tourist event in Jefferson.

Two years later, thirty-five local women formed the Jesse Allen Wise Garden Club and began to make plans to sponsor the first Jefferson Dogwood Trail.[17] This event covered a twenty-five-mile route and was held during the peak blossom season, April 7-24, 1940.

Jefferson hosted more than 500 visitors the first Sunday. The only home open to them was that of Mrs. Mary Alley Carlson, granddaughter of Daniel N. Alley, the co-founder of Jefferson who gave each of his ten children a gift of $10,000 and a house or materials for building one. One family has lived in the Alley-Carlson House since 1859 when Dan, Jr., received the place as a wedding gift from his father. The home still has original furnishings brought from New Orleans by steamboat.

Dressed in her 1895 wedding gown, Mrs. Carlson continued to welcome visitors to her home during each garden club event. This tradition continued until she died in 1967 at ninety-three.

When the second annual Dogwood Trail was held in 1941, there were so few dogwood blooms that regional newspapers advised the public not to come. According to Mrs. Carlson, a couple didn't see the ads and "came anyway." They asked why the people of Jefferson did not open up their historic houses to public tours. As a result, Mrs. Carlson and four other local women allowed the couple to visit their homes — and a grand idea was born.

The end of World War II brought renewed interest in tourism, and the garden club resumed the Dogwood Trail in 1948. This time, however, four historic homes, the Presbyterian and Episcopal churches, and the Excelsior House were opened to the public along with a seventeen-mile trail of blossoms. Visitors also enjoyed coffee and tea cakes served by club members at the Jefferson Country Club.

In February 1950, the garden club voted to change the name of the Dogwood Trail to the Jefferson Historical Pilgrimage and to expand the event from Saturday afternoon to all day Sunday, April 16. At a cost of $2 each, 1,983 visitors toured eight homes, the Excelsior House, and the Jefferson Historical Museum. The next year excursions from the Jefferson waterfront became a part of the pilgrimage when the sternwheel riverboat *Victory* offered rides on Big Cypress.

By 1955 the oldest historical pilgrimage in Texas was well established. That year the first two performances of "The Diamond Bessie Murder Trial" were presented in the Jefferson Playhouse on Friday and Saturday, April 22-23, at 8:30 P.M. The playhouse was the old Jewish synagogue recently purchased and restored by the garden club. The script for the original production was written by Mrs. Lawton Riley, wife of the Jefferson Episcopal minister. Mrs. Riley was a professional writer who wrote magazine articles under the pen name of Pat O'Neele.

Today the full cast comes together for three rehearsals before the opening night on Wednesday. At times all of the actors are Jefferson residents. There are shows scheduled Wednesday through Sunday. All performances are sold out weeks in advance. There has never been a cancellation of a performance. Tickets are priced at one-fourth the going rate for legitimate theater. Profits have been used to provide the nineteenth-century playhouse with a new roof, wall reinforcements, and fresh paint.

In the early years of the weekend pilgrimage, the sponsoring garden club used all the proceeds from tour ticket sales for local restoration projects, including the rebuilding of the Episcopal church bell tower, restoring the Jay Gould railroad car, and purchasing three historic structures — the Manse, the former residence of Presbyterian ministers, the Excelsior House, and the old Jewish synagogue.

Homeowners who took part in the early pilgrimages were paid as much as $100 by the garden club for cleaning, flowers, etc. Later the club divided profits into nine equal parts: one part for owners of the four houses on the morning tour, the same to the four owners on the afternoon tour, and one part to the garden club for planning and promotion. Homeowners use these funds for home improvements, furniture, landscaping, etc. The garden club pilgrimage committee selects the homes on the pilgrimage tour.

Initially, the tour was held on the second weekend after Easter. Since that date fluctuated, it was decided that the tour date would always be the first weekend in May.

Hundreds of residents and out-of-town volunteers have regular roles to play in the Jefferson Historical Pilgrimage. Women wear long, fancy dresses with bustles, and men don tie and tails. Schools are dismissed on Friday of tour weekend. There are also special additions of the *Jimplecute*, the Marion County Historical Commission *Jeffersonian*, and the Junior Historian *Riverboat Ledger*. As a result of these joint efforts, Jefferson has earned a national reputation as a historic showcase.

What is reputed to be the finest small town museum in America had its beginnings on July 6, 1948, when the Jefferson Historical Society and Museum was organized with 171 charter members. The museum opened on April 1, 1949, on the first floor of the Jefferson Carnegie Library. At that time the book collection was moved to the second floor. The first large collections — a total of almost 1,000 items — were given by Mrs. Lillie Warner McDonald and by Mrs. Dolly Bell Rutherford Key.

In 1962 an opportunity came to expand into larger facilities. At that time the Federal Building was closed when a new post office opened and the court moved to Marshall. Located at the corner of Austin and Market streets, the 1890 structure was the largest building in downtown Jefferson with 233,636 cubic feet of space.

On December 9, 1964, it was announced that the vacant Federal Building would be offered for public sale by competitive bids. The high bid of $8,100 was decided on by J. A.R. Moseley, the co-founder of the Jefferson Historical Museum. That bid was approved on February 4, 1965, and the Jefferson Historical Society moved into the Federal Building in September 1965.

On the main floor of the four-story red-brick building is the Lucille Blackburn Memorial Archives, some 1,200 volumes on Texas and northeast Texas history. There are also display cases of artifacts and documents connecting Jefferson to Sam Houston, Jay Gould, Diamond Bessie, Vernon Dalhart, Barry Benefield, Charles and David Culberson, J. A. R. Moseley, and Lady Bird Johnson.

Other main floor displays include cannon balls, shells, Civil War artifacts, Republic of Texas documents and money, a doll collection, a fan collection, papers of Sam Houston, old Bibles, rare china, pioneer doctors' instruments, and the Mabry exhibit.

A decorative staircase leads to the upper floors. On the second floor in the former courtroom is the Moseley Art Gallery, which is enhanced by 800 yards of red velvet draperies donated by couples from Dallas and Tyler. The art collection includes three nineteenth-century Godey prints donated by actress Greer Garson and five major paintings donated by W. L. Moody III.[18]

Smaller rooms on the second floor are devoted to rare antique furniture, the Hobart Key collection of Caddo Indian pottery and arrow points in the Indian Room, the McDonald gun and weapon collection, and the Bride's Room. The third floor includes the Children's Room and a display of children's clothing and toys. The museum basement has displays of early farm tools, a 200-year-old loom, a primitive kitchen, unique clothing, country store items, Annie Oakley's boot last, a full-size steam engine, and old Jefferson bottles.

The number of museum visitors increased from 15,000 in 1966 to 35,000 in 1981. The museum is open seven days a week. The largest attendance is during the first weekend of May for the annual pilgrimage.

As of 1983, there were 15,000 items on display in the museum catalogued and displayed by two volunteer curators, Mrs. Doris Koontz and Mrs. Lucille Ballard.

The museum building became a Texas Historic Landmark in 1965 and was entered in the National Register of Historic Places in 1969.

Since the creation of the Texas State Historical Survey Committee in 1953, Jefferson has been a key participant in the program. Ruth Lester of Jefferson was a board member for the Texas State Historical Foundation Committee. The RAMPS program was begun in 1964 with the goal of dedicating within five years 5,000 historical markers with inscriptions cast in aluminum plaques. In August of 1973, the survey committee was renamed the Texas Historical Commission with the same program for historical markers.

By 1983 there were more than sixty state historical markers in approximately ten square blocks in Jefferson, the largest concentration of markers anywhere in Texas. Forty-nine of these homes and buildings were also given recognition by the National Register of Historic Places. On August 7, 1971, Congressman Wright Patman announced that the National Register of Historic Places had designated several blocks between Big Cypress and Broadway as the Historic Waterfront District.

More than any other individual, Ruth Lester was responsible for Jefferson becoming a tourism center in the 1950s and 1960s. In recognition of her untiring efforts, Mrs. Lester was one of eighteen women in the United States invited to attend the first of Mrs. Lady Bird Johnson's "Women Doer's Luncheons" at the White House on January 25, 1966. At that time Ruth was invited to report on restoration work completed in Jefferson. She and her daughter were also overnight guests at the White House.

Ruth Lester died after a brief illness on August 30, 1968. To honor her memory, the highest award given by the Texas Historical Commission — that for the best restoration project — is designated as the Ruth Lester Award. The garden club has also dedicated the restored convent portion of the Jefferson Playhouse complex as the Ruth Lester Memorial.

The most interesting Jefferson legend of recent years involved the hidden treasure of a native son, Clarence C. Braden, who died on June 14, 1962, at age sixty-six. A lifelong bachelor, Braden was a former professor of mathematics at Texas A&M and Southern Methodist University. One of Jefferson's best-known citizens, he served as mayor, museum and historical society president, and Rotary Club president.

Clarence's mother, Mrs. L. G. (Nannie) Braden, was a large, brassy town character who made buggy deliveries of milk, buttermilk, and butter. After completing her first year of teaching in Huckaby, Mrs. Braden's daughter, Beulah, drowned in Big Cypress on July 3, 1916. Losing Beulah made Nannie Braden more eccentric and protective of Clarence.

Clarence Braden inherited what was left of the old Haywood House on Dallas Street. During its prime in the 1860s, it was considered the finest hotel west of the Mississippi. Clarence was the sole occupant of the part of the building still standing, living first in an upstairs apartment until September 1, 1956.

During the years he lived in the Haywood House, Braden stored away a cache of half a million coins. According to Jefferson residents who knew him, Clarence always paid for things with a bill and asked for change in silver. He never spent a coin, only bills. Many knew Braden was storing coins away, but his many acts of kindness caused him to be spared by thieves.

After his death the coins were scooped up with a shovel, boxed and carried in a two-ton flatbed truck to the First National Bank to be counted. The task kept clerks busy from Friday until Tuesday, and the total came to $55,337.82. Braden also had bank accounts in other towns and left an estate of more than $376,350 for forty-two recognized heirs.

The day before Braden's death, the Jefferson Rotary Club met at his bedside to preserve Clarence's thirty-two years of perfect attendance. His longtime home, the Haywood House, was renovated in 1981. The museum in the basement contains a display case with a shelf devoted to Braden.

In February 1971 the Jefferson Junior Historians were organized with thirteen charter members under the direction of David Robertson. Several years ago they purchased the old Masonic lodge building at No. 61 Dallas Street. Built in the late 1850s, this two-story "shell" building is the last remaining example of the commercial structures on Jefferson's Dallas Street wharf front during its heyday as an inland port.

After restoring the building, the Junior Historians renamed it "McGarity's Saloon." For more than twenty years, it has been the home of the lively, toe-tapping production of "You've Come a Long Way," which is preformed by the Junior Historians during Mardi Gras Upriver and the Jefferson Historical Pilgrimage. All members of the cast are either current or former members of the Jefferson Junior Historians. The McGarity Saloon Can-Can Line began performing in 1973 with only three members; there were twenty-five in the line in 1994.

Tourism in Jefferson received a boost in 1980, when newcomers Sandy and Ray Spalding restored the old Brown house and opened the state's first bed-and-breakfast inn. George Brown, the manager of an iron ore furnace in nearby Kellyville, built the two-story, gingerbread-trimmed house at 409 Broadway from a mail-order blueprint in 1888.

After being damaged by a fire in 1964, the vacant house sat neglected and decaying until the Spaldings restored the place and renamed it the Pride House for their son. The grand old home has four coal-burning fireplaces, nine-foot windows bordered with rainbow-colored glass, and ornately carved cast bronze hardware on the doors and windows.

The four upstairs guest rooms are handsomely decorated in antiques. Guests have a cozy downstairs parlor at their disposal and can serve themselves breakfast from a large armoire in the hallway.

Sandy's mother, Ruthmary Jordan, a successful Jefferson restaurateur, took over the Pride House in 1981. She is also the genteel proprietor of the Dependency, a two-story, four-room guest cottage behind the main house.

Jefferson is the birthplace — and capital — of the state's bed-and-breakfast industry. A 1994 directory listed thirty-four such inns, each with its own distinctive decor and ambience.

Perhaps the most colorful such inn is the Captain's Castle (the Rogers-McCasland home). The home was so named by Capt. Thomas J. Rogers, a Confederate officer and local pioneer banker. In the early 1870s, he chose to combine two older Jefferson houses. One was already located on the present site at 403 Walker Street (the back portion of the existing structure). The other house was an imposing Tennessee planter-style structure (the two-story front portion today). It was moved across town on rollers from the riverfront. This 1850s house had been an elegant bawdy house in its steamboat heyday.

The combined structure was first restored by Judge Joe McCasland. It is a history buff's delight with its original nineteenth-century furnishings.

The Captain's Castle offers three rooms for overnight lodging. Four rooms are also available in the nearby Carriage House and Cottage.

Many other bed-and-breakfast inns have their own special charm. Roseville Manor offers five guest rooms and has a vast, priceless collection of Roseville pottery. The Stillwater Inn has a chef-owned restaurant specializing in Continental cuisine, three upstairs guest rooms, and a private cottage. The McKay House, an 1850s cottage, has been cited as one of the most romantic B&Bs in the United States. The owners provide Victorian sleepwear for their guests — sleepshirts for gentlemen and Victorian gowns for ladies — along with period antiques, original wallpaper patterns, and an indoor "outhouse."

Other fine bed-and-breakfast inns in town include the Claiborne House, the Bluebonnet Inn, the Cottonwood Inn, the Steamboat Inn, and the Rowell House.

In late 1989, townspeople began to plan the revival of one of the great events of Jefferson's glory days. This new celebration was scheduled for mid-February and was to be known as Mardi Gras Upriver. Jefferson volunteers first organized themselves into a club or "krewe." Their Krewe of Hebe was named for the Greek goddess of youth whose statue rests atop the Sterne fountain near downtown Jefferson.

Extending over two weekends, the Mardi Gras Upriver festivities begin on a Saturday night with the Krewe of Hebe Queen Mab Ball, held on the top floor of the Carnegie Library. The following Friday night a small, torchlit "Do-Da" parade leads to the statue of

Hebe, where a ceremony ends with the proclamation, "Let the party begin!" At midafternoon on Saturday, Willie Smith and his Marching Cobras — a nationally known troupe of black youths from Kansas City — lead the mile-long Krewe of Hebe Grand Parade. During the parade the Mardi Gras king and queen roll by in a white, horse-drawn carriage.

Other Saturday events include two performances of an award-winning musical by the Jefferson Junior Historians, live entertainment from a riverfront stage at the corner of Polk and Dallas streets, and a nighttime Mardi Gras Dance at the Kellyville Community Center.

Sunday's activities are geared for the family and feature the Krewe of Hebe Children's Parade.

The three days of revelry also include elaborate parties, an arts and crafts fair, a homes tour, boat excursions down Big Cypress Bayou, and steam-engine train rides.

Another Jefferson attraction is the River Museum, located at 222 E. Austin Street. The museum has displays on every aspect of life aboard the great steamboats of the Mississippi system, including Big Cypress Bayou and Jefferson. One block behind the museum is the site of the Steamboat Turn Basin, where steamboats coming to Jefferson docked and turned around to return downstream.

The Jesse Allen Wise Garden Club sponsors two walking tours of historic Jefferson with each beginning at the Excelsior House. Historic Walk No. 1 has twenty-eight stops, and Historic Walk No. 2 offers twenty-three points of interest. A brochure includes an easy-to-read map for each tour.

The Jefferson Historic District embraces a forty-seven-block National Register District showcasing fifty-six restored buildings dating from the 1850s to the 1890s. Sixty-five Jefferson structures bear state markers from the Texas Historical Commission.

A 1994 Jefferson directory listed ten historic homes as being open for tours. They included the 1860s Beard House at the corner of Henderson and Vale, the 1850s Captain's Castle at the corner of Alley and Walker, the Culberson House at 403 N. Walnut, the Freeman Plantation a mile west of town on SH 49, Maison-Bayou (an authentic reproduction of an 1850s plantation overseer's house) on Bayou Street, Secession Hall at the corner of Jefferson and Alley, the Ruth Lester Memorial and Jefferson Playhouse at the corner of Market and Henderson, the 1872 House of the Seasons at the corner of Alley and Delta, Roseville Manor at 217 W. Lafayette, and the Alley-Carlson House and Museum at the corner of Main and Walker.

Three companies offer tours of Jefferson. The Polk Street Trolley provides an open-air, rubber-wheel trolley tour of over 100 points of interest. This narrated, one-hour tour departs three times daily from 101 Polk Street.

The Mullins Narrated Tours offer narrated forty-five-minute mule-drawn wagon and surrey tours of historic Jefferson. These tours begin at the intersection of Austin and Market streets.

The L.J. Carriage Service offers a narrated, horse-drawn carriage tour of historic Jefferson which begins from the corner of Austin and Vale streets.

The Jefferson & Cypress Bayou Railroad offers a steam locomotive pulling open-air passenger cars along the bayou and through historic areas. The depot for this narrow-gauge train is located at the east end of Austin Street.

The Jefferson Riverboat Landing and Depot is located across the Polk Street bridge from downtown. Four one-hour riverboat tours of Big Cypress Bayou are offered daily. Each tour begins in the Turning Basin and follows the last 2.5 miles that steamboats traveled. These boat tours are expertly narrated by licensed riverboat pilots.

In addition to the annual Jefferson Historical Pilgrimage and the Mardi Gras Upriver celebration, there is also an annual Jefferson Christmas Candlelight Tour the first two weeks in December. This tour includes four Victorian-style residences — the Culberson House, the Davanna House, Secession Hall, and Victorian Heights. Other tour events include Christmas choirs, English handbell choirs, and a Christmas craft bazaar and art show.

Visiting Jefferson today is like stepping back in time. Only Galveston has more homes and buildings carrying Texas historical medallions. Instead of yesteryear's steamboat horns and whistles, one hears carriages filled with camera-toting tourists clattering over the red brick streets. Such attractions as the Excelsior House, the *Atalanta,* the Jefferson Historical Museum, the year-round home tours, and the annual historical pilgrimage have combined to give this town of 2,200 residents its reputation as the "Williamsburg of Texas."

Success, however, has not spoiled the hospitable members of the Jesse Allen Wise Garden Club, who still refer to the tourist throng as "our guests" or "our visitors." Because of their unflagging effort and dedication, Jefferson remains the "town that wouldn't die."

Capt. William Perry, who brought the first steamboat to Jefferson.
— Photo courtesy Excelsior House, Jefferson, Texas

George Addison Kelly,
founder of the Kelly Iron Works and the Kelly Plow Co.
— Photo courtesy Jefferson Historical Museum, Jefferson, Texas

Diamond Bessie Moore, the victim of a sensational murder plot.
— Photo courtesy Excelsior House, Jefferson, Texas

Abe Rothschild, the accused murderer of Diamond Bessie Moore.
— Photo courtesy of Excelsior House, Jefferson, Texas

The Brooks House, the last address of Diamond Bessie Moore.
— Photo courtesy of Marion County Historical Commission

Sen. Charles Allen Culberson,
governor of Texas and long-time United States senator.
— Photo courtesy Jefferson Historical Museum, Jefferson, Texas

The Culberson House, built in 1880 — 403 N. Walnut St.
— Photo courtesy J. C. Hoke, Wharton, Texas

Jay Gould, who is said to have put a curse on Jefferson.

— Photo courtesy Jefferson Historical Museum, Jefferson, Texas

The Atalanta, *the private railroad coach car built for Jay Gould, located across from the Excelsior House.*

— Photo courtesy J. C. Hoke, Wharton, Texas

Jefferson Historical Museum, 1890 — formerly the Federal Building, located at corner of Austin and Market streets.

— Photo courtesy J. C. Hoke, Wharton, Texas

The Excelsior House, built in 1858 — facing Austin St.
— Photo courtesy J. C. Hoke, Wharton, Texas

The Freeman House (1850) — located a mile west of Jefferson on S. H. 49.
— Photo courtesy J. C. Hoke, Wharton, Texas

The House of the Seasons (1872) — corner of Alley and Delta streets.
— Photo courtesy J. C. Hoke, Wharton, Texas

Jefferson Cumberland Presbyterian Church, 1872 — corner of Line and Jefferson Streets.

— Photo courtesy J. C. Hoke, Wharton, Texas

Presbyterian Manse (1853) — corner of Alley and Delta streets.

— Photo courtesy J. C. Hoke, Wharton, Texas

Jefferson Carnegie Public Library (1907) — corner of Market and Lafayette streets.

— Photo courtesy J. C. Hoke, Wharton, Texas

Sterne Fountain (1913) — left front corner of library block.

— Photo courtesy J. C. Hoke, Wharton, Texas

Site of old Kahn Saloon, corner of Austin and Vale streets.

— Photo courtesy J. C. Hoke, Wharton, Texas

Confederate Monument, 1907, moved to courthouse lawn in late 1930s.

— Photo courtesy J. C. Hoke, Wharton, Texas

Haywood House, built in 1865 — Dallas at Market Street.

— Photo J. C. Hoke, Wharton, Texas

Jefferson Playhouse, the old Jewish Synagogue, corner of Market and Henderson streets.

— Photo courtesy J. C. Hoke, Wharton, Texas

Portrait of Ruth Lester, who was most responsible for Jefferson becoming a tourism center.

— Photo courtesy of Ruth Lester Memorial

Ruth Lester Memorial, the restored convent portion of the Jefferson Playhouse complex.

— Photo courtesy J. C. Hoke, Wharton, Texas

Steamboat Col. A. P. Kouns, *1875.*
— Photo courtesy Jefferson Historical Museum, Jefferson, Texas

Replica of steamboat Mittie Stephens.
— Photo courtesy Jefferson Historical Museum, Jefferson, Texas

Steamboats docking at Jefferson.
— Photo courtesy Marion County Chamber of Commerce, Jefferson, Texas

The Magnolias, built in 1867 — 209 E. Broadway St.
— Photo courtesy J. C. Hoke, Wharton, Texas

Alley-Carlson House and Museum (1861) — corner of Main and Walker.
— Photo courtesy J. C. Hoke, Wharton, Texas

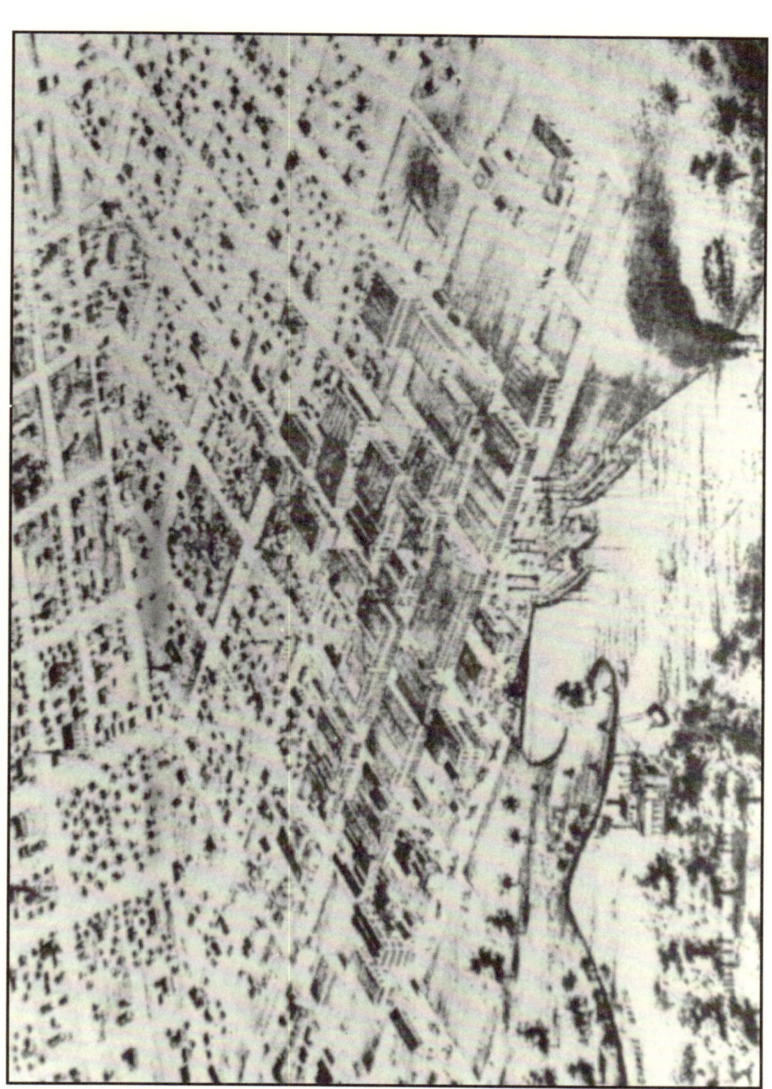

Map showing bird's-eye view of Jefferson, 1872.
—Photo courtesy Marion County Historical Commission

Ruins of gas works on Big Cypress.
— Photo courtesy Jefferson Historical Museum, Jefferson, Texas

Confederate clothing factory and Federal Building, 1890.
— Photo courtesy Jefferson Historical Museum, Jefferson, Texas

Barry Benefield, author of short stories, novels, and screenplays.
— Photo courtesy Jefferson Historical Museum, Jefferson, Texas

Vernon Dalhart (Marion Try Slaughter), the "Father of Country Music."
— Photo courtesy Jim Walsh, *Hobbies* magazine (from *Jefferson: Riverport to the Southwest* by Fred Tarpley)

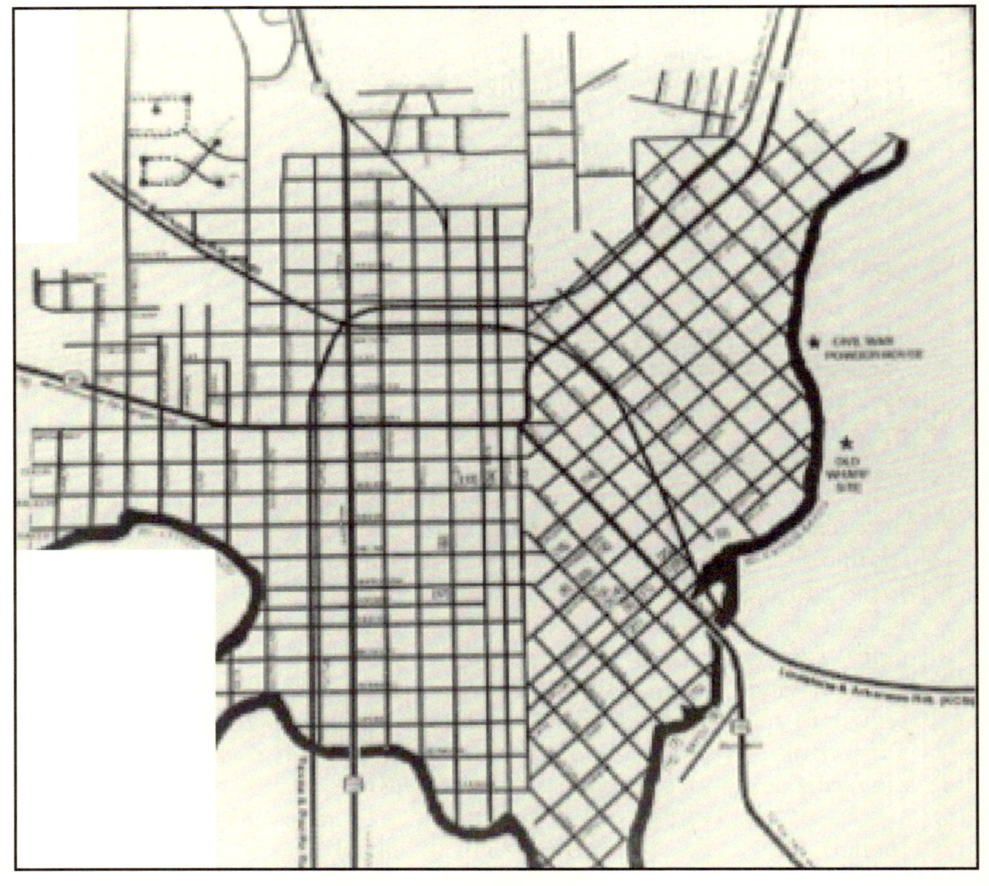

Map of Jefferson, Texas.

— Photo courtesy *The Jeffersonian*, Historic Jefferson Foundation, Jefferson, Texas

Notes

Chapter 1: Gonzales: The Lexington of Texas

1. In May 1827, Kerr received title to a league of land in present Jackson County as one of the "Old Three Hundred" and raised the first crop in the county. In August, Ben Milam executed a power of attorney to Kerr to manage the adjoining colony in his absence. After Green DeWitt and his colonists moved back to Gonzales in December 1827, James was left alone with little Mary Margaret at their home on the Lavaca. He remarried in September 1833, taking Sarah Grace Fulton, the foster daughter of John J. Linn of Victoria, as his bride.

Kerr played a leading role in Texas revolutionary politics. He was a delegate to both the Conventions of 1832 and 1833 and presided over the protest Lavaca-Navidad Meeting of July 1835. The formal protest signed there at Millican's gin house was the forerunner of the Texas Declaration of Independence. James was also elected to the Consultation at San Felipe in November 1835 but did not attend; at the time he was in the successful expedition against Lipantitlan, a Mexican fort on the Nueces River.

Upon returning from the frontier, Kerr was appointed a member of the General Council by the Consultation. He and his neighbor, Elijah Stapp, were elected delegates from Jackson municipality to the convention meeting at Washington-on-the-Brazos on March 1, 1836. The two drew straws to see which one would go or stay behind and lead their families to safety. Elijah won and went on to gain fame as a signer of the Texas Declaration of Independence. After Interim President David Burnet appointed him a major in the Texas army in March 1836, James sent his family to Missouri.

In 1838 Major Kerr represented Jackson County in the House of Representatives of the Third Congress. He then retired from public life to devote more time to his growing family; Thomas Richard was born February 15, 1841. Late in life James Kerr went to New Orleans to study medicine and spent his last years as a physician. After a brief bout with pneumonia, Dr. Kerr died at his old Lavaca home on December 23, 1850, and was buried on the premises beneath a handsome marble vault.

On January 26, 1856, Kerr County was created by the state legislature and named in his honor, with Kerrville as the county seat. A state historical marker has been placed near the old Kerr cemetery eight miles north of Edna on Farm Road 822.

2. Sarah Seely DeWitt was truly the mother of the colony. Her duties included entertaining visitors and travelers coming to the colony, but she would not prepare a hot meal on Sunday because of her religious beliefs. A traveler wrote in 1828 that she was "a most excellent Lady, kind and hospitable to Strangers."

Mrs. DeWitt lived to see all of her children reared and married: Eliza to Thomas Hardeman; Naomi to W. A. Matthews; Evaline to Charles Mason; C. C. to Narcissa Barrow; Clinton to Elizabeth Frazier; Minerva to Isham G. Jones.

Sarah died on November 28, 1854. Her body was placed on an oxen-drawn sled and carried to the hilltop called Santa Anna's Mound near her home. She was the first to rest in the DeWitt Burying Gound.

3. The location where the cannon was fired was later verified by David Sterling Hughes Darst, who was fifteen on October 2, 1835, and witnessed the burning of Gonzales. David was guest of honor on April 21, 1903, at ceremonies marking the dedication of the stone at the battle scene on the Dikes place at Cost, Texas, located seven miles southwest of Gonzales on Highway 97.

Jacob C. Darst, his wife Margaret, and son David came by ox-wagon from St. Charles County, Missouri, and joined old friends and neighbors in Gonzales on January 8, 1831. Jacob was granted twenty-four labors of land on the north side of the Guadalupe River, an area known today as the Darst Creek oil field.

Darst was one of the "Old Eighteen" at Gonzales and was one of the thirty-two Gonzales volunteers who died at the Alamo. His wife and son returned to Gonzales in 1839, and Margaret died in 1846.

David S. H. Darst took part in the Battle of Plum Creek. In 1845 he married Emeline Zumwalt, and they had two sons and a daughter. David was a member of the Old School Presbyterian Church and served as ruling elder for years.

He served as mayor of Gonzales from 1850 until 1853 and was a co-founder of the *Gonzales Inquirer* in June 1853. David was also one of the first merchants in Gonzales, a trustee of Gonzales College, and a charter member of the Masonic Lodge Royal Arch Chapter No. 51 in 1846.

Darst was elected county treasurer in 1859 and held that post for twelve years. In 1860 he built a brick home in Gonzales on grounds covering eighteen acres. In 1874 he built a mill and gin on East Avenue later known as the Vrazel Gin. David also contributed $500 toward bringing a railroad branch to Gonzales in 1882.

This pioneer Gonzales resident died at age eighty-four on June 14, 1906, and was buried in the Masonic Cemetery.

4. In late June 1936, during Texas' centennial year, a devastating flood hit Central Texas, and the small cannon was discovered by Lowell Cooper in a washed-out hole on the west bank of Sandies Creek. After being picked up by a rural mail carrier — the grandson of gunman John Wesley Hardin — the historic cannon was stored in the basement of the old Gonzales post office for thirty-two years.

When a new post office was built, the cannon was purchased at a Houston gun show by gun collector Henry Guerra of Reynosa, Mexico. In May 1979, Guerra displayed the cannon at a National Rifle Association meeting in San Antonio. The gun carried the simple inscription: "Small iron cannon dug up at Gonzales, Texas. The cannon probably dates back to Mexican period in Texas, 1821 to 1836."

The unsuspecting Robert Vance of Refugio, president of the Texas Gun Collectors Association, and son Johnnie traded for the cannon, then sold it to another gun collector, Shiner physician Patrick Wagner, for an undisclosed sum of money in December 1979. The next month Dr. Wagner read a copy of Noah Smithwick's classic book, *Evolution of a State or Recollections of Old Texas Days.* In the book was a drawing of the original "Come and Take It" cannon by Smithwick's daughter, Mrs. Nana Donaldson. The gun had a remarkable resemblance to the one Dr. Wagner had just purchased. Smithwick, a skilled blacksmith and gunsmith, had scoured out the cannon in John Sowell's workshop the day after the Battle of Gonzales. He also described bushing the cannon; that is, reducing the caliber size of the touchhole, which had been spiked by the Mexicans. The spike had been driven out, leaving a touchhole the size of a man's thumb.

Using his medical instruments, Dr. Wagner viewed and photographed the inside of the barrel and touchhole. He also had the cannon X-rayed and found that his gun had been spiked and bushed just as Smithwick described it. It was as if Noah had put his signature on a work of art.

With the help of two researchers (a rancher and a photographer), Dr. Wagner completed 134 qualitative and quantitative comparisons of the unearthed cannon and the one described in the Battle of Gonzales. "Dr. Pat" also traveled 7,000 miles and spent $50,000 in time and money in 1980. Through such painstaking efforts, he was able to authenticate his discovery of the old "Come and Take It" cannon, among the most important relics of Texas history.

Today it is displayed at the Gonzales Memorial Museum and at various sites around the state of Texas.

5. On November 17, 1837, John Fisher was back in the new city of Houston when he wrote to President Sam Houston asking to be appointed as notary public to Velasco, where he intended to live.

Fisher later assigned to Peter Grayson his rights for a headright certificate for one league and one labor he was entitled to. He soon left Texas for Virginia, intending to return with his family. He was forced to remain in Virginia, however, and care for two female relatives who were aged and blind.

John Fisher died on August 13, 1865, and was buried in the Hollywood Cemetery in Richmond. His wife, Margaret Connor McKim, also was born and died in that city.

6. The other members of the "Immortal Thirty-two" were Isaac Baker, John Cane, George Cottle, David Cummings, Squire Damon, Jacob Darst, John Davis, William Dearduff, Charles Despallier, William Fishbaugh, John Flanders, Dolphin W. Floyd, Galba Fuqua, John E. Garvin, John E. Gaston, James George, Thomas Jackson, Johnny Kellogg, Andrew Kent, John G. King, William P. King, Jonathan Lindley, Jesse McCoy, Thomas Miller (the wealthiest person in Gonzales), Isaac Millsaps, George Neggan, William Summers, George Tumlinson, Robert White, and Claiborne Wright.

7. During the civilian flight known as the Runaway Scrape, Susanna Dickinson and baby Angelina accompanied Sarah Nash Bruno in an ox-cart to her old home on Nash Creek in East Texas. Five weeks after the Battle of San Jacinto, the attractive, penniless widow and daughter moved to the new town of Houston. There she was befriended by Pamelia Mann, the owner of the most notorious brothel in the Republic of Texas.

In a desperate search for security, Susanna turned to a series of stormy marriages. She left the cruel John Williams within a year for her own safety. She lived with her next husband, Francis Herring, for five years before he died of drink.

On December 15, 1847, Susanna took her fourth husband, a drayman named Peter Bellows who was three years her junior. During this time she was operating a boardinghouse at Franklin and Crawford streets. In the summer of 1849, she became a "born-again" Christian and was baptized in Buffalo Bayou by Rufus Burleson, pastor of the First Baptist Church of Houston.

On July 8, 1851, Reverend Burleson married Angelina Dickinson and John Maynard Griffith, a no-nonsense, strait-laced farmer from Montgomery County. The pampered, pleasure-loving city girl hated the drudgery of country life. After innumerable spats, Angelina divorced her husband and sent their three children to live with their uncle and grandmother.

On June 15, 1857, Peter Bellows was granted a divorce from Susanna, charging her with adultery and "taking up residence in a house of ill fame."After selling Almeron's original league of land for $2,500, Susanna operated a small boardinghouse at Lockhart, where she met and married Joseph William Hannig, a German cabinetmaker, in 1857.

Using the money from her land sale, Susanna set Joseph up in his own business in Austin, a furniture and cabinet shop at 205 E. Pecan (now Sixth Street). The newlyweds moved into a rock house on Pine Street (now 501 E. Fifth Street), a place that still stands today.

This fifth marriage was the turning point in Susanna's life. She was finally to find true love, happiness, and repectability in Austin.

In the 1870s, Mr. Hannig's three-story furniture store on Pecan Street became "one of the largest in the state" with stock purchased in New York, Cincinnati, and Chicago. Joseph soon had another business venture: controlling interest in the Colorado Mills. Reflecting his stature as one of the richest men in Austin, Hannig in the mid-1870s built a comfortable two-story frame house at the corner of Duval and East 32nd streets.

Susanna Hannig had one final tribulation to endure, the tragic death of her only child. After her divorce, Angelina moved to New Orleans and married Oscar Holmes in 1864. Soon after baby Sallie was born in September 1865, Angelina simply deserted her husband and daughter and moved to Galveston, where she lived with and took the name of a railroader named James H. Britton.

According to her granddaughter, a yellow fever epidemic hit the island in 1869, and Angelina died after nursing others through the ordeal. However, a far different version of her death appeared on July 14, 1869, when *Flake's Daily Bulletin* of Galveston reported that ". . . Em. Britton. . . embraced the life of a courtezan and so died last night. . ." Four days later the *Bulletin* mortuary report said that Emma Britton, age thirty-seven, died of a uterus hemmorhage.

The years in Austin were Susanna Hannig's redemption, an opportunity to make amends for a checkered past. She made a good home for Joseph, was active in church functions, enjoyed concerts at Presslar's Gardens, and supported her husband in his civic and social efforts.

By terms of a law passed by the Texas Congress on December 21, 1837, descendants of those who participated in the defense of the Alamo could apply for 640 acres of land. Susanna and Angelina received four such land grants between 1839 and 1855. In making their own claims, many Alamo descendants appealed to Susanna for proof of their relatives' service, and she gave numerous such depositions throughout her life. She even returned to the Alamo ruins as a visitor on April 27, 1881.

Susanna Hannig was a huge woman in her last years. Her Alamo calf wound never healed and required periodic dressing. On October 7, 1883, she died of hemmorhage of the bowels at age sixty-eight. Joseph had her funeral services in their home and buried his legendary wife in Austin's Oakwood Cemetery.

Mr. Hannig opened a new furniture business in San Antonio and married Louisa Staacke there in 1884. He died of acute gastritis on June 6, 1890, leaving an estate valued at $300,000. As per his request, he was buried next to Susanna.

On March 2, 1949, the State of Texas dedicated a white marble slab over Susanna Hannig's grave. On March 6, 1976, a granite state marker recognizing her unique place in Texas history was unveiled in the State Cemetery in Austin.

The Gonzales homesite of Almeron and Susanna Dickinson is at the southeast corner of St. James and St. Michael streets. The brick cistern is purported to have been theirs. Nearby is a Texas historical marker.

8. Sarah Ann McClure Braches typifies the sturdy, fearless pioneer woman of her time. The oldest of twelve children, she was born in Shelby County, Kentucky, on March 12, 1811. Her father, John Miller Ashby, was a descendant of a son of Pocahontas and John Rolfe.

Sarah was seventeen when she married Bartlett D. McClure in 1828. They had three sons: Alex in 1829, John in 1833, and Joel in 1839.

In 1831 the McClure and Ashby families came to Texas together by coastal schooner. John Ashby, who would soon go blind, settled five miles south of present Halletsville while Bartlett McClure received a league of land east of Gonzales on Peach Creek. After their parents died, the six Ashby children went to live with the McClures.

Since their home was the nearest white settlement on the road to the Colorado River, Sarah McClure gave beeves and provisions to Jim Bowie's party when they began their San Saba expedition in November 1831.

In 1834 Barlett went to Bastrop on business, leaving a Down-East carpenter with Sarah to build an addition to their house. When lurking Indians were seen in the area, the frightened, cowardly carpenter was shamed into leaving by the feisty, armed woman.

In 1839 Bartlett and Sarah were returning by horseback from a visit to her father's home when they were chased by twenty-seven Comanche warriors. The two separated with Sarah galloping toward Boggy Creek and her husband riding in the opposite direction to an upper crossing. Sarah escaped by jumping her horse across the wide stream to the opposite bank. Her pursuers rode up to the same creek bank chasm but made no attempt to duplicate her feat. Several miles further on, her husband rejoined Sarah.

On March 2, 1843, Widow McClure married Charles Braches, a native of Rheim, Prussia, who had conducted a music school in Mississippi before coming to Texas. At the time of their marriage, Braches was representing his Gonzales district in the Republic of Texas Congress. He had also fought in the Battle of Plum Creek.

Both Charles and Sarah were active in the Cumberland Presbyterian Church and noted for their hospitality and refinement. In the early 1850s, stagecoaches, mail hacks, and ox-drawn wagons of German immigrants stopped for water at their plantation "big house."

Charles Braches died on July 7, 1889, and was buried in the family cemetery. During her twilight years, representatives of noted Texas historian John Henry

Brown spent weeks with Sarah correcting and verifying information he had assembled. Brown, a personal friend of Sarah, paid her a splendid tribute in his book, *Indian Wars and Pioneers of Southwestern Texas.*

Sarah McClure Braches was confined to bed in her last years and died at home on October 17, 1894.

The McClure-Braches home and the Sam Houston Oak stand today close to Highway 90A between Gonzales and Shiner. The home and original league of land are still owned by Sarah Ann's descendants.

9. Today only the main rooms of the original house remain. They are furnished by Mrs. Will Steiner in the pioneer period and are maintained by the Gonzales Chapter of the Daughters of the Republic of Texas, who serve as advisors and are in charge of the house. The Eggleston House is now located in a park in the 1300 block of East St. Louis Street. The dog run log cabin sits on grounds that were once a state park of Texas and public lands for cattle drives through Gonzales.

10. On August 23, 1854, William Hess and Sue Jones sold the property to Asa C. Hill and his wife. They rebuilt the house with material from the original Ponton house and pine from Pensacola, Florida, which was carted by ox team from Indianola to Gonzales. For twenty-two years the Hills conducted a girls' school in the house, using the dining room as an auditorium or study hall.

On December 20, 1876, the property was sold to Thomas Jefferson Ponton, Andrew's nephew, who raised the upper story and made it a mansard roof. Ponton's daughter, Mrs. Ed Lewis, was born there.

On February 4, 1885, the home was purchased by Mr. and Mrs. William Madden Fly, who modified the house to a full two stories and planted twin cedar trees on either side of the front steps.

When Ben Peck died in 1913, Warren Taylor became a full partner in the old firm of Peck and Fly. Warren and his wife, Mary Ella Fly, who was born in the house, came there to live.

Soon after the death of Mrs. Clara Fly in 1916, her tall cedar tree was blown down and uprooted. Her husband, William, died in 1944, and his tree lost its largest and highest branch two weeks later.

The old Fly House, located at 424 St. Peter Street, has been bricked over and is now the Buffington Funeral Home.

11. Matilda Lockhart was destined to play a key role in the bloody Council House Fight at San Antonio. She lived with the Comanches for two years, serving as a horse herder. Initially, her feet were branded to keep Matilda from running away. A chunk of fire was used to awaken the hapless captive, leaving her nose burned off to the bone and her entire body scarred and bruised.

In January 1840, three Comanche chiefs rode into San Antonio seeking peace and offering to return their white captive women and children. They promised to return in thirty days with their principal chiefs to make the final arrangements.

Secretary of War Albert Sidney Johnston then sent word that if the Comanches did not bring in all of their estimated 200 prisoners, they were to be held as hostages and used in an exchange of captives for chiefs.

On March 19, 1840, sixty-five Comanches rode into San Antonio led by twelve chiefs, but they brought only two prisoners: a small Mexican boy and Matilda Lockhart, who managed to inform the Texans that there were thirteen other captives in her camp. The white men were also incensed over her pathetic condition.

Once both sides gathered in the council house (courthouse) adjacent to the Main Plaza, an interpreter told the chiefs that they would be held as hostages, then ran for his life. The Comanches then drew their bows and a hand-to-hand fight broke out. After rushing out into the square, the Indians fled in all directions. In the chase that followed, thirty-three Comanches were killed, including all twelve chiefs, and the other thirty-two were captured and put in jail. Seven Texans died, including two judges and the county sheriff. Among the wounded Texans was Matthew Caldwell. The Council House Fight was described as a "day of horrors" by Mrs. Samuel Maverick, the wife of a local merchant.

Today a visitor to the Institute of Texan Cultures at San Antonio can observe a huge wall painting in the foyer depicting the Comanche peace party entering the city. The likeness of Matilda Lockhart is clearly visible in the mural.

12. In 1892 a local chapter of the United Confederate Veterans — Camp J. C. G. Key Number 156 — was organized at Gonzales. Unfortunately, the membership lists were destroyed when the courthouse burned the next year. The local chapter ceased to function in 1921.

On October 10, 1900, the *Inquirer* reported that a reunion of Terry's Texas Rangers was held in Gonzales. Among those in attendance were J. F. Miller of Company I, R. C. Pullen of Company I, J. H. Cobb of Company I, E. M. Steen of Company I, and D. B. Shuler of Company E — all of whom were from Gonzales.

As late as August 1907, the county commissioners court was still approving pensions for Confederate veterans or their widows.

13. Fort Waul is located southeast of Gonzales Pioneer Village near the intersection of Highways 90A and 183. This earthen embankment fort was the only Confederate fort commissioned to be built west of the Mississippi River.

14. In 1874 Melvin and Thankful Allis established a school at Moulton, Texas, known today as Old Moulton. The Moulton Institute was a day school for several hundred area pupils and was also a boarding school drawing students from San Antonio to Houston. The brochure of 1889 listed four faculty: Melvin as principal; Thankful as preceptress; Mrs. Laurette F. Price, primary department; Sarah M. McLean, music department.

Allis, a thin, scholarly figure, and "Aunt Thank" maintained strict discipline in their school, which was rebuilt twice after being destroyed by fire in 1876 and by a storm in 1886.

After Allis died in 1892, his wife closed Moulton Institute in 1895 and moved to San Antonio, where she was employed by the Peacock School for Boys for fifteen years. Thankful died at age ninety-four on January 1, 1937, and was buried by her husband in the Gonzales Masonic Cemetery.

15. The huge bronze doors of Littlefield's Austin bank are bas-reliefed with cattle, cowboys, a chuck wagon, and his LFD brand. The door handles are steers' heads. The tinted bank lobby walls are decorated with six range murals depicting scenes from the Yellow House Ranch and the apple orchard from his ranch near Roswell, New Mexico. Over the main entrance is a huge American eagle with outstretched wings from one of the ranches.

One of Littlefield's former drovers, Jeff Connolly of Lockhart, later went to the American National Bank while in Austin. After being told that the major —

then a millionaire — was in his private office, Connolly strode in and told Littlefield who he was. The cowpoke later recalled that ". . .he treated me as fine as any man was ever treated. . . , and that's what makes us common fellows like him."

When the Old Time Trail Drivers' Association was organized at San Antonio on February 15, 1915, Littlefield agreed to serve on the board of directors.

For years veterans of the major's old outfit, Terry's Texas Rangers, held their reunions in Austin. After scrutinizing history textbooks, the local John B. Hood Camp complained that such books were written with a Northern bias.

In December 1912, Dr. Eugene C. Baker of the University of Texas history department wrote a letter to regent Littlefield. Noting that the best known Southern historical collections reposed in the North, Dr. Barker proposed a simple solution: It was merely a matter of money to collect these materials and make them available for use.

Ever the Southern champion, Littlefield in April 1914, donated to the university $25,000 to be known as the Littlefield Fund for Southern History. He gave an additional $30,500 "to get the stuff" the university needed between 1916 and 1920. In his will George added $100,000 to the principal of the original gift. By 1939 the Littlefield Southern History Collection numbered 25,805 books and pamphlets with a capital fund of $146,368.

Regent Littlefield also paid $225,000 for the John Henry Wrenn Library of English literature, some 6,000 volumes dating from about 1500 to the nineteenth century.

An early campaign contributor of Governor Jim Ferguson, regent Littlefield belatedly broke with him and sided with President Robert E. Vinson when Ferguson sought political and budgetary control of the University of Texas. During the bitter dispute, the governor appointed a regents' majority willing to remove six faculty members. Ferguson's attempt to veto the university's two-year appropriation bill led to his impeachment and removal from office in August 1917.

In his will, Littlefield left $300,000 to build the Alice Littlefield Dormitory for freshmen girls, $500,000 for the construction of a Main Building, and $200,000 for a south campus entrance "arch" or monument commemorating Southern statesmen. (The regents "filled in the space between the two driveways" with Pompeo Coppini's Memorial Fountain.) The residue of his estate was left to his wife.

Littlefield had a strong dislike for a rival benefactor, George W. Brackenridge, who served as a university regent from 1886 until 1911. Brackenridge had left Jackson County to avoid service to the Confederacy. Convinced that the original forty-acre campus was too small, Brackenridge in 1910 gave the university an undeveloped, wooded, 500-acre tract of land on the Colorado River near Austin to be used as a new "Big Campus." President Vinson ardently pushed the proposal for years. The project collapsed, however, when Littlefield died in November 1920. His will provided that the Littlefield Dormitory property would revert to his estate if the main university moved within twenty-one years of his death.

16. The old structure was closed as a jail in 1975. At that time it became the Old Jail Museum and the Chamber of Commerce office, and was replaced by a new facility immediately to the southeast. Located at 414 St. Lawrence Street, the Old Jail Museum houses law enforcement artifacts from the 1800s on the first floor.

There were six hangings in the Gonzales jail. The first recorded execution took place in 1855. The last hanging, that of Albert Howard, took place on March 18, 1921. Legend has it that he paid strict attention to the courthouse clock through his jail cell window, intent on knowing the number of hours he had to live. Howard protested his guilt, proclaiming that his innocence would be shown by that clock; that it would never keep correct time again. His prophecy was fulfilled. Even though the clock works were later changed, none of the four faces keep the same time.

The old jail has both a Texas historical marker and a National Register of Historic Places marker.

The Old Jail Museum is open daily for tours from 8:00 A.M. until 5:00 P.M. On weekends it is open Saturday from 8:30 A.M. until 4:00 P.M. and on Sunday from 1:00 P.M. until 4:00 P.M.

17. After telling the children goodbye at the Duderstadt Ranch, Hardin lived in Junction and Kerrville before drifting to El Paso in April 1895. Since he had little law work, Wes soon reverted to his base nature and spent most of his time drinking, gambling, and writing his autobiography. He also became the town bully and took a local prostitute, Mrs. Beulah Morose, as his companion.

At 11:00 P.M. on August 19, 1895, Hardin was rolling dice at the bar of the Acme Saloon when he was shot to death by Constable John Selman. Ironically, he had just told friends that his story would be ended with one more day's work. Hardin died from a single bullet to the left eye and was buried in an unmarked grave in the Concordia Cemetery in El Paso.

His autobiography was published by Smith and Moore of Seguin in 1896. Finally, after twenty years of effort by the Hardin family and Western historian C. L. Sonnichsen, a granite-and-bronze marker was placed on Wes Hardin's grave on September 29, 1965. It is a simple marker like that of Jane Hardin, containing only his name and dates.

18. Cortez was a barber during his years in prison. Eventually, he won the esteem and personal friendship of prision officials, including the warden, who wrote the governor that he "would very much like to see this man pardoned."

On July 7, 1913, Governor O. B. Colquitt signed papers giving Gregorio Cortez a conditional rather than full pardon. He first settled at Nuevo Laredo, on the Mexican side of the border. In 1916 Cortez died at age forty-one at the home of a friend at Anson, Texas, north of Abilene. He was buried in a little cemetery eight miles from Anson.

Today Gregorio Cortez is revered as a legendary folk hero by the Mexican population along the Rio Grande. A well-known ballad, "El Corrido de Gregorio Cortez," was written about him. Many Anglo-Americans also see him as a victim of injustice and admire him for the extraordinary courage, skill, and endurance shown in his flight from Texas authorities.

19. Forty-six original documents are on display in the museum. These include a page from the ledger of James Kerr, the Constitution of Gonzales (1831), several slave bills of sale, an army order and a $500 bond signed by Antonio López de Santa Anna, letters signed by Sam Houston and Mirabeau B. Lamar, and the list of cattle brands of Gonzales County cattlemen who drove herds to Kansas in 1873.

Chapter 2: Columbus: A Walk Into a Proud Past

1. For an excellent and exhaustive treatment of this subject, refer to the fol-

lowing article by Bill Stein: "Beyond Boosterism: Establishing the Age of Columbus." *Nesbitt Memorial Library Journal,* Vol. 2, No. 2 (May 1992), pp. 71-90.

Bill Stein is the archivist of the Nesbitt Memorial Library in Columbus. He is also the editor of the *Nesbitt Memorial Library Journal.*

2. Sometime after 1829, Dewees married Benjamin Beeson's oldest daughter, Lydia G., who was listed as age fourteen in the 1823 census. The couple had one daughter, Emily, before Lydia's death in early 1847.

Before 1835, Dewees sold a portion of his land to Fayette Copeland. The 1840 census showed him owning 1,207 acres of land with another 887 acres under survey based on a grant. He also owned eleven slaves, thirty head of cattle, nine horses, a clock, a pleasure carriage, and two watches.

On March 7, 1847, William married Angelica Besch. The 1850 census showed two girls living with them, Emily (age nine) and Lydia (age two). Lydia later married Hugh J. Smith on May 22, 1865, and T. Kerr on March 15, 1874. William's son Bufford married Lizzie Burk on October 22, 1870.

In the early 1850s, Dewees and Emanetta Cara Kimball, a young schoolteacher in Columbus, wrote a book together. Using her pen name of Cara Cardelle, Miss Kimball compiled a series of contrived letters written by Dewees to a "dear friend" in Kentucky. There were thirty of these lengthy and detailed letters supposedly written between 1822 and 1845. These letters were actually reminiscences shared with Miss Kimball.

On October 7, 1852, a contract between Dewees and Kimball was filed in the Colorado County clerk's office. Their contract indicated that the two had also finished another book in manuscript form, *Life on a Frontier or Adventures of Will Dewees,* but it was never published. In 1852 Morton & Griswold of Louisville, Kentucky, published William's small volume under the title *Letters from an Early Settler of Texas to a Friend,* by W. B. Dewees.

Little else is known about Emanetta Cara Kimball. On June 12, 1855, she married Magus S. Crawford. It is possible that P. A. Kimball, the minister performing the ceremony, was her father.

3. The five Alley brothers were all members of the "Old Three Hundred" and came to Texas from Missouri between 1821 and 1824. Their ancestors were French Huguenots who came to the American colonies in 1749 and 1752.

Rawson Alley, the oldest son, was Austin's surveyor and arrived on the Colorado River in 1821. His three half-brothers — Abraham, Thomas and John — came to Texas from St. Genevieve County, Missouri, in the spring of 1822 and joined Rawson on their land grant at the Atascosita Crossing on the east side of the Colorado. William Alley followed his brothers to Texas in 1824. He never married and spent the rest of his life in what became Alleyton, Texas.

John Alley was killed by the Karankawas in the winter of 1822. Thomas drowned in the Brazos River during an Indian campaign in the spring of 1824. Rawson died of natural causes in May 1833.

On April 26, 1835, Abraham Alley married Miss Nancy Millar, whose father, Dr. John Millar, had come to Texas from Decatur, Alabama, in 1831. Abraham and Nancy settled on the east side of the Colorado near the Atascosita Crossing. The couple had nine children, but only five survived childhood.

Dr. Millar died of smallpox on October 21, 1831. His headstone bears the earliest date in the Alley Family Cemetery. His widow, Elizabeth, married Jacob Bettis shortly thereafter.

During the Texas Revolution, Abraham Alley was charged by Gen. Sam Houston with seeing to the safety of area women and children. After burning his cabin, Alley moved his family and the other civilians to the Trinity River. After the Battle of San Jacinto, he returned to his land in 1836 and immediately built a square notch two-room log cabin on the original site eight miles below Columbus. The cabin had limestone chimneys on each end. In the center was a stairway dovetailed into the wall which led to a loft room.

Abraham Alley registered the first cattle brand in Colorado County on March 11, 1837, and served on the jury of the first district court one month later. He was appointed by President Houston as president of the Board of Land Commissioners for Colorado County on December 19, 1837. He later served as county commissioner of Colorado County. On September 11, 1850, he deeded 1,000 acres of land to Rutersville College in Fayette County. Abraham died at age fifty-eight on May 16, 1862, and was buried in the Alley Family Cemetery.

In 1849 Nancy Alley received a legacy from a wealthy great aunt and used the money to remodel the family cabin in 1852. The place was sided with pine lumber from Bastrop, and two rooms were added to give the house an L-shaped appearance. Another fireplace was also added between the two new rooms.

After Abraham's death Nancy continued to live in the old homestead with her bachelor son, William W. Alley. Nancy was a quiet person who dressed simply and knitted constantly. She died at home at age seventy-six on October 28, 1893, and was buried beside her husband.

In 1976 the Alley Log Cabin was moved into Columbus, restored, and given to Magnolia Homes Tour, Inc., through the generosity of Abraham Alley's descendants. They also donated the cabin site at 1224 Bowie Street.

The Alley Log Cabin is the oldest structure in Columbus. The two rooms are 16x16 feet and 16x18 feet with two fireplaces and chimneys. Some of the original roof rafters are still in the two loft rooms.

The Alley Family Cemetery is near Farm Road 102 three miles east of Alleyton on a ninety-acre tract of land now owned by Mr. Leslie Koehl. The one-acre plot is next to the railroad tracks and was once owned by William Alley. As of 1993 there were forty-nine burial plots there.

4. William Demetrius Lacy, a native of Kentucky, came to Texas in 1831 and established a tanyard and saddle shop near the site of present Columbus. In 1832 he married widow Sarah Ann McCrosky. After the Civil War, Lacy moved his family to Trespalacios. On September 27, 1865, his daughter, Fanny, married Shanghai Pierce.

William Menefee of Egypt also served as a member of the General Council of the provisional state government in 1835. President Sam Houston appointed him the first chief justice of Colorado County in December 1836. Menefee then represented Colorado District for five terms in the House of Representatives of the Republic, serving in the Second, Third, Fourth, Fifth and Ninth Congress. Judge Menefee was elected to the five-man commission which chose a site to be named Austin as the capital of Texas in January 1839.

Menefee moved from Egypt to Fayette County in 1846, where the town of Oso developed around his home. He represented Fayette County in the House of Representatives of the Fifth Legislature.

Judge Menefee died on October 29, 1875, and was buried beside his wife Agnes in the Pine Springs Cemetery six miles from Flatonia. Their remains were reinterred in the State Cemetery at Austin in 1936.

5. In 1846 Reverend Ervendberg became pastor of the First Protestant Church in New Braunfels. After a severe fever epidemic hit the second wave of 5,000 German immigrants arriving at Indianola and Galveston, he and Louisa took nineteen orphaned children into their home. Louis then obtained several acres three miles north of town and named it "New Wied." In 1848 the Ervendbergs' West Texas Orphan Asylum was incorporated there.

In 1850 West Texas University was chartered at New Wied with Ervendberg as president and the only professor. During this period he also served as pastor and probate judge.

In 1855 Louis took his two sons and ran off to Mexico with Franziska E. Langer, a seventeen-year-old girl from the orphanage. In February 1863, bandits broke into his home, murdered Ervendberg, and took a large sum of money.

6. The Tait plantation house has been taken down and moved — board by board — to higher ground three times since 1847. Much of the original structure is preserved in what is now the headquarters of the 6,000-acre Tait Ranch.

In 1934 Robert Elbert Tait brought his new bride, the former Alice Nina Pohler of Shiner, to live in the old log house referred to as the Tait Ranch House. At the time the dog-run house had an open hall with a room on either side. A kitchen and bath had been added to the back, but there was no electricity or telephone. Several years later Alice Tait finally got her front door when the dog-run was closed with a window panel and two large double doors.

In the early years, Mrs. Tait cooked on a wood stove and warmed baby bottles on fireplace coals at night. Their first two children — Millycent Ann and Rita Louise — were fed in a scratchy old high chair with a seat of woven corn. The chinking on the log house consisted of rags, sticks, and moss and provided a breeding ground for scorpions. Although the house was quite primitive, Alice Tait was known for her hospitality and often hosted parties and barn dances.

In 1941 the old house was disassembled, and each log was numbered and moved by teams of mules to higher ground about a mile west of the old Tait ferry. At this time a bathroom, office, dining room, kitchen, and modern conveniences were added.

After nine years in the country, the Taits moved to Columbus. Four other children were born there: Roberta Asbury, Charla Williams, Robert Elbert (Bob), and Monica.

In May 1964, the old bell used on the steamboat *Moccasin Belle* was installed on the carport of the Tait Ranch House. At one time this steamer hauled cotton down the Colorado River from the Tait plantation to Galveston.

In 1969 and 1970, the Taits restored the ranch house, the double log barn, and a slave house for showing on the annual Magnolia Homes Tour. Original furniture in the house includes a rocking chair with the date "1853" and the inscription "C. Tait" carved on the back seat, a trundle bed, a chest dated "1855," several homemade bootjacks, and iron cooking utensils.

The Tait family cemetery is about one mile from the present site of the house. It is located on high gravel ground overlooking McKenzie Creek and is enclosed by a four-foot-high limestone wall. The wall surrounds the graves of C. W. and Louisa Tait and seven of their children. A tall monument centers the plot for the children, and each of their graves has an individual marker. To the west, outside the wall, are the graves of slaves and overseers.

To reach the Tait Compound, travel south from Columbus on State Highway

71 for six miles, then turn left on County Road 101 and travel south three miles to the Tait Ranch House.

7. After the war, Dr. Tait found his plantation intact and most of his sixty-eight free Negroes remaining. He practiced medicine among his family and on the plantation. By 1870 he had only $6,545 in cash. Dr. Tait died at age sixty-three on November 2, 1878, and was buried in the family cemetery on the plantation. His wife Louisa died on December 12, 1896.

After Tait's death the Columbus town house was occupied by his daughter Caroline and her husband, Wells Thompson. They were followed by another daughter, Louisa, and her husband, Sam Green. When the Greens moved to Houston in the early 1900s, Dr. Tait's son William and his wife, the former Mathilda Auerbach, took up residence in the mansion. His widow lived there until her death in 1956.

At that time Mathilda's son, Robert Elbert Tait and his wife Alice, began a major remodeling and redecorating of the twenty-two-room house, adding a wing all the way across the back with a dining room, kitchen, breakfast area, utility room, and bedroom. The Taits also added screened porches on either side of the house. After the restoration was completed, they moved into the house.

In March 1955, R. E. Tait moved the anchor of the *Moccasin Belle* from the courthouse square to the lawn of the town house. The anchor belonged to the Tait family.

On October 30, 1957, the John Everett Chapter, Daughters of the American Revolution, formally dedicated a bronze tablet marking the C. W. Tait home. At that time his great-granddaughter, Millycent Ann Tait, gave a history of the house.

Rancher R. E. Tait, the family archivist and operator of the Tait Ranch, died at age sixty-eight in September 1971. Since that time Alice Tait has occupied the grand old town house. The first two floors are furnished almost entirely with antiques and lovely family heirlooms.

In 1990 Alice Tait was named Outstanding Older Texan from Colorado County. In 1994 the Magnolia Homes Tour Visitor's Guide paid her special tribute for her sixty years of service to Columbus, Colorado County, and the St. Anthony Catholic Church.

Columbus has also perpetuated the memory of the family patriarch through the Col. Charles W. Tait Chapter No. 669, Children of the Confederacy.

8. Dilue Rose was born in St. Louis on April 28, 1825. Her father, Dr. Pleasant W. Rose, brought his wife Margaret and three children to Texas in April 1833. After living at Harrisburg a short time, the Roses rented a farm at Stafford's Point in December 1833.

In the spring of 1836, there was a panic civilian retreat from Santa Anna's advancing Mexican armies. Dilue's reminiscences of the "Runaway Scrape" provide an excellent contemporary account of the chaos and confusion:

> . . . We left home at sunset, hauling clothes, bedding, and provisions on the sleigh with one yoke of oxen. Mother and I were walking, she with the infant in her arms. Brother drove the oxen, and my two little sisters rode in the sleigh.

When the Harrises reached the San Jacinto River, "There were fully 5,000 people at the ferry. . . . Everyone was trying to cross first, and it was almost a riot." As the women and children crossed the Trinity, illness broke out and many died of measles, sore throat, and whooping cough. Among the victims was Dilue's baby sister, Missouri, who was buried at Liberty.

The Rose family had been on the road for five weeks when a horseback rider caught up with them on April 22, 1836, and shouted, "Turn back! Turn back! The Texian army has whipped the Mexicans! Turn back!" Dr. Rose then started for home in a little boat but stopped to survey the San Jacinto battle scene. According to Dilue, "We were glad to leave the battlefield, for it was a gruesome sight. We camped that night on the prairie, and could hear the wolves howl and bark as they devoured the dead."

Dr. Rose chose to relocate on a farm on Bray's Bayou, five miles from Houston. During the 1838 San Jacinto ball, fourteen-year-old Dilue was twice close enough to Gen. Sam Houston to dance with him, but two pretty young widows stepped in front of her.

On June 15, 1838, Flournoy Hunt, the son of Mrs. Pamelia Mann, married Miss Mary Henry in his mother's notorious Houston hotel, the Mansion House. Sam Houston served as best man, and Dilue was asked to be the maid of honor. However, Mrs. Holliday, a designing widow, asserted that Miss Rose was "too young and timid" and marched off on Houston's arm.

Although Dilue was frustrated once more, she did meet Ira A. Harris at the wedding, and the two were married on February 20, 1839.

9. Fannie Amelia Dickson Baker was born near Montgomery, Alabama, in September 1829. Her father, Moseley Baker, led a company of 127 men during the Texas Revolution, When General Houston ordered a retreat from the Colorado to the Brazos, Captain Baker challenged his authority on March 28, 1836, prompting Houston to assign Baker and his company to garrison duty at San Felipe. The next day Baker ordered that the town be burned after receiving a false scouting report that a Mexican army was approaching.

In the spring of 1837, Moseley brought his wife Eliza and little Fannie to Texas on the brig *Eldorado.* Fannie's sisiter, Eliza, was the first white child born on Galveston Island in 1838. For several years the Bakers spent the winter in Houston and the summer in Galveston. After her father was elected to the Texas Congress in 1838, Fannie attended the inauguration of President Mirabeau B. Lamar that December.

In 1842 she was sent back to Alabama, where she attended school until the spring of 1846. Fannie married William J. Darden, a lawyer from Norfolk, Virginia, on January 26, 1847. Darden graduated from Columbia College in Washington, D. C., at age nineteen.

William and Fannie had two sons: the older boy, William Raiford, was killed by a horse at Galveston at age three; the younger son, Albert Dickson, died of yellow fever at age twenty-three.

Fannie Darden's renowned father, Moseley Baker, died of yellow fever on November 4, 1848, after becoming a Methodist minister in Houston.

10. The Brunson Building was later called the Goldsmith Building, the Grogan Building, and the Wendel Building. After a nine-month fund-raising effort, it was purchased by the Live Oak Art Club in January 1986. Funds for restoration have come from the Nesbitt Memorial Trust.

The Gallery is open Tuesday through Saturday, year round, from 10:00 A.M.

to 5:00 P.M. Over 10,000 visitors have attended exhibits and studied in workshops since the opening exhibit, "Texas Visions," organized by the Houston Art League.

Now a cultural art center, the Brunson Building bears a Texas State historical marker and is part of the Columbus Historic Walking Tour.

11. After John Stafford was killed in July 1890, his widow Grace married Connie Byars. "Miss Gracie" lived in the Stafford ranch house until she died at age eighty-one on April 13, 1940.

At that time her son, Joe W. Stafford, and his wife, the former Carrie Estelle Townsend, moved into the mansion. After Joe Stafford died on May 29, 1949, Carrie moved out of the Stafford house, leaving it unoccupied.

For years Carrie Stafford lived in the Live Oak Hotel in Columbus. The last eighteen months of her life, "Cabbie" (as her grandchildren called her) was a resident of Parkview Manor Nursing Home. She died at age eighty-nine on June 19, 1971, in the Youens Hospital in Weimar.

The old Stafford ranch house stayed in the family until 1973, when it was purchased by Lewis Ransopher, a Houston realtor, and Jim Bishop, a Bellville architect. The two had hopes of restoring the home to its original grandeur. In the years that followed, however, the house began to crumble and fall into disrepair, and was stripped by vandals. Even the driveway became overgrown with brush and trees.

On the night of June 7, 1994, the historic old house was completely destroyed by a fire of a "suspicious nature." The sheriff's office suspected arson because a party had been held on the private property the night of the fire and there was no electricity to the building.

Mr. Bishop had already divested himself of the property a few years earlier. Ironically, owner Ransopher was negotiating with an Austin builder to begin restoration work at the time of the fire. He said that losing the house was a "difficult thing to confront. It's a tragedy for me, the people of Columbus, and the state."

12. Sarah Stafford lived in the family home at Columbus until 1908. She was a charter member of the Shropshire-Upton Chapter, United Daughters of the Confederacy. After the death of Myra's husband, George Early, she married Ike T. Pryor on June 8, 1893, and the couple moved to San Antonio. Sarah Stafford followed them in 1908 to be near her only surviving child.

Mrs. Stafford died at age seventy-nine on May 17, 1911. Funeral services were held in the former family home in Columbus then occupied by Mr. and Mrs. E. A. Hutchins. Sarah Stafford was buried beside her husband in the family burial ground in Columbus. In recognition of her generosity, a memorial window was later dedicated to her in the third Methodist church built in Columbus.

Bob Stafford's house was purchased by Mrs. Helena Miller in 1915. After her death in April 1936, the home was inherited by Ellis G. Miller. It remained in the Miller family but was unoccupied for three years prior to January 1993. At that time Allan and Jane Miller Hill began a major renovation of the house. After the project was completed in January 1994, the Hills moved into the Stafford-Miller House.

13. Seven families, all related by blood or marriage, contributed to a "reign of terror" in Columbus lasting intermittently from 1871 until 1907.

Carrie Townsend, Light's daughter, married Joe W. Stafford, John's son, in 1905 to help heal that bitter old family feud. By December 1907, only one member of the Townsend family remained in the Columbus area.

Jim Coleman, Will Clements, Herbert Reese, and Walter Reese all died violent deaths. Walter died in November 1919, while serving as chief of detectives on the El Paso police force. One night while returning from Ysleta with friends, his car missed the turn at the "suicide bridge." Reese lingered several days after the accident before dying.

14. The old water tower was abandoned until 1931. When dynamite demolition was unsuccessful, the Shropshire-Upton Chapter 361, United Daughters of the Confederacy, received county permission to convert it into an attractive Memorial Hall. The Daughters installed a second floor for a library with a winding stairway leading to it. They also made an addition on the east side of the tower for a kitchenette. The main floor, which is eighteen feet in diameter, contains a fireplace and furnishings. Once the conversion was complete, the U. D. C. and other clubs used the Memorial Hall as a meeting place.

In 1962 the structure was converted to the Confederate Memorial Museum. Memorabilia of early Texas life now fill the first two floors.

In 1966 the building was awarded a Texas State Historical Survey Medallion.

15. In 1965 the Raymond Rau family purchased the grand old home. It was completely restored by 1969 and renamed "Raumonda." The house is now occupied by Raymond Rau and his mother, Hope Heller Rau.

Raumonda is also open as an elegant bed and breakfast facility, complete with central heating and air-conditioning. The home has nine rooms, four baths, a butler's pantry, and glass gallery. Two stairways and an elevator connect the two floors.

Guests have a choice of three luxurious upstairs bedrooms: the Heller Guest Room, the Ilse Guest Room, and the Tanner Guest Room. All are decorated with antiques and collectibles. A continental breakfast is served on the glassed gallery, and television is available in the east Living Room. There is also an adjacent swimming pool.

Raumonda has a Texas State Historical Medallion and is listed on the National Register of Historic Places as part of the Colorado County Courthouse Historic District.

16. In 1968 Magnolia Homes Tour, Inc., purchased the home from the Brando heirs and restored it as a museum of nineteenth-century small-town life.

17. Bill Stein has done extensive research on the history of the opera house. His article, "Prime Circuit: The Glory Days of the Stafford Opera House," appeared in Volume 1, Number 4 (March 1990) of the *Nesbitt Memorial Library Journal.*

In Appendix A, pp. 119-122, Mr. Stein lists the dates of all the prime circuit performers and shows during the six seasons of the Stafford Opera House.

In Appendix B, he effectively destroys the local legend that famed actress Lillian Russell and magician-escape artist Harry Houdini once played the Stafford Opera House.

The historical marker on the opera house states that Lillian Russell gave the first performance at the theater in 1886, a play called "As In A Looking Glass." In fact, it was Louise Balfe who opened the opera house in the play "The Planter's Wife" on the night of October 28, 1887.

Mr. Stein points out that Miss Russell, the biggest star of the time, never set foot in the hall. No contemporary issue of the *Colorado Citizen* or the *Weimar Mercury* mentions her performing in Columbus. During this period she was drawing a salary of $3,150 per week, the largest in theater history. It is simply implausible that she would be booked into a rural theater with only 800 seats. The legend that Lillian Russell performed in Columbus first appeared in print in Oscar Zumwalt's *Brief History of Columbus* (1935).

Mr. Zumwalt also passed down the legend that Harry Houdini once played the Stafford Opera House. Stein observes that Houdini did not emerge as a star until around 1900, well after the opera house had closed. It is unlikely that a struggling teenage performer would have arranged booking in far off Columbus, Texas.

Zumwalt also started another opera house legend about the fate of the original hand-painted stage curtain. He contended that it was destroyed by E. C. Guilmartin, who purchased the building in 1916. According to Zumwalt, Guilmartin became enraged when someone in Columbus poisoned his bird dog. As an act of revenge against the town, he ripped down the $10,000 curtain and used it to cover his hog pens.

Mr. Stein, however, offers a more likely explanation of the fate of the curtain. After Frank Troxell purchased the opera house in 1922, he began to clean out the debris accumulated on the second floor. In February 1923, an insurance inspector notified him that the stage and scenery posed too great a fire hazard and invalidated his fire policy. When Troxell was ordered to either fireproof the items or remove them from the building, he appealed to the community for funds. When the request went unanswered, Troxell cleaned up the problem on his own by removing the objectionable items. Although there is no list of the items removed, it most probably included the stage curtain.

There is no documentation as to its fate, but the curtain was gone for certain by 1935, when Zumwalt wrote on the subject.

18. On February 6, 1940, Reverend Marmion testified before a subcommittee of the U. S. Senate Judiciary Committee in Washington, D. C. He was then assistant rector of the St. Albans Church in Washington. At the time the subcommittee was holding hearings on the "Crime of Lynching" and considering the passage of a federal anti-lynching bill.

In his statement Reverend Marmion admitted telling Texas Ranger Davenport that he thought he recognized three people in the lynch mob — a sixteen-year-old girl, a well-known businessman, and a young man. Marmion refused to give any names, however, since he could not positively identify the three individuals.

On February 24, 1940, E. R. Spencer, a lawyer from Columbus, wrote a letter to Senator Tom Connally of Texas, a member of the Senate committee. Spencer spoke of Reverend Marmion in condescending terms and asserted that the people of Columbus did not consider him a hero for his intervention in the lynchings. In seeking to discredit the testimony of his former pastor, Spencer said:

> . . . . He seemed to me decidedly deficient in pure love of country, and in his appreciation of native American institutions and traditions. His attitude with regard to government and social problems. . . had acquired a noticeably Marxist coloring. In a word, he was decidedly radical in his leanings. . . .

19. Some fifty years later, a story began to circulate that the third black suspect, dressed like a woman, had been picked up at Frelsburg. After he was taken to the river bridge, an angry crowd wrapped a chain around him and ordered him to

cross to the other side. As soon as he entered the water, the crowd literally shot him full of holes. His riddled, weighted body sank to the bottom and was never recovered.

Chapter 3: Jefferson: The Old South Revisited

1. Buying the Manse was the second local restoration investment made by the Jesse Allen Wise Garden Club in the 1950s. This former residence of Presbyterian ministers then became headquarters of the garden club for a time. It was then sold with the stipulation that the club would have first refusal if the house was ever sold by the new owners, Mr. and Mrs. Martin Jurow.

2. In the late 1930s oilman Lawrence Flannery of Longview purchased and restored the Freeman House. In 1934 it received a plaque from the Department of the Interior and was cited by the Historic Building Survey Committee as "possessing exceptional historic or architectural interest and as being worthy of most careful preservation for the benefit of future generations."

The Freeman House is listed in the National Register and bears a State Historical Medallion. The present owners are the Jesse M. "Duke" DeWare family. The house is open to tours at 2:30 and 3:30 P.M. except Wednesdays.

3. After 1900 the entire structure was vacant. In 1955 the Jesse Allen Wise Garden Club presented the first performance of the "Diamond Bessie Murder Trial" play, using the synagogue as their theater. Since that time the play has been performed there annually during the Jefferson Historical Pilgrimage.

During the 1960s, the garden club purchased all of the property. The Jefferson Playhouse is basically unchanged today. In 1969 the garden club began restoration of the original two-story structure, dedicating it to the memory of Ruth Lester, a driving force in the club. The Ruth Lester Memorial is beautifully furnished with Victorian antiques and memorabilia.

Members of the Jesse Allen Wise Garden Club now show these buildings together in a combined tour every Saturday and Sunday afternoon.

4. The Texas Highway Commission has erected a granite marker on the original site of the little plow shop at Four-Mile-Branch (Kellyville).

5. In 1932 Mrs. Mary Carlson ("Miss Mary") returned to the family home to care for her mother. Mrs. Carlson lived there until her death in 1967, at which time the home was inherited by her daughter, Miss Nione Carlson of Houston.

In 1991 the Alley-Carlson Cottage and its contents were purchased by the Jefferson Historical Society and Museum. Since that time the house has been renovated and opened for tours.

The Alley-Carlson House Museum reflects the lifestyles of three generations of family ownership. Among the original furnishings are a Mallard dresser and a lovely walnut half-tester bed in which Mrs. Mary Carlson and all her brothers and sisters were born.

6. After serving for years as a private residence, the Haywood House reopened in 1981 after extensive renovation. The first floor offered a charming country gift shop and art gallery. On the second floor was an after-dinner theater.

As of 1994, the Haywood House was scheduled to be the home of the Texas Heritage Archives and Library (T. H. A. L. Museum). The facility will include a multi-media presentation and house the largest privately held collection of Texas bank notes.

7. After having thirty-five owners in 116 years, the Magnolias was purchased from a Marshall couple by Preston and Dale Kirk in the fall of 1982. At that time they moved from Dallas to Jefferson to live in and operate a bed-and-breakfast operation in the house.

The Kirks served as costumed guides for a twice-a-day living history tours and added a touch of humor and local color during their hands-on tours. Magnolias in bouquets and paintings set the theme for the Kirks' inn.

The Magnolias featured a Victorian "fainting couch" restored in red velvet, an old Mathuschek square grand piano made of Brazilian rosewood and brought to Jefferson in 1872, an eight-foot-tall grandfather clock built in Scotland in the 1840s, hand-painted English china in the elegant dining room, and blue ceramic tiles brought from a London theater to border the fireplace. The grand old home has pine floors, cypress ceilings, and hand-made bricks.

In 1988 Mr. and Mrs. William Stewart purchased the Magnolias as a family dwelling.

8. The Queen Mab Ball was discontinued after being held once again by the garden club at the Excelsior House during the pilgrimages of 1974 and 1975.

In late 1989, townspeople began to plan the revival of one of the great events of Jefferson's glory days. This new celebration was scheduled for mid-February and was to be known as Mardi Gras Upriver. Jefferson volunteers first organized themselves into a club or "krewe." Their Krewe of Hebe was named for the Greek goddess of youth whose statue rests atop the Sterne fountain near downtown Jefferson.

Extending over two weekends, the Mardi Gras Upriver festivities begin on a Saturday night with the Krewe of Hebe Queen Mab Ball, held on the top floor of the Carnegie Library. The following Friday night a small, torchlit "Do-Da" parade leads to the statue of Hebe, where a ceremony ends with the proclamation, "Let the party begin!" At midafternoon on Saturday, Willie Smith and his Marching Cobras — a nationally known troupe of black youths from Kansas City — leads the mile-long Krewe of Hebe Grand Parade. During the parade the Mardi Gras king and queen roll by in a white, horsedrawn carriage. Other Saturday events include two performances of an award-winning musical by the Jefferson Junior Historians, live entertainment from a riverfront stage at the corner of Polk and Dallas streets, and a nighttime Mardi Gras Dance at the Kelleyville Community Center. Sunday's activities are geared for the family and feature the Krewe of Hebe Children's Parade.

The three days of revelry also include elaborate parties, an arts and crafts fair, a home tour, boat excursions down Big Cypress Bayou, and steam-engine train rides.

9. In 1971 the 300-pound bell of the *Mittie Stephens* went on display in the Jefferson museum. The relic is on permanent loan from Mrs. Susie H. Reid and was taken from the plantation of her father, Harold H. Huckaway, near Vivian, Louisiana.

Jesse M. "Duke" DeWare IV, chairman of the Marion County Historical Commission, has a scale model of the *Mittie Stephens* on display in the Jefferson Historical Museum. The model was researched and built by a Shreveport man, although no photo of the steamer has been found.

In 1983 the Mittie Stephens Foundation was established with Dallas entrepreneur Richard Collins as president and Jefferson attorney Duke DeWare as vice-president. Their goal was to raise a $250,000 search fund for locating and raising the *Mittie Stephens.* Much of the wood on the boat was thought to be intact since deterioration would be slower in the silt of Caddo Lake than in salt water.

The search team was led by principal investigator Ruby Lang, who has a master's degree in nautical archeology from Texas A&M. Field coordinator T. Shumway, a former garage mechanic, is from Mooringsport, Louisiana, only a mile from the disaster site. Archeologist Jim Tribble is under contract to produce film, and team member Lexie Palmer is the only woman pilot of the *Delta Queen.*

The search for the *Mittie Stephens* began in March 1983, but no trace of the steamer was found. However, the team did find pieces of iron and copper from the wreck sites of two other steamboats on the old New Orleans-Shreveport-Jefferson route.

Team divers found visibility to be only six inches to a foot in Caddo Lake. They also became bogged down in Spanish moss and lush aquatic growth. The debris from turn-of-the-century oil drilling platforms also interfered with their sensory equipment.

10. In 1988 the Culberson House was completely restored by Mr. and Mrs. John F. Stewart, the present owners and residents. The home bears a State Medallion from the Texas Historical Commission. It is open to tours on Friday, Saturday, and Sunday at 11:30 A.M. and 1:00 P.M.

11. In the 1970s Mr. and Mrs. Richard Collins of Dallas restored the House of the Seasons to its elegant condition and began to make Jefferson their second home. It is now open to daily tours.

Since 1993 the carriage house has been the Seasons Guest House Bed and Breakfast. There are two spacious suites, and guests are served a full breakfast in the House of the Seasons formal dining room.

12. There are two differing accounts as to Abe's future: He either spent the rest of his life in Europe or served twenty years in prison for theft and forgery against the Pacific Express Company.

Local residents believe that he returned to Jefferson several times before 1909. The caretaker of Oakwood Cemetery told of a handsome, elderly man with a black patch over one eye. After asking to see the grave of Bessie Moore, this mysterious visitor laid a sheaf of red roses on her resting place, knelt in prayer, and left money for the care of the grave.

A headstone was secretly placed on Diamond Bessie's grave in the early 1930s. During a newspaper interview in April 1941, the donor was finally revealed when E. B. McDonald, a retired foundry operator, said, "I placed it there one night because it did not seem right for Diamond Bessie to sleep in an unmarked grave."

The plot has also been enclosed by a wrought-iron fence erected by the Jesse Allen Wise Garden Club. A sign designating the grave was added in the 1960s.

13. Jay Gould was born in Roxbury, New York, on May 27, 1836. This short, frail "skunk" and "corsair" of Wall Street suffered from tuberculosis and neuralgia. A master of manipulation and stock-rigging, the soft-spoken Gould worked sixteen-hour days in coming to control the Erie, Union Pacific, Wabash, Manhattan Elevated, Burlington, Denver Pacific, Central Pacific, Missouri Pacific, and Texas & Pacific lines between 1867 and 1881.

His estate, Lindhurst, in Irvington, New York, overlooked the Hudson River. While inspecting his railroad holdings, Gould traveled in palatial private cars. A favorite destination was El Paso, where he could escape bomb threats at his Wall Street office and seek drier relief for an advanced tubercular condition. When he died in New York City on December 2, 1892, Gould left an estate of $72 million to four sons and two daughters.

14. In 1960 the city of Jefferson sold the Carnegie Library building to a private, nonprofit organization. At the time, the structure needed major repair and restoration. In recent years the "Friends of the Jefferson Carnegie Library," a new organization of over two hundred members, has raised funds for various library projects. Since the fall of 1993, the "friends" have offered book reviews by prominent Texas authors.

The Carnegie Library now houses over 6,000 volumes and is the permanent home of an antique doll collection from over twenty nations. A room is also set aside for regular storytelling and reading periods for small children.

The library is also home to the Marion County Genealogical Society. Thus an area of special research interest is genealogy and family history.

The Carnegie Library also hosts the annual Mardi Gras Ball.

15. In 1981 Vernon Dalhart was inducted into the Country Music Hall of Fame. That year a Texas historical marker citing his career was placed at the site of the Kahn Saloon on Austin Street in Jefferson.

16. There are daily tours of the Excelsior House at 1:00 and 2:00 P.M. The plantation breakfast is served to guests and those with reservations. Luncheon and dinner are served to groups of sixteen or more. Parties are served by reservation only.

17. The club was named for a petite, auburn-haired civic and church leader. Jesse Allen Wise was born in Jefferson in 1859 and died in 1938. During her lifetime she gave countless hours of volunteer service to the 1881 Club, the Texas and General Federation of Women's Clubs, the Episcopal church, and the Oakwood Cemetery Association.

18. The Moseley Art Gallery is filled to capacity with great European paintings, a sampling of some of America's greatest artists, bronzes, woodcarvings, Cloissone, Capo-di-Monte, French bisque, Belleek china and other art glass.

The appointments of the room include such other articles as lamps of Venetian glass, a Dresdan carriage pulled by white horses, a Flemish tapestry, Bokhara rugs, a delicate nineteenth-century French desk, an open-back French settee and matching chair, a French bisque clock, a platter from one of Napoleon's chateaus, and an 1810 example of multi-colored English embroidery.

Bibliography

Austin, William T. "Report of William T. Austin on the Battle of Gonzales." *A Comprehensive History of Texas, 1685 to 1897.* Dudley G. Wooten, ed. 2 vols. Dallas: William G. Scarff, 1898.

Bailey, Ouida. *First Baptist Church, Five-Fourths of a Century: A Pageant Commemorating Its One Hundred Twenty-fifth Anniversary.* Jefferson: 1980.

Barker, Eugene C. "James H. C. Miller and Edward Gritten," *Quarterly of the Texas State Historical Association* 13 (October 1909), 145-153.

———. *The Life of Stephen F. Austin: Founder of Texas, 1793-1836.* Austin: The Texas State Historical Association, 1949.

Beebe, Lucius. *Mansions on Rails.* Berkeley: Howell-North, 1959.

Bennet, Miles S. "The Battle of Gonzales, the 'Lexington' of the Texas Revolution." *Quarterly of the Texas State Historical Association 2 (*April 1899), 313-316.

Biesele, Rudolph L. *The History of the German Settlements in Texas, 1831-1861.* Austin: Von Boeckmann-Jones, 1930.

Brown, John Henry. *History of Texas: From 1685 to 1892.* 2 vols. Fac. Austin: Jenkins Publishing Co., 1970.

———. *Indian Wars and Pioneers of Texas.* Austin: L. E. Daniell.

Buie, Clarita Fonville. "'Come and Take It' Comes Home." *Texas Highways,* January 1981, pp. 40-45.

Cameron, Rebecca M., and Ruth Lester. *Jefferson on the Bayou.* Marshall: Demmer, 1966.

Carrington, Evelyn M., ed. *Women in Early Texas.* Austin: Jenkins Publishing Co., 1975.

Clements, Olen W. "Slayers of Columbus Girl Hanged After Leaving Houston Jail." *Houston Post,* Nov. 13, 1935, pp. 1,9.

Cloppers, J. C. "J. C. Cloppers's Journal and Book of Memoranda for 1828," *The Quarterly of the Texas State Historical Association* 13 (July 1909), 44-80.

Colorado County Historical Commission. Patricia Woolery-Price, comp. *Colorado County Chronicles.* 2 vols. Austin: Nortex Press, 1986.

"Come and Take It" Days Celebration Insert. *Gonzales Inquirer*, September 29, 1988.

"Come and Take It" Days Celebration Insert. *Gonzales Inquirer,* September 27, 1989.

Cousins, Kelly. "Terror in the Texas Pecan Grove." *Famous Detective Cases* 3, No. 5 (July 1936), 18-21, 98-103.

Cowdrey, Albert E. *The Delta Engineers: A History of the U. S. Corps of Engineers in the New Orleans District.*

Crawford, Ann Fears, and Crystal Sasse Ragsdale. *Women in Texas: Their Lives — Their Experiences — Their Accomplishments.* Austin: Eakin Press, 1982.

Cutrer, Thomas W. *Ben McCulloch and the Frontier Military Tradition.* Chapel Hill: University of North Carolina Press, 1993.

Darden, Fannie Amelia Dickson, File. Nesbitt Memorial Library Archives, Columbus, Texas.

Dean, Willie Mims. *Jefferson, Texas: Queen of the Cypress.* Dallas: Mathis Van Nort, 1953.

Dewees, W. B. *Letters from an Early Settler of Texas.* Reprint. Waco: Texian Press, 1968.

Dewees, W. B., File. Nesbitt Memorial Library Archives, Columbus, Texas.

DeWitt, Edna, comp. *Lest We Forget.* Gonzales, Texas: *Gonzales Inquirer.*

Dimick, Howard T. "The Bonfoey Case at Marshall." *Southwestern Historical Quarterly* 48 (April 1955), 469-483.

Dorsey, Florence L. *Master of the Mississippi: Henry Shreve and the Conquest of the Mississippi.* Boston: Houghton Mifflin, 1941.

Edward, David B. *The History of Texas; or, the Emigrant's, Farmer's and Politician's Guide. . .* Cinncinnati: J. A. James & Co., 1836.

Emmett, Chris. *Shanghai Pierce: A Fair Likeness.* Norman: The University of Oklahoma Press, 1953.

Family Profiles, 1840-1900. Jefferson: Carnegie Library Board, Vol. 1, 1981, Vol. 2, 1982.

From Ox-Teams to Eagles: A History of the Texas & Pacific Railway. Dallas: Texas & Pacific Railway, 1947.

Geiser, Samuel Wood. *Naturalists of the Frontier.* 2nd ed. Dallas: Southern Methodist University Press, 1948.

Gonzales Art Group. *Gonzales: "The Lexington of Texas."* Gonzales, Texas: 1975.

Gonzales County Historical Commission. *The History of Gonzales County, Texas.* Dallas: Curtis Media Corporation, 1986.

Greer, James K., ed. *A Texas Ranger and Frontiersman: The Days of Buck Barry in Texas, 1845-1906.* Dallas: Southwestern Press, 1932.

Grodinsky, Julius. *Jay Gould: His Business Career, 1867-1892.* Philadelphia: University of Pennsylvania Press, 1957.

Gross, Jean, and Anders Saustrup, ed. "From Coblenz to Colorado County, 1843-1844: Early Leyendecker Letters to the Old Country." *Nesbitt Memorial Library Journal* 1, No. 6 (August 1990): 171-206.

Haden, Walter Darrell. "Vernon Dalhart," in *Stars of Country Music,* Bill C. Malone and Judith McCulloh, ed. Urbana: University of Illinois Press, 1975.

Haley, J. Evetts. *George W. Littlefield, Texan.* Norman: University of Oklahoma Press, 1943.

Hall, Martin Hardwick. *Sibley's New Mexican Campaign.* Austin: The University of Texas Press, 1960.

Hamm, Madeleine McDermott. "Curtain Rises Again." *Houston Post*, October 6, 1990, Sec C, pp. 1,5.

Harris, Dilue Rose. "The Reminiscences of Mrs. Dilue Harris." *Quarterly of the Texas State Historical Association* 3 (October 1900); 4 (January 1901); 7 (January 1904).

Harrison, William Henry. *Alleyton, Texas: Back Door to the Confederacy.* Alleyton, Texas: Show-Me Type & Print, 1993.

———. *The History of Banking in Colorado County.* Eagle Lake, Texas: Unpublished manuscript, 1976.

Heine, Dorothy Jean. *Come, Reminisce With Me: A History of Glidden, Texas, 1885-1985.* Columbus, Texas: Colorado County Historical Commission, Privately Printed, 1985.

Hendrix, John M. "Gonzales, Texas Perpetuates the Epoch of Cattle — Gonzales is Rich in Cattle Lore." *Cattleman Magazine* 23 (June 1936).

Historic Jefferson Foundation. *The Jeffersonian.* Jefferson, Texas, Vol. 14, No. 1 (Spring/Summer, 1994).

Hochuli, Paul. "Two Negro Rapists Lynched Despite Pleading of Pastor." *Houston Press,* Nov. 13, 1935, pp. 1,4.

Hollon, W. Eugene, and Ruth Lapham Butler, ed. *William Bollaert's Texas.* Norman: University of Oklahoma Press, 1956.

Hopkins, Mary Elizabeth. "The Columbus Tap Railway." Garwood, Texas: Unpublished, n.d.

Hoskins, B. B. "Gonzales, 110 Years a Cow Country." *Cattleman Magazine,* 26 (October 1939).

Hoyt, Edwin P. *The Goulds, A Social History*. New York: Weybright and Talley, 1969.

Hunter, J. Marvin, ed. *The Trail Drivers of Texas.* 2nd ed. Reprint. New York: Argosy-Antiquarian Ltd., 1963.

Hunter, Robert Hancock. *The Narrative of Robert Hancock Hunter.* Austin: The Encino Press, 1966.

King, C. Richard. *Susanna Dickinson: Messenger of the Alamo.* Austin: Shoal Creek, 1976.

Kemp, Louis Wiltz. *The Signers of the Texas Declaration of Independence.* Salado, Texas: The Anson Jones Press, 1944. Reprint 1959.

Kuykendall, James Hampton. "Reminiscences of Early Texans." *Texas State Historical Association Quarterly* 6(April 1903): 236-253; 7(October 1903): 29-64.

"Letter from William B. Dewees to his Mother." *Nesbitt Memorial Library Journal,* Columbus, Texas, 1, No. 10(September 1991): 313-316.

Lord, Walter. *A Time to Stand.* New York: Harper, 1961.

Lukes, Edward A. *The DeWitt Colony of Texas.* Austin: Jenkins Publishing Co., 1976.

Maguire, Jack. *Talk of Texas.* Austin: Shoal Creek, 1973.

Mallory, Randy. "Mardi Gras Upriver." *Texas Highways,* February 1994, pp. 50-52.

McClung, Mildred Mays. *Caddo Lake: Mysterious Swampland.* South Texarkana, Arkansas: Southwest Printers and Publishers, Inc., 1974.

McDonald, Archie P. *Travis.* Austin: Jenkins Publishing Co., 1976.

McKay, Mrs. Arch, and Mrs. H. A. Spellings. *A History of Jefferson, Marion County, Texas.* Jefferson: Jimplecute Printing, 1936.

McKinstry, William C. *The Colorado Navigator*. Matagorda, Texas: *Colorado*

Gazette, 1840.
Mitchell, Hugh C., comp. *The Mitchell Family in Texas* (Major James Kerr). Washington, D. C.: Unpublished Manuscript, 1954.
Moseley, J. A. R. "The Citizens White Primary of Marion County." *Southwestern Historical Quarterly* 44 (April 1946), 524-531.
———. *The Presbyterian Church in Jefferson, Texas.* Austin: Texas State Historical Association, 1946.
Muir, Andrew Forest, ed. *Texas in 1837.* Austin: The University of Texas Press, 1958.
Nichols, James I. *The Confederate Quartermaster in the Trans-Mississippi.* Austin: University of Texas Press, 1964.
Nielsen, George R. "Matthew Caldwell." *Southwestern Historical Quarterly* 64 (April 1961), 478-502.
O'Connor, Richard. *Gould's Millions.* Garden City, New Jersey: Doubleday, 1962.
Paredes, Americo. *With His Pistol in His Hand: A Border Ballad and Its Hero.* Austin: The University of Texas Press, 1958.
Parmelee, Deolece M. "The Deadly Jewels of Diamond Bessie." Booklet sold at Excelsior House, Jefferson.
Rather, Ethel Zivley. "DeWitt's Colony." *Quarterly of the Texas State Historical Association* 8 (October 1904), 95-191.
Reese, John Walter, and Lillian Estelle Reese. *The Flaming Feuds of Colorado County.* Salado, Texas: The Anson Jones Press, 1962.
Roemer, Fedinand. *Texas.* San Antonio: Standard Printing Co., 1935.
Russell, Traylor. *The Diamond Bessie Murder and the Rothschild Trials.* Waco: Texian Press, 1971.
Sanders, Allison. "County Attorney Says Columbus Lynchings Were 'Will of People.'" *Houston Chronicle*, November 13, 1935, pp. 1,9.
Seaholm, Ernest Mae, and Bill Stein, comp. "Richard V. Cook and the Battle of Sabine Pass." *Nesbitt Memorial Library Journal* 1, No. 8 (February 1991): 243-260.
"Search for the Mittie Stephens." *The Houston Post,* September 4, 1983, Sec. G, pp. 1,6.
Shaw, Norma. "The Early History of Colorado County." San Marcos, Texas: M. A. thesis, Southwest Texas State Teachers College, 1939.
Simpson, Harold B. *Hood's Texas Brigade: Lee's Grenadier Guard.* Waco: Texian Press, 1970.
Smithwick, Noah. *The Evolution of a State or Recollections of Old Texas Days.* Reprint. Austin: The University of Texas Press, 1983.
Sonnichsen, C. L. *I'll Die Before I'll Run: The Story of the Great Feuds of Texas.* New York: Devin-Adair Co., 1962.
Spurlin, Charles D. *Texas Veterans in the Mexican War.* Victoria, Texas: The Victoria College, 1984.
Stafford Family File. Nesbitt Memorial Library Archives, Columbus, Texas.
Stein, Bill, and Elizabeth Schoellmann, comp. "A Handbook of Colorado County Newspapers." *Nesbitt Memorial Library Journal* 1, No. 9 (June 1991): 275-299.
Stein, Bill, et al. Transcribed "Excerpts from the Kirchenbuch of Louis Cachand Ervendberg." *Nesbitt Memorial Library Journal* 2, No. 1 (January 1992): 41-64.
Stein, Bill. "Beyond Boosterism: Establishing the Age of Columbus." *Nesbitt Memorial Library Journal* 2, No. 2 (May 1992): 71-90.

———. "Capital Punishment in Colorado County." *Nesbitt Memorial Library Journal* 1, No. 5 (June 1990): 131-166.

———. "Prime Circuit: The Glory Days of the Stafford Opera House." *Nesbitt Memorial Library Journal* 1, No. 4 (March 1990): 103-125.

Tait Family File. Nesbitt Memorial Library Archives, Columbus, Texas.

Tarpley, Fred. *Jefferson: Riverport to the Southwest.* Austin: Eakin Press, 1983.

Texas Historical Foundation. "Walking Tour Focuses On Columbus' Heritage." *Heritage,* Spring 1988, pp. 28-30.

Thomas, Henry Calhoun. "A Sketch of My Life." *Nesbitt Memorial Library Journal* 1, No. 3 (February 1990): 71-91.

Tinkle, Lon. *13 Days to Glory: The Siege of the Alamo.* New York: McGraw-Hill, 1958.

Torma, Tracy. "Jefferson — The Inn City." *Texas Highways,* February 1984, pp. 22-29.

Walters, Mahlon L. "Who Done It to Whom: Rothschild in Retrospect." *Texas Bar Journal,* February 1963.

Weisman, Dale. "Charming, Disarming Jefferson." *Texas Highways,* November 1991, pp. 4-11.

Wilbarger, J. W. *Indian Depredations in Texas.* Austin: Hutchings Printing House, 1889.

Wooten, James H., Jr., and Bill Stein. "Hospital Care in Columbus." *Nesbitt Memorial Library Journal* 1, No. 8 (February 1991): 261-270.

Wright, Marcus J., and Harold B. Simpson. *Texas in the War, 1861-1865.* Hillsboro, Texas: Hill Junior College Press, 1965.

Zumwalt, Oscar A. "A Brief History of Columbus." Columbus, Texas: *Colorado County Citizen,* 1935.

Index